Mysterious Ja

Julian Street

Alpha Editions

This edition published in 2024

ISBN : 9789361471681

Design and Setting By
Alpha Editions
www.alphaedis.com
Email - info@alphaedis.com

Contents

PART I

MYSTERIOUS JAPAN

Far lie the Isles of Mystery,
With never a port between;
Green on the yellow of Asia's breast,
Like a necklace of tourmaline.

CHAPTER I

A Day Goes Overboard—A Sunday Schism—A Desert Island—Water, Water Everywhere—Men with Tails—Anecdotes of the Emperor of Korea—Korean Reforms—Cured by Brigands—The Man who Went to Florida—The Black Current—White Cliffs and Coloured Sails—Fuji Ahoy!

A peculiar ocean, the Pacific. A large and lonely ocean with few ships and many rutty spots that need mending. Ploughing westward over its restless surface for a week, you come to the place where East meets West with a bump that dislocates the calendar. It is as though a date-pad in your hand were knocked to pieces and the days distributed about the deck. You pick them up and reassemble them, but one is missing. Poor little lost day! It became entangled with the 180th meridian and was dragged overboard never to be seen again.

With us, aboard the admirable *Kashima Maru*, the lost day happened to be Sunday, which caused a schism on the ship. In the smokeroom, where poker was a daily pastime, resignation was expressed, the impression being that with the lost day went the customary Sunday services. But in reaching this conclusion the smokeroom group had failed to reckon with the fact that missionaries were aboard. The missionaries held a hasty conference in the social hall, and ignoring the irreverent pranks of longitude and time, announced a service for the day that followed Saturday. Upon this a counter-conference was held around the poker table, whereat were reached the following conclusions:

That aboard ship the captain's will is, and of a right ought to be, absolute; that the captain had pronounced the day Monday; that in the eyes of this law-abiding though poker-playing group, it therefore *was* Monday; that the proposal to hold church services on Monday constituted an attempt upon the part of certain passengers to set their will above that of the captain; that such action was, in the opinion of the smokeroom group, subversive to the ship's discipline, if indeed it did not constitute actual mutiny on the high seas; that members of this group could not, therefore, be party to the action proposed; that, upon the contrary, they deemed it their clear duty in this crisis to stand back of the captain; and finally, that in pursuance of this duty they should and would remain in the smokeroom throughout the entire day, carrying on their regular Monday game, even though others might see fit to carry on their regular Sunday game elsewhere in the vessel.

Had this been the Atlantic crossing we should by now have landed on the other side; yet here we were, pitching upon a cold gray waste a few miles south of Behring Sea, with Yokohama a full week away.

Yet land—land of a kind—was not so distant as I had imagined. Early one morning in the middle of the voyage my steward, Sugimoto, came to my cabin and woke me up to see it. (A splendid fellow, Sugimoto; short and round of body, with flesh solid and resilient as a hard rubber ball, and a circular sweet face that Raphael might have painted for a cherub, had Raphael been Japanese.)

"Good morning, gentleman," said he. "Gentleman look porthole, he see land."

I arose and looked.

A flounce of foam a mile or two away across the water edged the skirt of a dark mountain jutting abruptly from the sea. Through a mist, like a half-raised curtain of gray gauze, I saw a wintry peak from which long tongues of snow trailed downward, marking seams and gorges. It was, in short, just such an island as is discovered in the nick of time by a shipwrecked whaler who, famished and freezing in an open boat, has drifted for days through the storm-tossed pages of a sea story. He would land in a sheltered cove and would quickly discover a spring and a cave. He would devise a skilful means of killing seals, would dress himself in their skins, and subsist upon their meat—preceded by the customary clam and fish courses. For three years he would live upon the island, believing himself alone. Then suddenly would come to him the knowledge that life in this place was no longer safe. About the entrance to his cave he would find the tracks of a predatory animal— fresh prints of French heels in the snow!

Austere though the island looked, my heart warmed at the sight of it; for there is no land so miserable that it is not to be preferred above the sea. Moreover I saw in this land a harbinger. The Empire of Japan, I knew, consisted of several large islands—to the chief one of which we were bound—and some four thousand smaller ones stretching out in a vast chain. This island, then, must be the first one of the chain. From now on we would no doubt be passing islands every little while. The remainder of the voyage would be like a trip down the St. Lawrence River.

Soothed and encouraged by this pleasant thought, and wishing always to remember this outpost of the Island Empire, I asked its name of Sugimoto.

"That Araska, gentleman," he answered.

"Are you glad to see Japan again, Sugimoto?"

"That Araska," he repeated.

"Yes. A part of Japan, isn't it?"

Sugimoto shook his head.

"No, gentleman. Araska American land."

"That island belongs to the United States?"

"Yes, gentleman. That Araska."

I had never heard of an island of that name. Surely Sugimoto was mistaken in thinking it an American possession.

"Could you show it to me on the map?" I asked.

From my dresser he took a folder of the steamship company and opening to a map of the Pacific, pointed to one of many little dots. "Aleutian Islands," they were marked. They dangled far, far out from the end of that peninsula which resembles a long tongue hanging from the mouth of a dog, the head of which is rudely suggested by the cartographic outlines of our northernmost territory. We had sailed directly away from our native land for a week, only to find ourselves, at the end of that time, still in sight of its outskirts. Like many another of his fellow countrymen, good Sugimoto had difficulties with his *l*'s and *r*'s. He had been trying to inform me that the island—the name of which proved to be Amatisnok—belonged to Alaska.

I began to study the map and look up statistics concerning the Pacific Ocean. It was a great mistake. It is not pleasant to discover that three quarters of the world is worse than wasted, being entirely given over to salt water. Nor is it pleasant to discover, when far out on the Pacific, that more than a third of the surface of the earth is taken up by this one ocean. Any thought of getting General Goethals to remedy this matter by filling up the Pacific is, moreover, hopeless, for all the land in the world, if spread over the Pacific's surface, would only make an island surrounded by twenty million square miles of sea.

Feeling depressed over these facts I now began to look for points of merit; for we are told to try to find the good in everything, and though I fear I pay but scant attention to this canon when in my normal state ashore, at sea I become another man.

On land I have a childish feeling that the Creator has not time to pay attention to me, having so many other people to look after; but a ship far out at sea is a conspicuous object. I feel that it must catch His eye. I feel Him looking at me. And though I hope He likes me, I see no special reason why He should. I am so full of faults, so critical, so prejudiced. Consider, for instance, the way I used to go on about President Wilson and Josephus Daniels and W. J. Bryan. I am afraid that was very wrong in me. Instead of studying their failings I should have remedied my own. I should have given more to charity. I should have been more gentle in expressing my opinions. I should have written often to my sister, who so enjoys getting letters from me. I should have looked for good in everything.

Immediately I begin to run about the ship looking for it. And lo! I find it. The ship is comfortable. It seems to be designed to stay on top of the water. The table is beyond criticism. The passengers are interesting. The very vastness of this ocean tends to make them so. Instead of being all of a pattern, as would be one's fellow passengers on an Atlantic liner, they are a heterogeneous lot, familiar with strange corners of the globe and full of curious tales and bits of information. Instead of talking always of hotels in London, Paris, Venice, Rome and Naples, they speak familiarly of Seoul, Shanghai, Peking, Hongkong, Saigon and Singapore. And amongst them are a few having intimate acquaintance with islands and cities so remote that their names sing in the ears like fantastic songs. Fragrant names. The Celebes and Samarkand!

There was a little Englishman who hunted butterflies for a museum. He told me of great spiders as big as your two hands, that build their webs between the trees in the jungles of Borneo—I think he said Borneo. But whatever the name of the place, he found there natives having tails from two to four inches long—I think he said two to four inches. But whatever the length of the tails, he had photographs to prove that tails there were. The latest theory of man's evolution, he told me, is not the theory of Darwin, but holds that there existed long ago an intermediary creature between man and ape, from which both are derived—the ape having, I take it, evolved upward into the treetops, while man evolved downward—down, down, down, until at last came jazz and Lenine and Trotzky.

Another man had lived for years in Korea. In the old days before it was taken over by Japan, he said, it was a perfect comic-opera country with the Emperor as chief comedian. He knew and liked the Emperor, and told me funny stories about him. Once when His Majesty's teeth required filling the work had to wait until the American dentist in Seoul could have a set of instruments made of gold, that being the only metal permitted within the sacred confines of the Imperial mouth.

The concession to build an electric street railway in Seoul was given to Americans on the understanding that they should import motormen from the United States and that these should be held in readiness to fly to the Emperor's aid in case of trouble. A private wire connected the Imperial bedchamber with that of the manager of the street-car company, so that the latter might be quickly notified if help was needed. For more than a year the wire stood unused, but at last late one night the bell rang. The manager leaped from his bed and rushed to the special telephone. But it was not a revolution. The Emperor had just heard about a certain office building in New York and wished to know if it had, in fact, as many stories as had been reported to him.

In his fear of revolution or invasion the Emperor built a palace adjoining the American legation. And when, as happened now and then, there came a *coup d'état*, threatening his personal safety, he would get a ladder and climb over the wall separating the back yard of the palace from that of the American minister. This occurring frequently, so embarrassed the latter, that in order to put an end to His Majesty's habit of informal calling, he caused the top of the wall to be covered with inhospitable broken glass.

Up to the time of the annexation of Korea by Japan, my informant said, the Koreans were entirely without patriotism, but the Japanese so oppressed them that a strong national feeling was engendered after it was too late. That the Japanese had been harsh and brutal in Korea, he said, was indisputable, but this was the work of militarists, and was contrary to the will of the people of Japan who, when they learned what had been going on, protested with such violence that newspapers had to be suppressed in Japanese cities, and there was clubbing of rioters in the streets by the police. This caused immediate reform in Korea. The brutal Governor General was recalled and was replaced by Admiral Baron Saito, a humane and enlightened statesman who has earnestly striven to improve conditions, with the result that Koreans are to-day being better educated and better governed than they have been within the memory of man. Also they are prospering. First steps are now being taken toward allowing them to participate in their own government, and if conditions seem to justify the extension of their privileges, it is hoped that they may ultimately have home rule.

From another passenger I got a story about an American who was captured by brigands in China. The victim was a civil engineer, very skilful at laying out railroad lines. The American International Corporation wished to send him to China to plan a railroad, but he demurred because he was in bad health. Finally, on being pressed by the company, he consented to go if his private physician was sent with him. This was agreed to.

In China brigands caught the civil engineer but not the doctor. They kept him for a long time. He was taken from place to place over the roughest country, walking all night, sleeping by day in damp caves, eating coarse and insufficient food. At last he was released. He returned in rugged health. The life of the brigand was just the thing that he had needed.

"Out here on the seas, without home newspapers," one thoughtful traveller remarked to me, "we lose touch with the world and never quite make up all that we have lost. When we land we hear about some of the things that have happened, but there are minor events of which we never hear, or of which the news comes to us long after, as a great surprise. I recall one example from my own experience.

"In the New England town in which I live there was a banker, a prominent old citizen with a reputation for being very close, and none too scrupulous in the means he sometimes took for making money.

"It had for years been his habit to go every winter to Florida, but his daughter, who kept house for him, liked the northern winter and remained at home.

"Some years ago, while I was in the Far East, this old man died, but I was gone for a long time and heard nothing of it. When I got back it was winter. One day I met the daughter and stopped to speak to her. It was snowing and a cold wind was whistling down the street. We had been having trouble with the furnace at our house and my mind was full of that. So when I met her I said:

"'One good thing—on a day like this you don't have to worry about your father. Furnaces don't get out of order down there where he is.'

"Now, when I am away, I have the newspapers saved, and on my return I read them all if it takes me a whole week."

Somewhere in those seas that lie between the islands of Formosa and Luzon there arises a wide tepid current, known as the Black Current which, flowing northward, tempers the climate of Hondo, the main island of Japan. "To this beneficent stream," remarks the guidebook, "the shores of Nippon owe their luxuriant greenness."

As we crossed the Black Current a certain greenness likewise was revealed upon my countenance. I did not find the stream beneficent at all. It was only about two hundred miles wide, however, and by morning the worst of it was past. I came on deck to find the *Kashima Maru* riding like a placid bulky water-fowl upon a friendly sunlit sea. And far away on the horizon lay a streak of mist that was Japan.

In an hour or two the mist attained more substance. It was like a coloured lantern-slide coming slowly into focus. Someone showed me a white dot upon the shadow of a hill and said it was a lighthouse, and some one else discerned a village in a little smudge of buff where land and water met. Gulls were circling around us—gulls with dark serrated margins to their wings; smaller than those we had seen on Puget Sound. Foreign gulls!

Since leaving Victoria we had sighted only one ship, but now an unladen freighter, pointing high and showing a broad strip of red underbody, reeled by like a gay drunkard, and was no sooner gone astern than we picked up on the other bow a wallowing stubby caravel with a high-tilted poop like that of the *Santa Maria*—a vessel such as I had never dreamed of seeing asail in sober earnest. And she was hardly gone when we overhauled a little fleet of fishing boats having the lovely colour of unpainted wood, and the slender graceful lines of viking ships. All of them but one carried a square white sail on either mast, but that one had three masts and three sails, two of which were yellow, while the third was of a tender faded indigo. It promised things, that boat with coloured sails!

Distant white cliffs, tall and ghostly like those of Dover, brought memories of another island kingdom, far away through the cheek of the world, whose citizens were at this moment sleeping their midnight sleep—*last night.* Presently the white cliffs vanished, giving place to a wall of hills with conical tops and bright green sides splattered with blue-green patches of pine woods. And when I saw the brushwork on those wrinkled cone-shaped hills, so unlike any other hills that I had seen, I knew that Hokusai and Hiroshige, far from being merely decorative artists, had "painted nature as they saw it."

The villages along the shore could now be seen more plainly—rows of one-story houses taking their colour from the yellow wood of which they were constructed, and the yellow thatch of their roofs, both tempered by the elements.

Then, as I was looking at a village on a promontory reaching out to meet us, some one cried:

"Fuji! Come and look at Fujiyama!" and I ran forward and gazed with straining eyes across the sea and the hilltops to where, shimmering white in the far-off sky, there hung—was it indeed the famous fan-shaped cone, or only a luminous patch of cloud? Or was it anything at all?

"Where's Fuji?"

"Right there. Don't you see?"

"No. Yes, now I think——"

"It's gone. No! There it is again!"

So must the chorus ever go. For Fuji, most beautiful of mountains, is also the most elusive. Later, in Tokyo, when some one called me to come and see it, it disappeared while I was on the way upstairs.

Splendid as Vesuvius appears when she floats in opalescent mist above the Bay of Naples with her smoke plume lowering above her, she is, by comparison with Fuji, but a tawny little ruffian. Vesuvius rises four thousand feet while Fuji stands three times as high. And although the top of Pike's Peak is higher than the sacred mountain of Japan by some two thousand feet, the former, starting from a plain one mile above sea-level, has an immense handicap, whereas the latter starts at "scratch." Thus it comes about that when you look at Pike's Peak from the plains what you actually see is a mountain rising nine thousand feet; whereas when you look at Fuji from the sea the whole of its twelve thousand and more feet is visible.

Aside from Fuji's size, the things which make it more beautiful than Vesuvius are the perfection of its contour, the snow upon its cone, and the atmospheric quality of Japan—that source of so much disappointment to snapshotting travellers who time their pictures as they would at home.

A Japanese friend on the ship told me that though Fuji had been quiescent for considerably longer than a century there was heat enough in some of its steaming fissures to permit eggs to be boiled. Eighteen or twenty thousand persons make the climb each year, he said, and some devout women of seventy years and over struggle slowly up the slope, taking a week or more to the ascent, which is made by able-bodied men in half a day or less.

Peasants of the region speak of Fuji not by name but merely as *O Yama*, "the Honourable Mountain," but my Japanese friend added that though the honorific *O*, used so much by his countrymen, was translated literally into English as "honourable," it did not have, in the Japanese ear, any such elaborate and ponderous value, but was spoken automatically and often only for the sake of cadence.

Peasants of the region speak of Fuji not by name but merely as *O Yama*, the "Honourable Mountain"

"We say *O* without thinking," he explained, "just as you begin with 'dear sir,' in writing to a stranger who is not dear to you at all."

For Fuji, however, I like the full English polysyllabic of respect. It is indeed an "honourable mountain." The great volcanic cone hanging, as it sometimes seems, in thin blue air, has an ethereal look suggesting purity and spirituality, so that it is not difficult for the beholder from another land to sense its quality of sacredness, and to perceive its fitness to be the abiding place of that beautiful goddess whose Japanese name means "Princess-who-makes-the-Blossoms-of-the-Trees-to-Flower."

"There are two kinds of fools," says a Japanese proverb: "—those who have never ascended Fuji and those who have ascended twice." To this category I would add a third kind of fool, the greatest of them all: the fool who fails to appreciate the spectacle of Fuji. A creature who would be disappointed in

Fuji would be disappointed in any spectacle, however grand—be it the Grand Cañon, the Grand Canal, or the Grand Central Station.

CHAPTER II

The satisfying thing about Japan is that it always looks exactly like Japan. It could not possibly be any other place. The gulls are Japanese gulls, the hills are Japanese hills, Tokyo Bay is a Japanese bay, and if the steamers anchored off the port of Yokohama are not all of them Japanese, many of them have, at least, an exotic look, with their preposterously fat red funnels or their slender blue ones. Even the little launches from which the port authorities board you as you lie in the harbour are not quite like the launches seen elsewhere, and though the great stone pier, to which at last you are warped in, might of itself fit the picture of a British seaport, the women and children waiting on the pier, trotting along beside the ship as she moves slowly to her berth, waving and smiling up at friends on deck, are costumed in inevitable suggestion of great brilliant flower-gardens agitated by the wind. Amongst these women and children in their bright draperies, the dingy European dress of the male is almost lost, so that, for all its pantaloons and derby hats, Japan is still Japan.

Through this garden of chattering, laughing, fluttering human flowers we made our way to—score one for New Japan—a limousine, and in this vehicle were whirled off through the crowd: a jumble of blue-clad coolies wearing wide mushroom hats and the insignia of their employers stamped upon their backs, of rickshas, and touring cars, and motor-trucks, and skirted schoolboys riding bicycles, and curious little drays with tiny wheels, drawn by shaggy little horses which are always led, and which, when left to stand, have their front legs roped. Over a bridge we went, above the peaked rice-straw awnings of countless wooden cargo boats; then up a narrow road, surfaced with brown sand, between rows of delightful little wooden houses, terraced one above the other, with fences of board or bamboo only partly concealing infinitesimal gardens, and sliding front doors of paper and wood-lattice, some of which, pushed back, revealed straw-matted floors within, with perhaps more flower-like women and children looking out at us—the women and the larger children having babies tied to their backs. By some of the doors stood pots containing dwarf trees or flowering shrubs, by others were hung light wooden birdcages from which a snatch of song would come, and in front of every door was a low flat stone on which stood rows of little wooden clogs. Dogs of breeds unknown to me sat placidly before their masters' doors—brown dogs to match the houses, black and white dogs, none of them very large, all of them plump and benignant in expression. Not one of them left its place to run and bark at our car. They were the politest dogs I have ever seen. They simply sat upon their haunches, smiling. And the women smiled, and the children smiled, and the cherry blossoms smiled from branches overhead, and the sun smiled through them, casting over the brown roadway and brown houses and brown people a lovely splattering of light and shadow.

And what with all these things, and a glimpse of a *torii* and a shrine, and the musical sound of scraping wooden clogs upon the pavement and the faint pervasive fragrance, suggesting blended odours of new pine wood, incense, and spice—which is to me the smell of Japan; though hostile critics will be quick to remind me of the odour of paddy fields—what with all these sights and sounds and smells, so alluring and antipodal, I began to think we must be motoring through a celestial suburb, toward the gates of Paradise itself.

But instead of climbing onward up the hill to heaven we swung off through a garden blooming with azaleas white, purple, pink, and salmon-colour, and drew up at a pleasant clubhouse. There we had luncheon; and it is worth remarking that, though prepared by Japanese, both the menu and the cooking were in faultless French. The Japanese gentlemen at this club were financiers, officials and prominent business men of Yokohama. One or two of them wore the graceful and dignified *hakama* and *haori*—the silk skirt and coat of formal native dress—but by far the larger number were habited in European style: some of the younger men in cutaways, but the majority in frock-coats, garments still widely favoured in Japan, as are also congress gaiter shoes—a most convenient style of footwear in a land where shoes are shed on entering a house.

Luncheon over, we drove to the station of the electric railroad that parallels the steam railroad from the seaport to the capital—which, by the way, will itself become a seaport when the proposed channel has been dredged up Tokyo Bay, now navigable only by small boats.

From the car window we continued our observations as we rushed along. The gage of the steam railway is narrower than that of railways in America and Europe; the locomotives resemble European locomotives and the cars are small and light by comparison with ours. The engine whistles are shrill, and instead of two men, three are carried in each cab. This we shall presently discover, is characteristic of Japan. They employ more people than we do on a given piece of work—a discovery rather surprising after all that we have heard of Japanese efficiency. But Japan's reputation for efficiency is after all based largely on her military exploits. Perhaps her army is efficient. Perhaps her navy is. Certainly the discipline and service on the *Kashima Maru* would bear comparison with those on a first-rate English ship. Yet why three men on a locomotive? Why several conductors on a street car? Why three servants in an ordinary middle-class home which in America or Europe would be run by one or two? Why fifteen servants in a house which we would run with six or eight? Why so many motor cars with an assistant sitting on the seat beside the chauffeur? Why so few motors? Why men and women drawing heavy carts that might so much better be drawn by horses or propelled by gasolene? Why these ill-paved narrow roads? Why this watering of streets with dippers or with little hand-carts pulled by men? Why a dozen or more coolies operating a hand-driven pile-driver, lifting the weight with ropes, when two men and a little steam would do the work so much faster and better? Why, for the matter of that, these delightful rickshas which some jester of an earlier age dubbed "pull-man" cars? Why this waste of labour everywhere?

Can it be that in this densely populated little country there are more willing hands than there is work for willing hands to do? Must work be spread thin in order to provide a task and a living for everyone? But again, if that was it, would people work as hard as these people seem to? Would women be at work beside their husbands, digging knee deep in the mud and water of the rice fields, dragging heavy-laden carts, handling bulky boats? And would the working hours be so long? Here is something to be looked into. But not now.

It is a hand-embroidered country, Japan, though the embroidery is done in fine stitches of an unfamiliar kind. The rural landscape is so formed and trimmed and cultivated that sometimes it achieves the look of a lovely little garden, just as the English landscape sometimes has the look of a great park. Here, much more than in England, every available inch of land is put to use. Where hillsides are so steep that they would wash away if not protected, tidy walls of diamond-shaped stone are laid dry against them; but whenever possible the hillsides are terraced up in a way to remind one of vineyards along the Rhine and the Moselle, making a series of shelf-like little fields, each doing its utmost to help solve the food problem.

It is hard to say whether the towns along this line of railroad are separated by groups of farms, or whether the groups of farms are separated by towns, so even is the division. The farms are very small so that the open country is dotted over with little houses—the same low dainty houses of wood and paper that delighted us when we first saw them, and which will always delight us when, from the other side of the world, we think of them. For there is something in the sight of a neat little Japanese house with its few feet of garden which appeals curiously to one's imagination and one's sentiment. It is all so light and lovely, yet all so carefully contrived, so highly finished. To the Western eye—at least to mine—it has a quality of fantasy. I feel that it cannot be quite real, and that the people who live in it cannot be quite real: that they are part—say a quarter—fairy. And I ask you: who but people having in their veins at least a little fairy blood would take the trouble to plant a row of iris along the ridges of their roofs?

The houses, too, are often set in elfin situations. One will stand at the crest of a little precipice with a minute table-land of garden back of it; another will nestle, half concealed, in a small sheltered basin where it seems to have grown from the ground, along with the trees and shrubbery surrounding it—the flowering hedges and the pines with branches like extended arms in drooping green kimono sleeves; still another rises at the border of a pond so small that in a land less toylike it would hardly be a pond; yet here it is adorned with grotesquely lovely rocks and overhanging leaves and blooms, and in the middle of it, like as not, will be an island hardly larger than a cartwheel, and on that island a stone lantern with a mushroom top, and reaching to it from the shore a delicate arched bridge of wood beneath which drowsy carp and goldfish cruise, with trading fins and rolling ruminative eyes.

Just as one better understands Hokusai and Hiroshige for having seen the coastal hills, one understands them better for having seen these magic little houses with their settings resembling so charmingly those miniature landscapes made with moss, gravel, small rocks, and dwarf trees, arranged in china basins by a Japanese gardener, who is sometimes so kind as to let us see his productions in a window on Fifth Avenue. Often one feels that Japan herself is hardly more than such a garden on a larger scale. Over and over again one encounters in the larger, the finish and fantastic beauty of the smaller garden. And when one does encounter it, one is happy to forget the politics and problems of Japan, and to think of the whole country as a curiously perfect table decoration for the parlour of the world.

And the children! Children everywhere! Children of the children Kipling wrote of thirty years ago, when he called Japan

"... the land of Little Children, where the Babies are the Kings."

With his drum and his monkey he is Japan's nearest equivalent for our old-style organ-grinder

Of course we had heard about the children. Everyone who writes about Japan, or comes home and talks about Japan, tells you about them. Yet somehow you must witness the phenomenon before you grasp the fact of their astonishing profusion. Even the statistics, showing that the population of Japan increases at the rate of from 400,000 to 700,000 every year, don't begin to make the picture, though they do make apparent the fact that there are several million children of ten years or younger—about two thirds of whom go clattering about in wooden clogs, while the remainder ride on the backs of their parents and grandparents and brothers and sisters. All in a country smaller than the State of California.

Children alone, children in groups of three or four, children in dozen lots. Children in all sizes, colourings, attitudes, and conditions. Children blocking the roads, playing under the trees or in them, romping along paths, swarming over little piles of earth like bees on bell-shaped hives. Children watching the passing cars, children in tiny skiffs, children wading in ponds. Children glimpsed through the open wood and paper *shoji* of their matchbox houses, scampering on clean matted floors or placidly supping—the larger of them squatting before trays and operating nimble chopsticks, the smaller nursing at the mother's breast. (Sometimes those children nursed at the breast are not so very small—which is the reason why so many Japanese have over-prominent teeth.) Children brown and naked, ragged children, children in indigo or in bright flowered kimonos and white aprons. Demure children, wild rampageous children, children with shaved heads, children with jet-black manes bobbing about their ears and faces as they run. Chubby children with merry eyes and cheeks like rosy russet apples. Children achieving the impossible: delighting the eye despite their dirty little noses.

Can it be that they pile the children on each others' backs, making two layers of them, because there isn't room upon the ground for all of them at once? Babies riding on their mothers' backs travel in comparative dignity and safety. Under their soft little mushroom hats they sleep through many things—street-car trips, shopping expeditions and gabbling parties in the tea-rooms of department stores. But those who ride the shoulders of their elder brothers lead lives of wild adventure. Their presence is not allowed to interfere with the progress of young masculine life. The brother will climb trees, walk on stilts and even play baseball, seemingly unconscious of the weight and the fragility of the little charge attached to him by ties of blood and cotton. If the drowsy baby head drops over, getting in the way, the brother alters its position with a bump from the back of his own head. When the small rider slips down too far, whether on the back of child or adult, its bearer stoops and bucks like a broncho, tossing baby into place again. Through all of which the infant generally sleeps. Are its dreams disturbed, one wonders, when big brother slides for second-base? I doubt it. Knowing no cradle, no easy-riding baby carriage, the Japanese baby is from the first accustomed to a life of action. It seems to be a fatalist. And indeed it would appear that some special god protects the baby, for it always seems to go unscathed.

Sometimes in the streets the children outnumber their elders by two or three to one. Contemplating them one can easily fall into the way of looking upon adults as mere adjuncts, existing only to wash the children, see that they wear aprons, and give them their meals.

CHAPTER III

Growing Tokyo—Architecture and Statuary—The Westernization of Japan—The Story of Costumes—Women's Dress Advantages of Standardized Styles—Selection and Rejection

As you reach the outskirts of Tokyo you think you are coming to another little town, but the town goes on and on, and finally as the train draws near the city's heart large buildings, bulking here and there above the general two-story tile roofline, inform you in some measure of the importance of the place. In 1917 Tokyo ranked fifth among the cities of the world, with a population almost equal to Berlin's, and it seems likely that when reliable statistics for the world become available again we shall find that the population of Berlin has at most remained stationary, while that of Tokyo has grown even more rapidly than usual, owing to exceptional industrial activity and to the influx of Russian refugees, whose presence in large numbers in Japan has created a housing problem. Nor shall I be surprised to hear that Tokyo has passed Chicago in the population race, becoming third city of the world.

The central railroad station exhibits the capital's modern architectural trend. It is conveniently arranged and impressive in its magnitude as seen across the open space on which it faces, but there its merit stops. Like most large foreign-style buildings in Japan, it is architecturally an ugly thing. Standing at the gate of Japan's chief city, it has about it nothing Japanese. Its façade is grandiose and meaningless, and as one turns one's back upon it and sees other large new public structures, one is saddened by the discovery that the Japanese, skilful at adaptation though they have often shown themselves, have signally failed to adapt the requirements, methods, and materials of modern building to their old national architectural lines. One thing is certain, however: there will be no new public buildings more unsightly than those already standing. This style of architecture in Japan has touched bottom.

In twenty years or so I believe the ugliness of these modern piles will have become apparent to the Japanese. It will dawn upon them that they need not go to Europe and America for architectural themes, but to the castle of Nagoya, the watch-towers above the moat of the Imperial Palace, the palace gates, and the temples and pagodas everywhere.

When this time comes the Japanese will also realize how very bad are most of the bronze statues of statesmen and military leaders throughout the world, and how particularly bad are their own adventures in this field of art.

Until I saw Tokyo I was under the impression that the world's worst bronzes were to be found in the region of the Mall in Central Park, New York; but there is in Tokyo a statue of a statesman in a frock coat, with a silk hat in his hand, which surpasses any other awfulness in bronze that I have ever seen.

Looking at such things one marvels that they can be created and tolerated in a land which has produced and still produces so much minute loveliness in pottery, ivory, and wood. How can these people, who still know flowing silken draperies, endure to see their heroes cast in Prince Albert coats and pantaloons? And how can they adopt the European style of statuary, when in so many places they have but to look at the roadside to see an ancient monument consisting of a single gigantic stone with unhewn edges and a flat face embellished only with an inscription—simple, dignified, impressive.

All nations, however, have their periods of innovation-worship, and if Japan has sometimes erred in her selections, her excuse is a good one. She did not take up Western ways because she wanted to. She wished to remain a hermit nation. She asked of the world nothing more than that it leave her alone. She even fired on foreign ships to drive them from her shores—which, far from accomplishing her purpose, only cost her a bombardment. Then, in 1853, came our Commodore Perry and, as we now politely phrase it, "knocked at Japan's door." To the Japanese this "knocking" backed by a fleet of "big black ships," had a loud and ominous sound. The more astute of their statesmen saw that the summons was not to be ignored. Japan must become a part of the world, and if she would save herself from the world's rapacity she must quickly learn to play the world's game. Fourteen years after Perry's visit the Shogunate, which for seven centuries had suppressed the Imperial family, and itself ruled the land, fell, and the late Emperor, now known as Meiji Tenno—meaning "Emperor of Enlightenment"—came from his former capital in the lovely old city of Kyoto, the Boston of Japan, and took up the reins of government in Yedo—later renamed Tokyo, or "Eastern Capital"—occupying the former Shogun's palace which is the Imperial residence to-day.

The Meiji Era will doubtless go down as the greatest of all eras in Japanese history, and as one of the greatest eras in the history of any nation. To Viscount Kaneko, who is in charge of the work of preparing the official record of the reign for publication, President Roosevelt wrote his opinion of what such a book should be.

"No other emperor in history," he declared, "saw his people pass through as extraordinary a transformation, and the account of the Emperor's part in this transformation, of his own life, of the public lives of his great statesmen who were his servants and of the people over whom he ruled, would be a work that would be a model for all time."

Under the Emperor Meiji, Japan made breathless haste to westernize herself, for she was determined to save herself from falling under foreign domination. Small wonder, then, if in her haste she snatched blindly at any innovation from abroad. Small wonder if she sometimes snatched the wrong thing. Small wonder if she sometimes does it to this day. For she is still a nation in a state of flux; you seem to feel her changing under your very feet.

But because Japan has accepted a thing it does not mean that she has accepted it for ever. In great affairs and small, her history illustrates this fact. A case in point is the story of European dress.

More than thirty years ago, when the craze for everything foreign was at its height, when the whole fabric of social life in the upper world was in process of radical change, European dress became fashionable not only for men but for women. When great ladies had worn it for a time their humbler sisters took it up, and one might have thought that the national costume, which is so charming, was destined entirely to disappear.

Men attached to government offices, banks, and institutions tending to the European style in the construction and equipment of their buildings, had some excuse for the change, since the fine silks of Japan do not wear so well as tough woollen fabrics, and the loose sleeves tend to catch on door-knobs and other projections not to be found in the Japanese style of building.

But in Japan more than in any other country, "woman's place is in the home," and just as the Japanese costume is not well suited to the European style of building, so the European costume is not well suited to the Japanese house and its customs. For in the Japanese house instead of sitting on a chair one squats upon a cushion, and corsets, stockings and tight skirts were not designed to squat in. Equally important, clogs and shoes are left outside the door of the Japanese house in winter and summer, and as in the winter the house is often very cold, having no cellar and only small braziers, called *hibachi*, to give warmth, the covering afforded the feet by the skirts of a Japanese costume is very comforting. Moreover, the Japanese themselves declare that European dress is not becoming to their women, being neither suited to their figures nor to the little pigeon-toed shuffle which is so fetching beneath the skirts of a kimono.

What was the result of all this?

The men who found foreign dress useful continued to wear it for business, although those who could afford to do so kept a Japanese wardrobe as well. But the women, to whom European dress was only an encumbrance, discarded it completely, so that to-day no sight is rarer in Japan than that of a Japanese woman dressed in other than the native costume.

If a Japanese lady be cursed with atrocious taste, there is practically no way to find it out, no matter how much money she may spend on personal adornment. The worst that she may do is to carry her clothes less prettily than other women of her class. The lines she cannot change. The fabrics are prescribed. The colours are restricted in accordance with her age. Her dress, like almost every other detail of her daily life, is regulated by a rigid code. If she be middle-aged and fat she cannot make herself absurd by dressing as a débutante. If she be thin she cannot wear an evening gown cut down in back to show a spinal column like a string of wooden beads. Nor can she spend a fortune upon earrings, bracelets, necklaces. She may have some pretty ornamental combs for her black lacquer hair, a bar pin for her *obi*, a watch, and perhaps, if she be very much Americanized, a ring and a mesh bag. A hairdresser she must have, both to accomplish that amazing and effective coif she wears, and to tell her all the latest gossip (for in Japan, as elsewhere, the hairdresser is famed as a medium for the transmission of spicy items which ought not to be transmitted); but her pocketbook is free from the assaults of milliners; hats she has none; only a draped hood when the cold weather comes.

The feminine costume is regulated by three things: first, by the age of the wearer; second, by the season; third, by the requirements of the occasion. The brightest colours are worn by children; the best kimonos of children of prosperous families are of silk in brilliant flowered patterns. Their pendant sleeves are very long. Young unmarried women also wear bright colours and sleeves a yard in length. But the young wife, though not denied the use of colour, uses it more sparingly and in shades relatively subdued; and the pocket-like pendants of her sleeves are but half the length of those of her younger unmarried sister. The older she grows the shorter the sleeve pendants become, and the darker and plainer grows her dress.

In hot weather a kimono of light silk, often white with a coloured pattern, is worn by well-dressed women. Beneath this there will be another light kimono which is considered underwear—though other underwear is worn beneath it. Japanese underwear is not at all like ours, but one notices that many gentlemen in the national costume adopt the Occidental flannel undershirt, wearing it beneath their silks when the weather is cold—a fact revealed by a glimpse of the useful but unlovely garment rising up into the V-shaped opening formed by the collar of the kimono where it folds over at the throat.

As with us, the temperature is not the thing that marks the time for changing from the attire of one season to that of another. Summer arrives on June first, whatever the weather may be. On that date the Tokyo policeman blossoms out in white trousers and a white cap, and on June fifteenth he confirms the arrival of summer by changing his blue coat for a white one. So with ladies of fashion. Their summer is from June first to September thirtieth; their autumn from October first to November thirtieth; their winter from December first to March thirty-first; their spring from April first to May thirty-first. In spring the brightest colours are worn. Those for autumn and winter are generally more subdued.

Young ladies wear brilliant kimonos for ceremonial dress, but ceremonial dress for married women consists of three kimonos, the outer one of black, though those beneath, revealed only where they show a V-shaped margin at the neck, may be of lighter coloured silk. On the exterior kimono the family crest—some emblem generally circular in form, such as a conventionalized flower or leaf design, about an inch in diameter—appears five times in white: on the breast at either side, on the back of either sleeve at a point near the elbow, and at the centre of the back, between the shoulder-blades. Because of these crests the goods from which the kimono is made have to be dyed to order, the crests being blocked out in wax on the original white silk so that the dye fails to penetrate. Even the under-kimonos of fashionable ladies will have crests made in this way.

With the kimono a Japanese lady always wears a neck-piece called an *eri* (pronounced "airy"), a long straight band revealed in a narrow V-shaped margin inside the neck of the inner kimono. The eri varies in colour, material, and design according to the wearer's age, the occasion and the season, and it may be remarked that embroidered or stencilled eri in bright colourings make attractive souvenirs to be brought home as gifts to ladies, who can wear them as belts or as bands for summer hats.

If the weather be cold the haori, an interlined silk coat hanging to the knees or a little below, is worn over the kimono. This is black, with crests, or of some solid colour, not too gay. A young lady's haori is sometimes made of flowered silk. Men also wear the haori, but the man's haori is always black; and while a man will wear a crested haori on the most formal occasions, a woman *en grande tenue* will avoid wearing hers whenever possible for the reason that it conceals all but a tiny portion of the article of raiment which is her chief pride: namely the sash or obi.

The best obi of a fashionable woman consists of a strip of heavy brocaded or hand-embroidered silk, folded lengthwise and sewn at the edges making a stiff double band about thirteen inches wide and three and one third yards long. This is wrapped twice around the waist and tied in a large flat knot in back, the mode of tying varying in accordance with the age of the wearer, and differing somewhat in divers localities. The average cost of a fine new obi is, I believe, about two hundred dollars, and I have heard of obi costing as much as a thousand dollars. Some of the less expensive ones are very pretty also, and many a poor woman will have as her chief treasure an obi worth forty or fifty dollars which she will wear only on great occasions, with her best silk kimono.

A Tokyo lady notable for the invariable loveliness of her costumes gives me the following information in response to an inquiry as to the cost of dressing.

"As our style never changes," she writes, "we don't have to buy new dresses every season, as our American sisters do. When a girl marries, her parents supply her, according to their means, with complete costumes for all seasons. Sometimes these sets will include several hundred kimonos, and they may cost anywhere from two thousand to twenty thousand yen. [A yen is about equal to half a dollar.]

"So if a girl is well fitted out she need not spend a great deal on dress after her marriage. A couple of hundred yen may represent her whole year's outlay for dress, though of course if she is rich and cares a great deal for dress, she may spend several thousand.

"Our fashions vary only in colour and such figures as may be displayed in the goods. Therefore they are not nearly so 'busy' as your fashions. And we can always rip a kimono to pieces, dye it, and make it over."

Some other items I get from this lady: When a Japanese girl is married it is customary for the bride's family to present obi to the ladies of the groom's family. For a funeral the entire costume including the obi, is black, save for the white crests. Ladies of the family of the deceased wear white silk kimonos without crests, and white silk obi. The Japanese ladies' costume, put on to the best advantage, is not so comfortable as it looks. It is fitted as tight as possible over the chest, to give a flat appearance, and is also bound tight at the waist to hold it in position. The obi, moreover, is very stiff, and to look well must also be tight.

The more select *geisha* are said to attain the greatest perfection of style; which probably means merely that, being professional entertainers whose sole business it is to please men, they make more of a study of dress, and spend more time before their mirrors than other women do.

The speed with which women reverted to the lovely kimono after their brief experiment with foreign fashions, may have been due in part to a lurking fear in Japanese male minds that along with the costume their women might adopt pernicious foreign ways, becoming aggressive and intractable, like American women who, according to the Japanese idea, are spoiled by their men—precisely as, according to our idea, Japanese men are spoiled by their women.

But whatever the reasons, the fact remains that the Japanese revealed good practical judgment. They kept what they needed and discarded the rest. It is their avowed purpose to follow this rule in all situations involving the acceptance or rejection of western innovations, their object being to preserve the national customs wherever these do not conflict with the requirements of the hideous urge we are pleased to term "modern progress." This is a good rule to follow, and if we but knew the story of the period when Chinese civilization was brought to Japan, nearly fourteen centuries ago, we might perhaps find interesting parallels between the two eras of change.

CHAPTER IV

Quakes and the Building Problem—Big Quakes—Democracy in Architecture—Narrow Streets and Tiny Shops—The Majestic Little Policeman—The Dread of Burglars—What to Do in a Quake—The Man Who Went Home—"Fire!"—A Ricksha Ride to the Wrong Address—A Front-Porch Bath

Have I given the impression that Tokyo is a disappointing city to one in search of things purely Japanese? If so it was because I tarried too long in the district of railroad stations and big business. Moreover, to the practical commercial eye, this portion of the city must look promising indeed, because of the wide streets and the new building going on. And it is building of a kind to be approved by the man of commerce, for in her new edifices Tokyo is adopting steel-frame construction.

That she is only now beginning to build in this way is not due to inertia, but to the fact that earthquakes complicate her building problem. The tallest of her present office buildings is, I believe, but seven stories high, and I have heard that twice as much steel was employed in its construction as would have been employed in a similar building where earthquakes did not enter into the calculations of the architect.

It would be difficult to overestimate the part that earthquakes play in establishing the character of Japanese cities. There will never be skyscrapers in Japan, or apartment buildings with families piled high in air. The family, not the individual, is the social unit of the land, and the private house is the symbol of the family. Even in the congested slums of Japanese cities, or in the quarters given over to the pitiful outcast class called *eta*, each family has its house, though the house may consist only of a single room no larger than a woodshed and may harbour an appalling number of people, as miserable and as crowded as those of the poorest slums in the United States.

Though the seismograph records an average of about four earthquakes a day, most of the shocks are too slight to be felt. Tokyo is however, conscious of about fifty shocks a year. But she has not had a destructive earthquake since 1894, nor a great disaster since 1855, when most of the city was shaken down or burned, and 100,000 persons perished.

Minor shocks receive but little attention. In fact by many they are regarded with favour, on the assumption that they tend to reduce pressure in the boiler-room, preventing savage visitations. However, these do occasionally occur and on the seacoast they are sometimes accompanied by tidal waves which ravage long stretches of shore, wiping out towns and villages.

Earthquake shocks are sometimes accompanied by terrifying subterranean sounds. Scientists have their ways of accounting for all these things, but the man who really knows is the old peasant of the seacoast village. He can tell you what really causes the earth to tremble. It is the wrigglings of a pair of giant fish called *Namazu*, whiskered creatures somewhat resembling catfish, which inhabit the bowels of the earth and support upon their backs the Islands of Japan.

Even though the quakes are slight, they serve to keep in people's minds certain unpleasant possibilities; and these possibilities are, as I have said, acknowledged in the structure of Japanese houses. Two stories is the maximum height for a residence, and even tea-houses and hotels are seldom more than three stories high. This, together with the fact that everyone who can afford it has a garden, causes Japanese cities to spread enormously.

On the other hand, the Japanese requires fewer rooms than we do; his home life is simple and he is less a slave to his possessions than any other civilized human being. The average family can move its household goods in a hand-cart. Even the houses of the rich are not blatant except in a few cases in which florid European architecture has been attempted. The difference between the houses of the rich and of the poor is in degree, not in kind. As with the Japanese costume, the essential lines do not vary.

The Japanese is not a slave to his possessions. The average family can move its household goods in a hand-cart

This democracy in architecture is restful to the eye and to the senses. It gives the streets of Tokyo—excepting the important thoroughfares—a sort of small-town look. Nor is a great metropolis suggested by the old narrow streets, with their bazaar-like open shop fronts, their banner-like awnings of blue and white, and their colourful displays of fish, fresh vegetables, fruits, wooden clogs, curios, and many other objects less definable, the possible uses of which entice the alien wayfarer to speculation or investigation.

I never got enough of prowling in the narrow streets of Tokyo, staring into shops (and sometimes, I fear, into houses), watching various artisans carrying on home industries, wondering what were the legends displayed in Chinese characters on awnings, banners and lacquered signs; stumbling now upon an ancient wayside shrine, now upon a shop full of "two-and-a-half-puff pipes," tobacco pouches for the male and female users of such pipes, and *netsuke* (large buttons for attaching pipe-cases and pouches to the sash) carved in delightfully fantastic forms; now upon a tea-shop full of tall coloured earthenware urns, shaped like the amphoræ of ancient Rome and marked with baffling black ideographs. Now I would discover a tea-house on the brink of a stream, its balconies abloom with little geisha, its portals protected from impurity by three small piles of salt; now it would be a geisha quarter I was in, and I would hear the drum and flute and *samisen*; or again I would discover a little shop with Japanese prints for sale, and would enter and drink green tea with the silk-robed proprietor, bagging the knees of my trousers and cramping my legs by squatting for an hour to look at his wares.

Heavy wheeled traffic was not contemplated when the narrow streets of Tokyo were laid out. From the most attenuated of them, automobiles and carriages are automatically excluded by their size, while from others they are excluded by the policeman who inhabits the white kiosk on the corner. The policeman has discretionary power, and if you have good reason for wishing to drive down a narrow street he will sometimes let you do so, granting the permission coldly. He is a majestic little figure. He wears a sword and is treated as a personage.

Naturally, the first consideration in the construction of a Japanese house is flexibility. In an earthquake a house should sway. Earthquakes are thus responsible for the general use of wood, which is in turn responsible for the frequency of fires. And next to earthquakes, fires are regarded by the Japanese as their greatest menace.

Third on the list of things feared and abhorred comes the burglar. I doubt that there are more burglars in Japan than elsewhere, or that the Japanese burglar is more murderous than the average gentleman of his profession in other lands, but for some reason he is more thought about. This may be because of the vicious knife he carries, or it may be because Japanese houses are so easy to get into. In the daytime one would only have to push a hand through the paper shoji and undo the catch—which is about as strong as a hairpin. At night one might need a cigar-box opener. At all events, it is for fear of burglars that the Japanese householder barricades himself, after dark, behind a layer of unperforated wooden shutters, which are slid into place in grooves outside those in which the shoji slide. If the shutters keep out burglars they also keep out air; and even though you may be willing to risk the entrance of the former with the latter, the police will not permit you to leave your shutters open—not if they catch you at it.

I made some inquiries as to the course to be pursued in the event of burglary, fire, or severe earthquakes.

In earthquakes people act differently. I asked our maid, Yuki, what she did, and found that, when in a foreign-style house, she would crouch beside a wardrobe or other heavy piece of furniture which she thought would protect her if the ceiling should come down.

"But what if the wardrobe should fall over on you?" I asked.

Yuki, however, was not planning for that kind of an earthquake.

In a Japanese house one need not worry about the ceiling, as it is of wood; and as a matter of fact most of the ceilings in foreign-style houses are of sheet metal.

It seems to me that the most intelligent thing to do in an earthquake is to stand in the arch of a doorway; certainly it is a bad plan to try to run out of the house, as many people, attempting that, have been killed by falling fragments.

One night I got a letter from a friend at home. "Try to be in a little earthquake," he wrote. "They build their houses for them, don't they?"

In the middle of that same night a little earthquake came, as though on invitation. The bed-springs swung; the doors and windows rattled.

At breakfast next morning I asked my hostess, an American lady who has lived most of her life in Japan, whether she had felt the tremor.

"I always feel them," she said. "They bother me more and more. In the last few years I have got into the habit of waking up a minute or two before the shocks begin."

"What do you do then?" I asked.

"I lie still," she said, "until the shaking stops. Then I wake my husband and scold him."

The husband of this lady told me of a man he knew, an American, who came out to Japan some years ago on business, intending to stay for a considerable time. On landing in Yokohama he went directly to the office of the company with which he was connected, and had hardly stepped in when the city was violently shaken.

By the time the shocks were over he had changed all his plans.

"Nothing could induce me to stay in a country where this sort of things goes on," he said. "I shall take the next boat back to San Francisco."

He did—and arrived just in time for the great San Francisco quake.

The course to take in case of fire is the same the world over. Shout "Fire!" in the language of the country and try to put the fire out.

But if you find a burglar in your room don't shout the Japanese word for "burglars," even if you know it—which I do not. The thing to shout is "Fire!"—so I am advised by a Japanese friend, who, I am sure, has my best interests at heart. For if you shout "Fire!" in the middle of the night, the neighbours, fearing that the fire will spread to their own houses, rush to your assistance; whereas if you cry "Burglars!" it merely gives them gooseflesh as they lie abed.

Many times it happened in Tokyo that when I was bound on a definite errand somewhere, the chauffeur or the ricksha coolie would land me miles from my intended destination. There are three reasons why this happened so often. First, Tokyo is a very difficult place in which to find one's way about. Second, addresses in Tokyo are not always given by street number, but by wards and districts, and there are tricks about some addresses, as, for instance, the fact that 22 Shiba Park isn't on Shiba Park at all, but is a block or two distant from the park's margin. And third, though the language in which I told the chauffeur or the *kurumaya* where to go, was offered in good faith as Japanese, it was nine times out of ten not Japanese, but a dead language—a language that was dead because I myself had murdered it.

In some other city I might have felt annoyance over being delivered at the wrong address. But in Tokyo I never really cared where I was going, I found it all so charming.

Once a kurumaya trotted with me for three hours around the city to reach a place he should have reached in one. I knew I would be hours late for my appointment. I knew I ought to fret. But did I? No! Because of all the things that I was seeing.

I saw the bean-curd man jogging along the street with a long rod over his shoulder, at each end of which was suspended a box of *tofu*, which he announced at intervals by a blast on a little brass horn: "Ta—ta: teeya; *tee-e-*

e—ta!" I saw a thicket of bamboo. I saw a diminutive farmhouse, with mud walls and a deep straw thatch, and in the doorway was a bent old white-haired woman seated at a wooden loom, weaving plaid silk. And behind the bamboo fence and the flowering hedge, stood a cherry tree in blossom.

It began to rain. In any other land I might have felt annoyance over so much rain as we were having. But not so in Japan. Japan could not look gloomy if it tried. Rain makes the landscape greener and the flowers fresher. It makes the coolies put on bristling capes of straw which shed the water as a bird's feathers do, and transform the wearer into a gigantic yellow porcupine. It makes the people leave off the little cotton shoes, called *tabi*, and go barefoot in their clogs. It makes them change their usual clogs for tall ones lifted up on four-inch stilts; and these as they scrape along the pavement give off a musical "clotch-clotch," which is sometimes curiously tuned in two keys, one for either foot. It brings out huge coloured Japanese umbrellas of bamboo and oiled paper, with black bull's-eyes at their centres, and a halo of little points around their outside edges. And as you go splashing by them with your kurumaya ringing his little bell, the women turn their great umbrellas sidewise, resting the margins of them in the road to keep their kimonos from being splattered. And even then they do not look at you severely. They understand that you can't help it. And are you not, moreover, that lordly creature, Man, whereas they are merely women?

All these things I saw while I was lost, that afternoon. Then, just when I might have begun to wonder if I was ever going to reach my destination, what did I see?

Under the eaves of a thatched house beside the way a bronze young mother and three children, all innocent of clothing and self-consciousness, preparing to get into a great wooden barrel of a bathtub. You never saw a sweeter family picture!... Yes, the Japanese are peculiarly a clean race. It is not merely hearsay. It is a front-porch fact.

The bath of the proletariat consists of a large barrel with a charcoal stove attached. Frequently it stands out of doors

Could any man lose patience with a kurumaya who can get him lost and make him like it?

CHAPTER V

Reversed Ideas—Some Advantages of Old Age—Morbidity and Suicide—High Necks and Long Skirts—Language—Chinese Characters and Kana—Calligraphy as a Fine Art—The Oriental Mind—False Hair—The Mystery of the Bamboo Screens—A Note on Cats at Cripple Creek—The Occidental Mind

On the day of my arrival in Japan I started a list of things which according to our ideas the Japanese do backwards—or which according to their ideas we do backwards. I suppose that every traveller in Japan has kept some such record. My list, beginning with the observation that their books commence at what we call the back, that the lines of type run down the page instead of across, and that "foot-notes" are printed at the top of the page, soon grew to considerable proportions. Almost every day I had been able to add an item or two, and every time I did so I found myself playing with the fancy that such contrarieties ought in some way to be associated with the fact that we stand foot-to-foot with the Japanese upon the globe.

The Japanese method of beckoning would, to us, signify "go away"; boats are beached stem foremost; horses are backed into their stalls; sawing and planing are accomplished with a pulling instead of a driving motion; keys turn in their locks in a reverse direction from that customary with us. In the Japanese game of *Go*, played on a sort of checkerboard, the pieces are placed not within the squares but over the points of linear intersection. During the day Japanese houses, with their sliding walls of wood and paper, are wide open, but at night they are enclosed with solid board shutters and people sleep practically without ventilation. At the door of a theatre or a restaurant the Japanese check their shoes instead of their hats; their sweets, if they come at all, are served early in the meal instead of toward the end; men do their *saké* drinking before rather than after the meal, and instead of icing the national beverage they heat it in a kettle. Action in the theatre is modelled not on life but on the movements of dolls in marionette shows, and in the classic *No* drama the possibility of showing emotion by facial expression is eliminated by the use of carved wooden masks.

Sawing and planing are accomplished with a pulling instead of a driving motion

Instead of slipping her thread through the eye of her needle a Japanese woman slips the eye of her needle over the point of her thread; she reckons her child one year old on the day it is born and two years old on the following New Year's Day. Thus, when an American child born on December thirty-first is counted one *day* old, a Japanese child born on the same day is counted two *years* old.

Once when I was dining at the house of a Japanese family who had resided for years in New York, their little daughter came into the room. Hearing her speaking English, I asked:

"How old are you?"

"Five and six," she answered. Then she added, by way of explanation, that five was her "American age" and six her "Japanese age."

Old age is accepted gracefully in Japan, and is, moreover, highly honoured. Often you will find men and women actually looking forward to their declining years, knowing that they will be kindly and respectfully treated and that their material needs will be looked after by their families. Old gentlemen and ladies are pleased at being called grandfather and grandmother—*o-ji-san* and *oba san*—by those who know them well, and elderly unmarried women like similarly to be called *oba san*—aunt. The same terms are also used in speaking to aged servants and peasants whom one does not know, but to whom one wishes to show amiability.

The duty of the younger to the older members of a family does not stop with near relatives, but includes remote ones, wherefore poorhouses have until quite recently been considered unnecessary.

It seems to me that one of the most striking differences between the two nations is revealed in the attitude of Japanese school and college boys. Instead of killing themselves at play—at football and in automobile accidents—as is the way of our student class, Japanese boys not infrequently undermine their health by overstudy, and now and then one hears that a student, having failed to pass his examinations, has thrown himself over the Falls of Kegon at Nikko. Undoubtedly there is a morbid strain in the Japanese nature. Translations of the works of unwholesome European authors have a large sale in Japan, and suicides are by no means confined to the student class. Poisoning, and plunging before an oncoming locomotive are favourite methods of self-destruction. Once when I was riding on an express train I felt the emergency brakes go on suddenly. A moment after we had stopped I saw a woman running rapidly away on a banked path between two flooded rice-fields with a couple of trainmen in pursuit. They caught her, but after a few minutes' agitated talk during which they shook her by the sleeves as though for emphasis, let her go. We were told that the engineman had seen her sitting on the track. Two or three days later I read in a newspaper that a woman had committed suicide beneath a train at about the place where I witnessed this episode. Her husband, the paper said, had deserted her. I suppose it was the same woman.

Another curious inversion is to be found in the Japanese point of view concerning woman's dress—and undress. I have been told that our style of evening gown, revealing shoulders, arms and ankles (to state the matter mildly), does not strike the Japanese as modest. Certainly the mandate of the Japanese Imperial Court is not the same as that of the French *modiste* (how curiously and inappropriately the word suggests our word "moddest"!) for whereas, at the time of writing, the latter decrees skirts of hardly more than knee length, the former decrees, for ladies being presented at court, skirts that touch the ground. Considering the foregoing facts it is, however, somewhat perplexing to the Occidental mind to find that men and women often dress and undress, in Japanese inns, with their bedroom shoji wide open, and that furthermore they meet in the bath without, apparently, the least embarrassment.

Like the English, the Japanese are persistent bathers, but whereas the English take cold baths the Japanese bathe in water so hot that we could hardly stand it. And when they have bathed they dry themselves with a small, damp towel, which they use as a sort of mop.

Also like the English they drive to the left of the road. There is much to be said for that, but some of their other customs of the road surprise one. Wherever they have not been "civilized" out of their native courtesy you will find that one chauffeur dislikes to overtake and pass another. Surely to an American this is an inversion! When a procession of automobiles is going along a road and one of them is for some reason required to stop, the cars which follow do not blow their horns and dash by in delight and a cloud of dust, but draw up behind the stationary car; and if it becomes necessary for them to go on, the chauffeurs who do so apologize for passing. This custom, which is dying out, comes, I fancy, from that of ricksha-men, who never overtake and pass each other on the road, but always fall in behind the slowest runner, getting their pace from him, protecting him against the complaints which his passenger would make if others were continually coming up behind and going by.

Of all differences, however, none is more pronounced than that of language. Instead of a simple alphabet like ours, the fairly educated Japanese must know two or three thousand Chinese ideographs, and a highly cultivated person will know several thousand more. To be sure, there is a simple way of writing by a phonetic system, not unlike shorthand, which is called *kana*. Every Japanese can read kana, which is sometimes also mastered by foreigners long resident in Japan. There are but forty-eight characters in kana, and as the characters have in themselves no meaning, but signify only a set of sounds, they can be used to write English names as well as Japanese words. My own name is written in kana characters having the following sounds: *Su-tō-rii-tō*—which being spoken in swift succession produce a sound not unlike "Street."

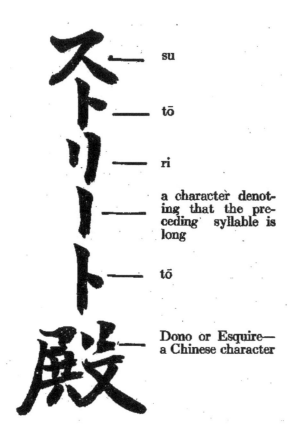

su

tō

ri

a character denoting that the preceding syllable is long

tō

Dono or Esquire—
a Chinese character

The Chinese ideographs used by the Japanese have the same forms as the characters used in China, but are pronounced in an entirely different way, so that the Japanese and Chinese can read each other's writing, yet cannot talk together. Books and newspapers published in Japan are printed in a mixture of Chinese characters and kana, and there is, moreover, beside each Chinese character in newspapers a tiny line of kana giving the sound of the word represented. In this way a reader of newspapers gets continual instruction in the written language and finally comes to know the most frequently used words from the ideographs, without referring to the kana interpretation. Thus there are actually two ways of reading a Japanese paper. A thoroughly educated man reads the ideographs, while a poorly educated one reads the kana, which gives him the sound of a word that he knows by ear, though he does not know it by sight when it is written in the classic character. These conditions, of course, eliminate the use of our sort of typewriter, though there is an extremely complicated and slow Japanese typewriter which is used chiefly where carbon copies are required. Also, they render the use of the linotype impracticable, and make hand-typesetting an extremely complicated trade. The difficulty of learning the Chinese characters, moreover, makes it necessary for students to remain in school and college several years longer than is the case with us. There is a movement on foot to Romanize the Japanese language, just as in this country there is a movement to adopt the metric system; but practical though such improvements would be in both cases, the realization of them is, I fear, far distant, because of the difficulties involved in making the change. And, indeed, from the standpoint of picturesqueness, I should be sorry to see the Chinese characters discarded, for they are fascinating not only in form but by reason of the very fact that we never, by any chance, know what they mean.

The Japanese write with a brush dipped in water and rubbed on a stick of India-ink; they seem to push the brush, writing with little jabs, instead of drawing it after the hand, even though they write down the column. Calligraphy is with them a fine art; and beautiful brushwork, such as we look for in a masterly painting, is a mark of cultivation. Because of their drilling with the brush almost all educated Japanese can draw pictures. Short poems and aphorisms written in large characters by famous men are mounted on gold mats and hung like paintings in the homes of those so fortunate as to possess them. A scription from the hand of General Count Nogi or Prince Ito would be treasured by a Japanese as we would treasure one from the hand of Lincoln or Roosevelt—possibly even more so, for where a letter from one of our great men has a sentimental and historical value, a piece of writing from one of their great men has these values plus the merit of being a work of art. Such bits of writing bring large prices when put up at auction, and forgeries are not uncommon.

In its structure the Japanese language is the antithesis of ours. Lafcadio Hearn declares that no adult Occidental can perfectly master it. "Could you learn all the words in the Japanese dictionary," he writes, "your acquisition would not help you in the least to make yourself understood in speaking, unless you learned also to think like a Japanese—that is to say, to think backward, to think upside down and inside out, to think in directions totally foreign to Aryan habit."

The simplest English sentence translated word for word into Japanese would be meaningless, and the simplest Japanese sentence, translated into English, equally so. To illustrate, I choose at random from my phrase book: "Please write the address in Japanese." The translation is given as: *Doka Nihon no moji de tokoro wo kaite kudasai.* But that sentence translated back into English, word for word, gives this result: "Of beseeching Japan of words with a place write please." And there is one word, *wo*, which is untranslatable, being a particle which, following the word *tokoro*, "a place," indicates it as the object of the verb.

I shall mention but one more inversion. The Japanese use no profanity. If they wish to be insulting or abusive they omit the customary honorifics from their speech, or else go to the opposite extreme, inserting honorifics in a manner so elaborate as to convey derision.

Numerous and curious though these reversals be, they are but the merest surface ripples upon the deep, dark, pool of Japanese thought and custom.

At first I did not quite grasp this fact. In my early days in Japan, when I was asking questions about everything, it sometimes looked to me as if the average Japanese was constitutionally unable to give a direct and simple answer to a direct and simple question, and my first impression was that this was due to some peculiarity of the far-famed Oriental Mind. But that impression soon changed—so much so that I am now disposed to doubt that such a thing as the Oriental Mind exists in Japan, if by that term is meant a mental fabric constitutionally different from that of Occidental peoples. That is to say, I believe the average Japanese child starts out in life with about the same intellectual potentialities as the average American, English, French or Italian child, and that differences which develop as the child grows older are not differences in mental texture, but only in the mental pattern produced by environment. My contention is not that Japanese brains are never imperfect or peculiar, but that their imperfections and peculiarities are precisely those found everywhere else in the world. And the same rule applies, of course, when one compares the great intellects of Japan with the great intellects of other nations. At bottom we are much more of a piece with the Japanese than either they or we generally suppose. The differences between us, aside from those of colour, size, and physiognomy, are almost entirely the result of our opposite training and customs and the effect of these upon our respective modes of thought. Neither nation has a corner on brains nor on the lack of them.

In a hotel in Kobe a lady of my acquaintance ordered orange juice for breakfast. The Japanese "boy"—waiters and stewards are all "boys" in the Far East—presently returned to say that there was no orange juice to be had that morning. But he added that he could bring oranges if she so desired.

The Oriental Mind? Not at all. The Orient has no monopoly of stupid waiters. The same thing might have happened in our own country or another. And that is the test we should apply to every incident which we are inclined to attribute to some basic mental difference between the Orientals and ourselves.

Granted the same background, could not this thing have happened in an Occidental country?

Never, in Japan, was I able to answer that test question with a final, confident "No."

Sometimes, however, I thought I was going to be able to.

One day on the Ginza, the chief shopping street of Tokyo, I saw a well-dressed young lady strolling along the walk with her long, beautiful hair hanging down her back, and false hair dangling from her hand. She was evidently returning from the hairdresser's where she had been for a shampoo. The situation, from my point of view, was precisely as if I had seen a similar spectacle on Fifth Avenue. But when I spoke about it to Yuki, who besides being our maid was our guide, philosopher, and friend, she assured me that the young lady was quite within the bounds of custom.

"We Japanese no think it shame to have false hair," she said.

Once I thought I had the Oriental Mind fairly cornered, and had I not later chanced to discover my mistake I should probably be thinking so still.

I was driving in an automobile with a Japanese gentleman, a director in a large pharmaceutical company. Parenthetically, I may say that he had been telling me how, when his company bought three hundred thousand *hectares* of land in Peru, for the purpose of raising plants from which some of their products are manufactured, the anti-Japanese press of the United States took up the story, falsely declaring that here was a great emigration scheme backed by the Japanese Government. But that is by the way.

Presently we came to a place where a large building was being erected. The framework was already standing and was surrounded by screens of split bamboo which were attached to the scaffolding. Having noticed other buildings similarly screened, I asked about the matter.

"Ah," said the gentleman, "the screens are to prevent the people on the streets from seeing what is going on inside."

"But what goes on inside that they ought not to see?" I asked, mystified.

My informant gazed at me gravely for a moment through his large round spectacles. Then he said, as it seemed to me cryptically: "It is not thought best for the people to see too much."

I pondered this answer for a moment, then noted it down in my little book, adding the memorandum: "The Oriental Mind!"

Doubtless I should now be making weird deductions from that brown-eyed gentleman's explanation of the screens, had I not chanced to mention the matter to another Japanese with whom I was more intimately acquainted.

"But that is not correct," he said, smiling. "The screens are not there to prevent people from seeing in, but to prevent things from falling on their heads as they pass by."

The bamboo screens, in other words, served precisely the protective purpose of the wooden sheds we erect over sidewalks before buildings in process of construction. The pharmaceutical gentleman did not know what they were for, just as we do not know the uses of a great many things we see daily on the streets of cities in which we live; he was anxious to be helpful to me; he did not wish to fail to answer any question I might ask him; so he guessed, and guessed wrong. But as any reporter can tell you, the practice of passing out the results of guessing in the guise of accurate information is by no means exclusively a Japanese practice. Reporters sometimes guess at things themselves, but that is not what I mean. I mean that a conscientious reporter now and then finds himself deceived by misinformation coming from some source he had supposed reliable.

In writing about American towns and cities I have more than once been so deceived. An old inhabitant of Colorado told me that the altitude of Cripple Creek was so great that cats could not live there. Later, however, I learned that cats can perfectly well live in Cripple Creek despite the altitude. Indeed some cats having but little regard for the character of their surroundings do live there. It is only the more critical cats who cannot stand the place.

Every American knows that he could be asked questions about his own country and its ways which he could not answer accurately offhand, but in a foreign land he expects every resident of that land to be able to explain anything and everything. I wonder if the Japanese expect as much of us when they question us.

"Why do you say 'Dear me!'?" I once heard a Japanese gentleman inquire of an American lady. And though the lady explained why she said "Dear me!" I doubt that the Japanese gentleman was able to understand. I know that I was not.

Another Japanese who had been in New York wished to know why we called a building in which there were no flowers "Madison Square *Garden*," and why ladies called a certain garment, once generally worn by them, a "petti*coat*," although it is distinctly not a coat, but a skirt.

My answers to these questions were, to put it mildly, vague, and I suppose my questioner said to himself as he listened to me:

"Ah, the Occidental Mind! How curiously it works!"

CHAPTER VI

Interlocking Ideas—Customs and Symbolism—Simplicity versus Complexity—Flower Arrangement—Teaism—The Egg-Shaped God—The Feudal Era—Ceremonial Tea—Household Decoration—Keys to Japan—The Seven Blind Men

When I had been several weeks in Japan, striving continually to gain some comprehension of the people and their ways, I began to feel a little bit discouraged. Never had I been so fascinated by a foreign land. Never in so short a time had I seen and heard so much that was new and strange and charming. Yet never had my observations been so fragmentary, so puzzling. My notebooks made me think of travelling-bags packed with unrelated articles of clothing. With the stockings belonging to one theme I had, as it were, packed the shoes of another. Here was a full dress coat; here a pair of overalls. Nothing was complete and no two things seemed to match. I could help to dress an army of ideas, but I wondered if I could fully clothe one.

I kept asking questions, but frequently the answers led me far afield, and were incomplete and unsatisfactory.

After a time, however, I began to understand why a Japanese so often fails to give a simple and direct answer to a simple and direct question about things Japanese. It is because, in many instances, no such answer is possible. Nor is this impossibility due to any mental kink in the Japanese of whom the question is asked. It is due to the fact that the thing asked about is not a simple, self-contained unit, but is a minute part of some great mass of thought or custom which must be in a general way understood before any single detail of it can be understood. It is as though you were to ask a question about a coloured pebble only to find yourself thereby involved with cosmos.

Japan is a land of customs. Her customs are based on principles which are rooted in traditions, which in turn frequently rest upon foundations of history, religion, superstition, or perhaps a mythology involving all three. Thus it often seems that every little word and act of a Japanese can be accounted for in some curious, complex yet essentially logical manner—that every thought in the Japanese mind has, so to speak, a genealogy, which, like the genealogy of the Japanese Imperial Family, reaches back into the mists of antiquity. Symbolism, moreover, plays an immense part in the daily life of Japan, and this fact enormously complicates matters for the foreigner who aspires to understand the country and the people. These are some of the reasons why in an article recently written for a magazine, I called Japan "The Isles of Complexities."

Yet when I mentioned the title of that article to an American friend who has lived for many years in Japan, he wrote me that he considered it a misnomer.

"I should call Japan 'The Isles of Simplicities,'" he declared, "just because life there is so different from life in our own artificial civilization. I am speaking particularly of our false modesty as compared with the more natural ideas of the Japanese concerning natural functions and unnatural emotions—or emotions unnaturally excited. If you will get down to fundamentals I think you will find that we are the complex people and they the simple people. Can you, for instance, project yourself into the mind of a Martian visiting this earth for the first time, taking a trip through the dance-halls, cabarets, and midnight frolics of New York and Chicago, then going to Japan and seeing the class of entertainment there provided for natives and foreigners alike? Let such an unprejudiced outsider watch the street scenes of Japan, note the frank customs of the people, including those revealed in the community baths, and I think he would say the Japanese are essentially simple as compared with us, that they are purer in thought and action, and (though I know I am inviting contradiction) that they have on the average a higher sense of real morality."

My friend makes out a good case and I agree with much that he says, but he is thinking along one line while I am thinking along another. He is thinking of the outward simplicities of Japanese life, while I am thinking of its inward complexities, especially with regard to the relation of one fact to another—I might almost say of every fact to every other fact.

Let me illustrate:

That grouping of flowers in a bamboo vase, which you find so satisfying, is not the result of any fancy of the moment, but is the product of an elaborate art, dating back at least five centuries. Flower Arrangement is a part of the curriculum of girls' schools and is one of the accomplishments of every lady. Hundreds of books have been written on the art and there are thousands of professional teachers of it. It has, you are informed, a philosophy of its own. Confucianism is invoked. The Universe is represented by three sprays of different height—an effect often found also in plantings in Japanese gardens. The tallest spray, standing in the middle, symbolizes Heaven; the shortest, Earth; the intermediate, Man. There may be five, seven or nine sprays, but the principle of Heaven, Earth and Man must be preserved. There must never be an even number of sprays, and four is a number to be avoided above all others, since *shi*, the Japanese word for "four", also means "death."

Significance likewise attaches to the species of blooms and branches used. The plum blossom, which is sent to brides, symbolizes purity, and also, because it flowers when snow is on the ground, stands for courage in adversity.

But just when you begin to flatter yourself that you have acquired some understanding of Flower Arrangement you meet some one who does not follow the tenets of the particular school of Flower Arrangement you have heard about—which, let us say, is the popular Ikenobo school—but believes in the teachings of the Enshiu school, the Koriu school, or the Nagéire—"thrown in"—school. Or perhaps he favours the kindred art called Morimono—"things-piled-up"—which deals with compositions of fruit and vegetables; or the Morihana school, which applies the "things-piled-up" principle to flowers; or that other kindred art which teaches the making of "tray landscapes"—pictures drawn on the flat surface of a tray in pebbles and various kinds of sand.

The essential point in all Flower Arrangement is that there shall be form and balance, yet that the composition shall not be perfectly symmetrical, as perfect symmetry is not found in nature. In order to attain the desired effects the flower-stalks and branches used are carefully bent and twisted, and this work is done with such delicacy and dexterity as to conceal the fact that their forms have been altered by artificial means. I have seen a Flower Master make waterlilies stand upright on their stalks by forcing water up through the stalks with a syringe. He then set them on one of those flat metal flower-holders we have lately been learning to use in this country, so arranging them in a shallow bowl that there was an open space between the stems, which he said was "for the fish to swim through"—though the fish was in this case purely a creature of his imagination.

Many methods of making flowers draw water are also taught. Especially in the case of chrysanthemums, the ends of the stalks are burned; the end of a hardwood branch is often crushed so that it admits water more freely; certain flowers are put in hot water; others are dipped in a solution of strong tea and pepper.

The origin of Flower Arrangement is traced by Okakura to a time when ancient Buddhist saints "gathered the flowers strewn by the storm and, in their infinite solicitude for all living things, placed them in vessels of water." We are told that Soami, a painter of the Ashikaga period, was an adept, and that Juko the Tea Master was his pupil. Flower Arrangement thus became a recognized art in the fifteenth century, albeit not an independent art, since it was at first a branch of Teaism.

Teaism? They tell you you cannot understand Flower Arrangement unless you also understand Teaism. What is Teaism?

Here is unfolded to you a further range for study. You knew, of course, that the first thing which happens when you pay a call in Japan, be it a business or social call, is the arrival of a cup of clear Japan tea, and that the second and third things which happen are the arrival of the second and third cups. You knew that the tea of Japan is green tea, and that it is taken without cream or sugar from cups having no handles. You knew, perhaps, that such tea is made with hot—*not* boiling—water. But were you aware that tea is in its highest sense not a beverage, but a creed, a ritual, a philosophy?

The discovery of the brew is said to have been made by the Chinese Emperor Chinnung, in the year 2737 B.C., but the mythology of Buddhism traces the creation of the tea-bush itself to the diverting god Daruma—that amusing egg-shaped fellow often represented in a child's toy which, when pushed over, persists in rolling back to an upright position, thereby symbolizing unflagging aspiration. "Down seven times—up eight times," the Japanese say of Daruma.

Having meditated day and night for weeks, Daruma fell asleep. On awakening he was so vexed with his drowsy eyelids that he cut them off and flung them to the ground, where they sprouted into plants from the leaves of which a sleep-destroying beverage might be made.

The seeds of the tea-plant were brought to Japan from China in the year 805 A.D., but the initiation of the habit of tea-drinking is generally dated from the time, about four centuries later, when the priest Eisai, of the Zen sect of Buddhists—a favourite sect among artists and tea-drinkers to this day—wrote a treatise on "The Salutary Influence of Tea-Drinking," which he presented, along with a cup of tea, to one of the early *shoguns*, who was ill. Thus tea was first taken as a medicine "to regulate the five viscera and expel evil spirits."

Not long after this we find the drinking of tea becoming a pastime of the nobility, and by degrees we see the development of aesthetic practices in connection with it. Art objects were displayed when people met for tea; sumptuous tea-parties were given by *daimyos*, and one writer tells us that there came a period of decadence in the Feudal Era when warriors would lay down the sword in favour of the teapot, and die cup in hand when their castles were taken by their enemies.

———————

Let me digress here to speak briefly of the Feudal Era, the most interesting era of Japanese history. It lasted from the twelfth to the middle of the nineteenth century—that is, throughout the period during which Japan was ruled not by its Emperors, but by several successive families of shoguns, or as for reasons given later they were sometimes called, *tycoons*. Though the shoguns usurped Imperial power it is a noteworthy fact that they did not usurp the throne itself nor attempt to destroy the Imperial family, but were content to keep the successive emperors in a state of impotence. Under the shoguns were the daimyos, powerful feudal lords acting in effect as provincial governors; and each daimyo had his *samurai*, or fighting men, holding rank in several grades. There was also a class of samurai known as *ronin* who acknowledged no lord as their master, but were independent fighters and trouble-makers. I give this outline because these various terms confused me at first. There was but one shogun at a time; the daimyos numbered between two and three hundred, and it has been estimated that there were some two million samurai. With a very few exceptions—among them rich farmers and swordmakers—no one below the rank of samurai could wear a sword. The sword-wearing class was the ruling class, and ordinary workers were regarded as of little consequence. A samurai could strike down with his sword any plebeian who jostled him by accident, or who as much as looked at him in a manner which he found distasteful.

The rank of samurai corresponded with that of knights in feudal Europe, and Japanese families who are descended from samurai are proud of the fact, precisely as some European families, and indeed some American families, are proud of having sprung from knightly forbears.

But to return to our tea. A Zen priest named Shuko is said to have originated the idea of associating with the habit of tea-drinking the cultivation of "the four virtues"—urbanity, purity, courtesy, and imperturbability—and this conception, originating about the middle of the fifteenth century, is to this day a tradition of the Tea Ceremony, or *cha-no-yu*.

The great soldiers Nobunaga and Hideyoshi, chief figures of the latter half of the sixteenth century, were addicts of the Tea Ceremony. It was Hideyoshi who caused the Tea Master, Sen-no-Rikyu, to consider the various schools of Ceremonial Tea which had developed, and codify them.

The keynote of the ceremony prescribed by Sen-no-Rikyu was "simplicity" of a most elaborate kind. There must be a special teahouse in the garden—though in recent times a special tearoom in the house is considered adequate. The teahouse was required to be small. Its exact dimensions were given, down even to the height of the doorway, which was so low as to compel guests to enter with bowed heads. The house must be simple in the extreme, yet built of the choicest woods. The character of the tea equipment was specified, as was the nature of the decorations.

This was where Flower Arrangement originally came in. A *kakemono*—one of those Oriental paintings mounted on a vertical panel of silk arranged to roll up on a cylindrical piece of wood and ivory attached to its lower margin—must hang in the shallow alcove which is the place of honour in every Japanese room; and beneath the kakemono must be displayed an object of art or an arrangement of flowers having a certain relationship to the painting.

For example, if the painting be that of a lion the suitable flower to be displayed beneath it is the peony, because the lion is the king of beasts and the peony the king of flowers. This is merely one simple instance of an artistic association of ideas, infinite in number and sometimes complicated in character. Yet these decorative affinities are understood not only by the highly educated Japanese, but by a large proportion of the people—for the feeling for art is, I believe, distributed more widely amongst the people of Japan than amongst those of any other nation. The Japanese do not jam their homes with furniture and decorations as we so often do, but exhibit their art treasures a few at a time, keeping most of them put away. It is said that Japanese rooms look bare to the average foreigner. To me, however, their rooms do not look bare, but have an air of exquisite refinement seldom found in an American or English room.

Some Americans who have learned to appreciate the Japanese idea of decoration, and who imitate it superficially, nevertheless achieve assemblages of art objects which, because of the lack of relationship between them, offend the trained Japanese eye precisely as a discord offends a trained musical ear. As Chamberlain points out, the Japanese have few mere "patterns." They don't make "fancy figures" merely for the sake of covering up a surface. Their decoration means something—as indeed decoration has in its highest periods in all countries.

There have been many Tea Masters since Sen-no-Rikyu, and the names of not a few of them are remembered to this day with veneration. The chief treasure of a friend of mine in Tokyo is a little teahouse, standing in his garden, which belonged some three hundred years ago to Kobori-Enshiu, Tea Master to the third Tokugawa shogun. If you would know how such associations are valued in Japan, go to an auction when some piece of Ceremonial Tea equipment, once the property of a famous Tea Master, is coming up for sale.

Ceremonial Tea has practically nothing to do with ordinary tea-drinking. The very tea used for the purpose is not like other tea. It comes in the form of fine green powder which is placed in a special sort of bowl in a special sort of way, whereafter water of exactly the right temperature and quantity is added, and the mixture is whipped to a creamy froth with a tiny bamboo brush, manipulated in a special manner. Great stress is laid upon the frame of mind brought into the tearoom, as well as on the etiquette and technique governing every detail connected with the making and drinking of the tea. The bowl is passed and received according to exact rules, and there is profound bowing back and forth. First it circulates as a loving-cup amongst the guests; later a special bowl is served to each in turn. On accepting the bowl the guest revolves it gently in both hands; then with as much of the calm dignity of a Zen Buddhist as he is able to exhibit, he raises it and takes a large sip. Removing the bowl from his lips he pauses meditatively; then repeats the process. Etiquette demands that when three large sips have been taken there shall remain in the bowl enough tea to make a small sip. In disposing of this final draught great gusto must be shown. The head is thrown back in indication of eagerness to drain the last drop, and the tea is drawn into the mouth with a sucking sound which advertises the delight of the drinker.

Nor is the potency of Ceremonial Tea diminished by the fact that it is served by a lovely little Japanese hand

The second night afterward he may be able to sleep. Ceremonial Tea is potent. Nor is its potency diminished by the fact that the hand which makes and serves it is a characteristically exquisite little Japanese hand, set off by the long soft sleeve of a flowered silk kimono.

Obviously you cannot understand Japan without understanding the Japanese woman—the nation's crowning glory. But as Lafcadio Hearn tells you, she is not to be understood without an understanding of the organization of Japanese society, which in turn, is not to be understood without a comprehension of Shintoism, the State religion.

You cannot understand Japan without understanding the Japanese woman, who is the nation's crowning glory

Everyone has a prescription for understanding Japan. One friend told me I could never understand it until I had grasped the attitude of the people toward the Imperial House. But that is only another way of saying that Shintoism must be understood. Many, naturally, speak of Buddhism. Others mention the feudal system, with its clan loyalty, as the touchstone, and still others assured me that a knowledge of the Tea Ceremony and the No drama were essential.

"Fujiyama is the key-note of Japan," wrote Kipling. "When you understand the one you are in position to learn something about the other." Sir Charles Eliot, long before he became British Ambassador at Tokyo, wrote that it is hopeless to attempt to understand Japan without first recognizing "the peculiar spirituality of the Japanese"; but there are not wanting others to deny the existence of any such spirituality as Sir Charles describes, and who, instead, harp upon the alleged Prussianism of Japan as explaining everything.

Doctor Nitobé, the gifted Japanese author, who, like Okakura, writes delightfully in English, gives us as the key to Japan the doctrine of *bushido*, or "military knight ways"; but again there are students of Japan who affirm that the system of practical ethics attributed by the doctor's patriotic pen to the samurai of old, would astound those doughty warriors could they hear of it. The book "Bushido," declare these critics, is less a key to Japan than to Doctor Nitobé.

Is not the interdependence of facts, of which I spoke earlier, illustrated in the trend of this chapter, all of which, remember, grew out of a discussion of a bunch of flowers in a bamboo vase? Do you see why I called Japan "The Isles of Complexities"? And do you see that I might also call it "The Isles of Contradictions"?

Perhaps you will not be surprised, then, at my confession that after having spent several weeks in Japan I found myself fascinated but also puzzled. Why, I asked myself, had I so gaily set forth under an agreement to write about Japan? Why hadn't I made it a mere pleasure trip? For it is one thing to see and be satisfied with seeing, and quite another to attempt interpretation.

It has often been said that if a man stays in Japan six or eight weeks he can write a book about it; that if he stays a year or two he may write a single article for a magazine; but that if he stays several years he will be afraid to write at all.

"To get the Japanese background," one friend told me, "you ought to have a month or two in Korea, and at least a year in China. Then you should come back and rent a house and live in Japanese fashion for a while."

"Say about two hundred years?" I suggested.

My friend smiled.

"One hundred and fifty years might do," he said, "if you made every minute count."

Then, perhaps because he read in my face the signs of my discouragement, he reminded me of an old fable:

> Seven blind men went to "see" an elephant. One of them, bumping into the great beast's side, said, "Here is a creature resembling a wall." Another, feeling the trunk, likened the elephant to a serpent; another, touching a tusk, announced that the animal resembled a spear; and still another, grasping an ear, compared the elephant to a large leaf. The one who

got hold of the tail likened it to a rope, while he who embraced a leg thought of a tree, and he who crawled over the back declared that an elephant resembled a hill.

There in a paragraph you have Japan and her interpreters.

PART II

CHAPTER VII

The Lyric Impulse—A Man-Made Product—The Remoteness of Woman Suffrage—Efforts Toward Progress—Divorce—Marriage and the Go-Between—The Rising Generation—Japanese-American Duality—Leprosy

Lafcadio Hearn tells us that training in the Tea Ceremony "is held to be a training in politeness, in self-control, in delicacy—a discipline in deportment"; but Jakichi Inouye, a searching and sincere Japanese writer, goes even further, declaring that "the calm, sedate gracefulness of the Japanese lady of culture is the result of the study of the Tea Ceremony...."

My one quarrel with Mr. Inouye is over that statement. To say that the study of the Tea Ceremony assists young ladies to attain poise is safe enough; but to say that the fine bearing of the Japanese lady is *the result* of studying the Tea Ceremony seems to me to be going altogether too far.

The bearing of the Japanese lady is a thing too exquisite to have been produced by the practice of any artificial social ritual. Such a bearing is not, in my opinion, to be classed as a mere accomplishment, though it may have been so a thousand years ago. Rather it is the reflection of an incomparably lovely spirit, the flower of countless generations of such spirits, reaching back through ages of tradition, centuries of self-abnegation. It is the crowning product and proof, not of any Tea Ceremony, but of the disciplined civilization of Old Japan.

Whenever I find my thoughts reverting to the Japanese woman, I feel stirring within me a tendency to lyricism. Let Lafcadio Hearn, whose wife was a Japanese lady, speak for me. "Before this ethical creation," he writes, "criticism should hold its breath; for there is here no single fault save the fault of a moral charm unsuited to any world of selfishness and struggle.... Perhaps no such type of woman will appear again in this world for a hundred thousand years: the conditions of industrial civilization will not admit of her existence."

The fact that the Japanese woman is in no small degree a man-made product does not fill me with admiration for Japanese men, as would some insentient product of their art. For whereas the artist has a right to carve what he will in wood or ivory or lacquer, to mould what he will in wax or clay or bronze, I doubt his moral right to use the human soul as a medium for his craftsmanship in making an ornament for his own home, however exquisite that ornament may be.

I am well aware that in this case the end may be said to justify the means, but I am enough of an individualist to believe in our American system, even though I must admit that it has not produced so sweet and delicate an average of womanhood as has the Japanese system. Women as we produce them exhibit a much wider range of types than may be found in Japan, and though a vulgar American woman, be she rich or poor, attains a degree of vulgarity such as is not even faintly approximated in Japan, we also know that we produce types of women as fine as the world can show. And while I cannot speak with absolute certainty of the intellectual attainments of Japanese women, I am inclined to think that our more liberal attitude toward the sex, the greater freedom of companionship between American women and men, and the growth of the American woman's interest and share in public matters may tend to make her, at her best, a more completely satisfying comrade—not because her brains are necessarily better brains than those of the women of Japan, or of other countries, but because she has been encouraged to exercise them in a larger way.

From my point of view, however, the basic question here is not the question of which system produces the highest specimens of womanhood, but that of the inherent right of the individual to develop, let the results be what they may.

The Japanese woman is not allowed this freedom, since it is obviously to the interest of the Japanese man to keep her as she is. Lately there has been some agitation in Japan for what is called "universal suffrage," but it must not be supposed that by that term woman suffrage is meant. The proposal involves only the extension of the ballot to all males, as against the present system which requires that a man shall pay taxes above a certain amount in order to have a vote. Woman suffrage is not even in sight. When I was in Japan a few progressive women were asking, not for the vote, but for the abrogation of the rule which denied their sex the right to attend political meetings. They were successful. The rule was recently abrogated. A movement had also been started by some advanced women led by Mrs. Raicho Hiratsuka, for laws compelling men who wish to marry to obtain medical certificates declaring them mentally sound and free from diseases of a kind likely to be communicated to a wife. I heard that seventy out of three hundred girls employed by the railway administration in Kyoto had organized an association to aid in the advancement of the measures proposed, vowing never to marry unless their would-be husbands complied with the requirements for which Mrs. Raicho Hiratsuka and her associates were endeavouring to obtain legal recognition.

Another matter that wants mending is the legal status of married women. So far as I know there has been made no serious effort to improve the present situation. Under Japanese law a woman, upon contracting marriage, is debarred from civil rights, having practically the standing of a minor. A wife cannot transfer her own real estate, bring an action at law, or even accept or reject a legacy or a gift, without the consent of her husband. Laws not dissimilar to these exist, I believe, in some of the more backward states of our own Union. According to the law of Japan a widow cannot succeed her husband as head of the family if she has a child who can take the succession. In matters of inheritance an elder sister gives place to a younger son, even to an illegitimate son recognized by the father.

A husband may divorce a wife for adultery, but a wife cannot divorce a husband for this cause—or rather, she can do so only when he has offended with a married woman whose husband has therefore brought action for divorce. Thus it will be seen that a husband may even take a concubine to live in his home, along with his wife and children, without giving ground for divorce. Concubinage, I am told, is still to some extent practised in Japan, though popular opinion is against it. In one respect, however, the Japanese divorce laws are more enlightened than our own. A husband and a wife who agree in desiring a divorce may easily obtain it by stating the fact to the court.

Somehow or other I came to the subject of divorce before that of marriage. The Orient and the Occident are nowhere farther apart than in their views and customs as to the mating of men and women. In Japan marriages for love rarely occur, though it is said that the tendency of young people to marry to suit themselves is growing. Young Japanese girls, I am told, often look with envy upon women of other nations, where marriage for love is the general rule. Probably they suppose that such matches are invariably happy; that the love is always real love, and that it endures for ever. No doubt our system, viewed from afar, looks as rosy to a Japanese girl as their system looks appalling to an American girl. Yet each has certain merits. The Japanese system does not suggest romance, it is true; but is romance, after all, the most essential stone in the foundation for a happy married life? Romantic notions figure too largely in some of our matches, and too little in some of theirs. And while the mature judgment of older people is with them the determining factor in the making of a match, it is too often with us no factor at all.

Marriages in Japan are generally brought about by older married couples who act as go-betweens. There is a popular saying that everyone should act as a go-between at least three times. The go-between, knowing a young man and a young woman whom he regards as suitable to each other, proposes the match confidentially to the parents of both. If preliminary reports are mutually satisfactory to the two families, a meeting of the young couple and their parents and relatives is arranged on neutral ground. Any intimation of the real purpose of this meeting is tactfully avoided at the time, though the purpose of it is, of course, fully understood by all concerned. Under this arrangement either family may, without giving offence, drop the matter after the first meeting, but if the results of the preliminary inspection are satisfactory to both sides, the parents meet again and definitely arrange the match, which is made binding by an exchange of presents.

Chamberlain says that while, in theory, the betrothal may not be concluded if either young person objects, in practice the two are in the hands of their parents, and that "the girl, in particular, is nobody in the matter."

This generalization was doubtless accurate a few years ago, and may be accurate to-day in remote parts of Japan where Western ideas have not crept in, but among the educated classes in large cities a distinct change has come over the rising generation. There is as great a gap between the older and the younger generations in Japan as in the United States, and as with us, the older people over there complain that youth is getting altogether out of hand, while youth complains that its aspirations are not understood by parents and grandparents. This does not mean that Japanese young men and young women run practically wild, as so many of our young people now are doing, but merely that the slight personal freedom they are demanding represents in Japan as great a novelty as is exhibited in the United States by the change from moderate parental control to no control at all.

Yet the cults and traditions of Old Japan are vastly powerful, and though they may yield a little here and there, they will not soon be broken down. This fact is made apparent in the quick reversion to type of Japanese men and women who have lived for years in the United States, and who, when in the United States, seem to have become quite like Americans. Meet them in Japan and you see that their Occidentalism was only skin-deep. While among us they gracefully adapted themselves to our ways, and doubtless enjoyed them, but always in the back of their minds was the knowledge that they were Japanese and that they would ultimately return to Japan, there to become a part of the finely adjusted mechanism of Japanese homogeneity. I know many such men and women and find them very interesting. They have passed through an extraordinary mental and spiritual experience, generally without being confused by it. Instead of mixing their Japanese and American selves, they acquire a perfect duality. They can sit on either side of the fence, as it were, and look over calmly and interpretatively at the other side.

I discussed this subject with one young matron who spent the first twenty years of her life in the United States, and who, when she moved to Japan, spoke her native tongue with an American accent.

"My brothers and sisters and I went to American boarding schools," she said. "We dressed like Americans, had American boy and girl friends, went to house-parties, and grew up outwardly, just as they were growing up. But always we were taught by our parents to understand that this was not to go on for ever.

"When I came to Japan and married I saw that the best thing to do was to show people that I was as Japanese as any of them. If I had kept up my foreign ways it would have been resented. So I became completely Japanese, and for a number of years did not even meet Americans who came here. Then when I had made clear my attitude and felt I was established, I began to see Americans again and entertain them."

In another case a young Japanese in an American university used to tell his college friends that when he went back to Japan he would show his emancipation from old Japanese tradition by marrying as he pleased. Soon after reaching home, however, he was married by his parents to a bride he hardly knew. He speaks fluent English, I am told, and has an American side which he can show at will, but the inner man is essentially as Japanese as though he had never been away. And rightly so, of course. The Japanese who throws himself as an impediment against the movement of the great machine of national conventions is not likely to break so much as a single tooth in the smallest of its wheels, but will surely break himself.

But to return to the subject of marriages:

Having arranged the match, the go-between naturally takes pride in its success. He befriends the young couple; if they are unhappy he mediates between them, endeavouring to settle their difficulties; and if their unhappiness continues, and divorce is spoken of, it becomes his duty to exhaust every resource to prevent their acting rashly.

Before arranging the match, however, the go-between takes precautions to provide against such dangers as may be foreseen. He must, for example, make discreet investigations as to the health of both families for several generations back, to insure against hereditary taints, among which the most dreaded is leprosy.

The Japan Year Book, in most cases a useful reference work, is curiously silent on the subject of leprosy, though several pages are devoted to tuberculosis and other diseases. It was reported recently that a million Japanese have tuberculosis, but leprosy, though less contagious and consequently much less frequent, is more feared. An authority has told me that there are probably two million lepers in the world and that the only countries free from the disease are England and Scotland, from which it has been eradicated by segregation. It is estimated that New York City has one hundred lepers, and that there are cases of it in most, if not all states in the Union. Yet according to the government report only three states—California, Louisiana, and Massachusetts—make provision for the segregation and care of sufferers from this most terrible of diseases. Some people give the number of lepers in Japan as under twenty thousand. The Home Office sets the figure at sixty-four thousand. Specialists, however, say that even the latter figure is far too low, and that the actual number is nearer one hundred thousand.

The first leprosarium in Japan was started twenty-eight years ago by Roman Catholic missionaries. A few years later a second leper hospital was founded by Miss H. Riddell, an Englishwoman who has been probably the greatest single influence in bettering conditions for the Japanese lepers. Miss Riddell's leprosarium at Kumamoto, south Japan, was, I believe, used by the Japanese Government as a model for the State leprosariums of which there are now five. Other such institutions are operated by missionaries and private individuals, but the work must be greatly extended if it is hoped to check the spread of the disease, to say nothing of stamping it out.

A Japanese friend of mine who has frequently acted as go-between in arranging matches for employees of a large company of which he is an official, tells me that girls in families tainted with leprosy are often exceptionally beautiful, and that they frequently have very white skins. In certain parts of Japan where leprosy is common there are, he tells me, rich families having beautiful daughters for whom it is impossible to find husbands in the neighbourhood because of rumours that the dread disease is in their blood. Such families occasionally move to the great cities where they seek to find husbands for their daughters through matrimonial agents or by personal advertisements in newspapers. The custom of advertising for a husband or a wife has of late years grown considerably, and as has happened in this country, rascalities are sometimes discovered behind such advertisements, wherefore the police keep an eye on matrimonial agencies.

One reason why accurate statistics on leprosy are hard to get, not only in Japan, but in all countries, is that families in which a case occurs will often go to great lengths to conceal it. In Japan this is particularly true because there a leper cannot marry, and leprosy is cause for divorce not only in the case of the individual actually afflicted, but in that of the victim's blood relations including those as far removed as second cousins.

No wonder the go-between feels a sense of responsibility!

CHAPTER VIII

Wedding Gifts—A Wife's Duties—Adopted Son-Husbands—Women in Business and Professional Life—Actresses—The "New Woman"—Kissing as a Business Custom—Film Censorship—"Oi, Kora!"—Women of Old Japan—The Change is Coming

Though the Japanese system of arranged marriages is sometimes likened to the French system, the two are quite different. In France the great point is the bride's dowry, but the Japanese bride is not necessarily expected to bring a dowry of money. Her wedding present from her parents consists as a rule of furniture and clothing which they give according to their purse.

The ceremonies connected with a Japanese wedding are extremely interesting, but are too elaborate to be gone into here. There is no wedding trip. The bride moves at once to the home of her husband's parents, unless she has married a younger son sufficiently prosperous and enterprising to set up a home of his own. The rule is that the eldest son continues to live under the parental roof after his marriage. Along with her name and residence the bride transfers her allegiance absolutely to the husband's family. Particular stress is laid upon her duty to her husband's mother.

This fact is recognized in a textbook issued by the Imperial Department of Education for use in the higher girls' schools, which says:

> Absence of harmony is often witnessed between a husband's mother and her daughter-in-law, and this is often traceable to the latter's disobedience and undutifulness. The mother-in-law may be too conservative to get on smoothly with the young daughter-in-law trained in new ideas, but dutifulness, patience, and sincerity on the latter's part will bring on peace and harmony.... If, on the contrary, the daughter-in-law, while tolerant of her own weaknesses, is critical toward her husband's mother and complains of her heartlessness, she will only betray her own unworthiness. These points should always be kept in mind by young girls.

Young Japanese heiresses are doubly fortunate since their affluence provides, among other comforts, a means of escaping the dreaded mother-in-law. Instead of moving to her husband's home, an heiress will often bring her husband to the shelter of her own paternal roof, where by adoption he becomes a son of her family, taking the family name. One hears that the bed of roses sought by some of these *muko-yoshi*, or adopted son-husbands, does not prove always to be free from thorns, and there is a Japanese proverb which advises: "If you have left so much as a pound of bad rice, don't become a muko-yoshi." The muko-yoshi is not, however, always married to an heiress. Poor families having daughters, but no sons, will often take in a muko-yoshi to perpetuate the family line under the ancestral roof.

A laundry on the river's brim

When all is said, there is no question that the condition of Japanese women is slowly improving, although the woman movement there is still in the academic stage. Little by little the example of women in America and England is making itself felt, and the educational opportunities open to women are gradually increasing. The average college for women is not, to be sure, comparable with the ordinary college for men, but there is said to be one university of really high standing which is open to women, and a number of other co-educational institutions are listed as fairly good. Waseda College is now opening its doors for the first time to women as well as men, and though women cannot graduate from Tokyo Imperial University, I am informed that they are permitted to attend lectures there.

Women are going more and more into business and professional life. Great numbers of them are now employed in the government postal and railway offices, in the offices of prefectures and municipalities, and, of course, in the telephone service, as well as by private companies of all kinds. Employers report steady improvement in the standard of intelligence and capability among their woman employees. Women, they say, do their work well and are usually content with small salaries. In seeking positions they generally declare that they wish to occupy themselves profitably between the time of leaving high school and that of marrying.

Eliminating, for the time being, the geisha, who because of her curious occupation will be separately discussed, and who does not in any case fit into a discussion of woman's progress, since she is in some measure a barrier to it, we find that the medical profession is probably the most profitable field for woman workers. There are some seven or eight hundred woman doctors in Japan, of whom almost half are graduates of the Tokyo School for Women, founded by a woman physician, Dr. Y. Yoshioka.

Trained nursing is also a popular occupation, and many girls have lately been leaving office and telephone work to take it up, chiefly for the reason that trained nurses receive from $1 to $1.25 per day, which is considered good pay.

Until ten or a dozen years ago there were no actresses in Japan, female rôles invariably having been played by men, but the octogenarian Baron Shibusawa (lately created Viscount), who has done so much toward liberalizing the thought of Japan in many lines, founded a school for actresses, with the result that there is now a place for them, and that a few have come to be well known, although none is as yet so popular as are the best-known actors. Actors hold in Japan a social position similar to that held by Occidental players a century or more ago. They are distinctly a lower caste, and while they are admired for their art, and are adored by young girls as matinée idols are with us, they are considered as belonging to a social stratum in which geisha and wrestlers figure.

There are now perhaps a dozen or more women working as reporters and special writers on the various Tokyo newspapers. Miss Osawa, who started work on the *Jiji Shimpo* twenty-one years ago, is, I believe, the dean of Japanese woman journalists.

There are more than twenty well-known monthly magazines for women, many of them edited by women and largely contributed to by woman writers. Authorship is a traditional occupation for women in Japan, women's names being among the greatest in the nation's ancient literature—in which connection it is interesting to note the fact that some of the old-time authoresses were courtesans.

One hears a good deal of talk of the "new woman" in Japan, and perhaps the surest indication that she is coming into being is the fact that supposedly humorous postcards are sold on the Tokyo streets, in which the new woman is shown in various dictatorial attitudes before a cringing husband. Once, at a dinner I attended in Osaka, a woman who runs a business training school for girls, arose and made a short speech. I noticed that while she spoke not a few of the men smiled pityingly. From this item American women old enough to recall the early days of the woman movement in this country will have no difficulty in estimating the distance that the Japanese woman has yet to go.

Japanese ladies who have the time and the inclination for charitable activity accomplish a great deal. The W. C. T. U. is active in Japan, Mrs. Yajima, its president, a lady who, in 1920, at the age of eighty-eight, went to England for the International W. C. T. U. Convention, being perhaps the leader among progressive women of the land. The Red Cross has a large membership, and the Y. W. C. A., like the Y. M. C. A., has a firmly fixed and useful place, carrying on a wide variety of activities. Among these are classes to teach young girls the ways of the business world which is so rapidly opening to them. As an indication of the need for such instruction, a lady who works in the Y. W. C. A. in Tokyo told me of a case in which a Japanese girl who came for instruction reported that she was in the habit of kissing her foreign employer good morning and good night, in the belief—a belief we must suppose to have been inculcated by him—that such was the general business custom.

It is often said that the Japanese never kiss. Bowing is the national form of salutation, though those accustomed to meet foreigners shake hands with them. The fact as to kissing is that one never sees it, even between mother and child, and that this is interpreted as signifying that kissing is unknown. That is not the case. I own an old print by Utamaro which shows a man and a woman kissing with the greatest zeal. The Japanese simply do not kiss indiscriminately or in public places.

The feeling against demonstrations of affection in public is so strong that when American motion pictures were first taken to Japan, audiences would hoot at those tender passages so much enjoyed by some persons in this country. For several years past, however, all such representations have been cut from American films intended for exhibition over there. This work is done by an American who lives in Japan, and who has made up what is probably one of the strangest films in the world by assembling all the cuts into one awful reel of lust and osculation, in which figure most of the widely known American movie stars. This film he sometimes runs off privately for his friends, and it is said to leave those who witness it in a frame of mind to vote kissing a capital offence.

In a rather pitiful list of ten requests made by a Japanese wife to her husband, and exhibited as a poster at the Girls' Industrial School of Tokyo, was the appeal: "Please stop saying '*Oi, kora,*' when you call me."

Oi, the expression used by most Japanese husbands when they call their wives, is about equivalent to our "Hallo!" or "Hey!" Sometimes a husband will call his wife by name, but one more often hears "*Oi*," or "*Oi, oi*," even among persons of position. *Oi* is more familiar than rude. A man would say it to his close friend. But a woman would never say it to her husband. *Kora* is really objectionable, being an exclamation addressed only to inferiors. Naturally, then, wives do not like it, whether they make bold to declare the fact or not. For a wife may not even call her husband by his first name, but must address him as *anata*, which is a respectful form for "you."

It has been declared that the peasant woman who works beside her husband in the fields or fishing villages, or who helps him push a cart, or navigate a boat on the rivers and canals, is the happiest woman in Japan, being a real companion to him. However, that may be, there is much room for improvement in the attitude of the average middle-class Japanese toward his wife. He gets into automobiles and railroad trains ahead of her and has the air of ignoring her in public.

It should be said, though, that the attitude of such husbands does not necessarily mean that they do not care for their wives. Rather it means that they are old-fashioned—that the ancient notion of woman's position, based on the teachings of Buddhism and Confucianism, has clung to them. But most of all, I think, it reveals their fear of being thought ridiculous. For if a man showed his wife what we should call ordinary civility, the old-school Japanese thought him henpecked.

Strangely enough the position occupied by women in the days of Japan's early antiquity was much higher than it has since become. In olden times women took part in war, had a voice in politics, and in other ways held their own with men. In the eighth century successive Empresses occupied the Imperial throne, and the influence of certain able women was strongly felt at court; two centuries later we find a great era of literary women many of whose names are famous to this day.

But soon after the introduction of Buddhism and Confucianism all this was changed. The Buddhist doctrine called women creatures of sin, treacherous and cruel; and says Confucius: "When a boy is born let him play with jewels; when a girl is born let her play with tiles." So it came about that woman's position declined until it was possible for a famous moralist to write a treatise on the Duty of Woman, containing such maxims as these:

> A woman should look upon her husband as if he were
> Heaven itself, and never weary of thinking how she may
> yield to him, and thus escape celestial castigation. Let her
> never dream of jealousy. If her husband be dissolute she
> must expostulate with him but never either nurse or vent

her anger. Should her husband become angry she should obey him with fear and trembling and not set herself up against him in anger and frowardness.

An endless quantity of such quotations may be taken from the writings of moral teachers, and in them is indicated the debt of the women of Japan to Chinese doctrines. In view of which it seems strange indeed to visit a Buddhist temple and there be shown coils of thick black rope which was used in the erection of the building, and which was made entirely from the hair of devout women who sacrificed their prized tresses for this purpose, being too poor to give aught else.

Thus, while the Occident was teaching men to be chivalrous toward women, the Orient was teaching women to be, as one might put it, chivalrous toward men. But in both cases the modern tendency is toward change. The growth of woman's economic independence in this country, making her man's competitor, tends to make man less polite in his general casual contacts with her. Having elected to be his equal she must take her chances with him in the subway rush and in the scramble for street-car seats.

Fifty years hence, Japan will perhaps have reached this pass, but the present rudeness of men to women is not that of equals to equals, but of superiors to inferiors; that is the thing that must be changed.

And it will be changed. Slowly, very slowly, the attitude of the Japanese man toward the Japanese woman is improving. I found that evening classes were being held at the Y. W. C. A. in Tokyo for the purpose of teaching young husbands and wives how to enjoy social life together, and there is no doubt that in fashionable society the better type of modern young husband treats his wife with much more consideration and courtesy, and makes much more a companion of her, than was customary or even possible under the old régime. Twenty-five years ago it was well enough for a man to walk on the street with a geisha, but the man who walked in public with his wife was jeered at, and might even find himself a target for missiles. Though that is no longer the case, the tradition that man should assume a superior air still to some extent survives among the masses, so that for a husband to treat his wife with perfect courtesy before strangers requires, singular though it may seem, real moral courage.

CHAPTER IX

Baseball in Japan—The National Sport—Wrestling and Shintoism—Fans—Wrestlers' Earnings—The National Game Building—Formalities Before the Matches—The Super-Champions—Peculiarities of Japanese Wrestling—Days Off

Though the grip of the American national game upon Japan is sufficiently strong to have brought a Japanese university team to this country and to have taken one or two American university teams to Japan for return games, there is as yet no professional baseball in Nippon, and the kind of wrestling known as *sumo* still maintains its ancient prestige as the national sport.

Having been in Tokyo at the time of an election and again during the annual spring wrestling season, I could not but be struck by the fact that the street crowds watching the bulletin boards for the results of the physical contests were larger and more enthusiastic than the crowds which assembled to learn the results of the political struggle.

The average Japanese knows, I believe, about as much and about as little of domestic politics as the average American. He has a loose idea of the structure of the government and of political machinery; he follows political leaders rather than causes, and like us he is prone to read rich meanings into the glib banalities of politicians.

Wrestling he understands much better. He knows all its fine points. His enthusiasms on this subject are informed enthusiasms, and unlike the baseball fan, he inherits them from a long line of ancestors—for compared with wrestling, baseball is a brand-new sport. When the Greeks and Romans wrestled, the Japanese were wrestling, too. In the ninth century the Japanese throne was wrestled for. A Mikado died and left two sons, and these, instead of going to war against each other, left their claims to be settled by a wrestling match.

The sport is, furthermore, associated, in a manner more or less diaphanous, with Shintoism. Certain Shinto traditions are connected with it, and the matches used to be held in the grounds of Shinto temples—as indeed amateur matches often are today in country districts.

For many years past it has been customary to hold wrestling meets in Tokyo twice yearly, in January and May. Prior to the construction of the Kokugikwan, or National Game Building, the large steel and concrete structure in which the meets are now held, they occurred in the grounds of the Eko-in temple. January is a cold month in Tokyo and even May is often chilly, wherefore, the audience was none too comfortable at these open-air matches. Moreover, Japan is a rainy land; the old open-air matches had frequently to be declared off because of bad weather; sometimes it took twenty days to run off a ten-day meet. But the Kokugikwan has put an end to these difficulties. The modern Japanese wrestling fan keeps warm and dry, with the result that the sport now has more devotees than ever.

During the wrestling season Tokyo is profoundly excited. Men of large affairs have a way of disappearing mysteriously from their offices. Officials of banks and large corporations are vaguely reported to be "out of town for a few days." Prince Tokugawa, President of the House of Peers, suddenly becomes a difficult gentleman to find—unless, perchance, you happen to know where to look for him. So, too, with many a man of smaller consequence. If he can afford it—often whether he can afford it or not—he drops his work and vanishes. But he does not always vanish; for if his enthusiasm for wrestling verges on dementia he may adorn himself in an eccentric manner and make himself conspicuous in the auditorium by his antics and his cries. Thus certain wrestling fans of Tokyo have come to be considered privileged characters—as, for instance, the one who always appears at the great matches in a coat of scarlet silk, which his father wore before him, and whose habit it is to prance down the aisle before the wrestlers as they march in solemn procession to the ring.

When I inquired about tickets for one of the days of the great meet I was strongly reminded of our World Series baseball games. It seemed that tickets were not to be had. Eventually, however, I managed to secure them in the way such things are secured the world over—by means of "pull." I found a friend who had a sporting friend who knew a wrestler who could get seats.

The attitude of the sporting Japanese gentleman toward wrestlers resembles that of the sporting American or Englishman toward pugilists and jockeys. It is *chic* to know them, but not as equals. One is very genial with them and at the same time a little patronizing, whereas they are expected to assume a slightly deferential manner. Perhaps the attitude of the Japanese sporting gentleman toward his favourite wrestlers is rather more like that of the Spanish sporting gentleman toward bullfighters, for in both countries it is customary for the wealthy patron to give expensive presents to the hero. But whereas in Spain handsome jewelry is sometimes thrown to the bull-fighters in the ring, it is the custom in Japan for the fan to throw his hat, coat, pocketbook, cigarette case, or whatnot to the popular idol, who later sends the trophy back to the owner, receiving in exchange a valuable gift— frequently a gift of money.

Hence, though the actual pay of wrestlers is small, perquisites make the profession profitable to those fairly successful in it, and poor parents, having a son of unusually large proportions, are likely to look with resignation upon the Japanese theory that great size is generally accompanied by stupidity, and to rejoice in the dimensions of their offspring because of a fond hope that he may become a champion wrestler and grow rich.

My friend the Japanese sporting gentleman (who, by the way, was a graduate of the University of Michigan) did more than obtain tickets for me. He called with his automobile and took me to the amphitheatre.

"Our mode of wrestling is not at all like yours," he said, "and I want to explain it to you."

It was about eleven in the morning when, after traversing several streets strung with rows of Japanese lanterns, and filled with hurrying throngs, we reached the great circular concrete building into which an eager crowd was pouring through many portals—an audience which, though made up for the most part of men, contained not a few women and some children. Many, though by no means all of the women were geisha, for wrestlers have about the same rank as geisha in the social scale, and they are often the heroes as well as the intimates of the fair entertainers.

As we approached the amphitheatre the thought came to me that there is a curious sameness in the atmosphere surrounding great sporting events the world over, however little the various sports themselves may resemble one another. To approach this great building in Tokyo during wrestling week is quite like approaching the Plaza de Toros in Madrid, or the building in which *jai alai* is played in Havana, or the Polo Grounds in New York, or the Yale Bowl, or the Harvard Stadium.

The Kokugikwan is a circular building roofed with glass and seating fourteen or fifteen thousand persons. At the centre is a mound of earth with a flat top on which the ring is marked with a border of woven straw. Over the ring is a kiosk supported by four heavy posts which are respectively red, green, black, and white in colour, and are considered to symbolize the four corners of the earth. The kiosk has a roof somewhat resembling that of a temple and is embellished with curtains of purple-and-white silk which hang down a few feet below the eaves.

The main floor of the amphitheatre is banked up toward the back. The seats at the ringside are reserved for the participant wrestlers; behind these are some tiers of chairs which are presumably occupied by the most frantic fans, and behind the chairs comes a great area of boxes, each seating from four to six persons. These boxes, like those of a typical Japanese theatre, do not contain chairs, but are floored with thick straw mats on which are cushions for the occupants to squat on. The only division between the boxes is a railing about a foot high. Above the main floor are two galleries running all the way around the building. The Imperial box is in the first gallery. People in the galleries sit in chairs, in front of which are narrow shelf-like tables from which luncheon may be eaten—for wrestling matches, like the old-style theatrical performances, last practically all day.

During the first part of the morning, bouts between numerous minor wrestlers are run off, but at about eleven the building fills up, for everyone wishes to see the two groups of champions march in. One group represents East Japan, the other West Japan; each group contains about twenty men, and their seats are at the eastern and western sides of the ring, respectively. This representation of East and West is not literal, but is the traditional division. A man from an Eastern province may be champion of the West, and vice versa.

Gross-looking creatures, naked to the waist, they enter in single file, each wearing a long velvet apron, elaborately embroidered and tasselled. These aprons, which are given to them by their patrons, are removed before the contests, a loin-cloth and short skirt of fringe being worn beneath them.

Marching into the ring the champions form a circle and go through a series of set exercises, clapping their hands in unison, raising their legs high and stamping their feet violently upon the ground to exhibit their muscular flexibility. After these exercises they march out again.

Next enter the supreme champions of the Eastern group and of the Western group—the two great wrestlers of Japan—popular idols who, by reason of having remained undefeated throughout three or more successive wrestling meets, are entitled to wear not only the elaborate velvet apron, but a very thick white rope wound several times about their waists and knotted in a certain way.

Each of these super-champions is attended on his march to the ring by two other wrestlers. The one who precedes him is known as the *tsuyu harai*, or dew-brusher. In theory, he clears the way, brushing dew from imaginary grass before the feet of the mighty one. The attendant who brings up the rear is the *tachi mochi*, or sword-bearer; for according to old Japanese custom no wrestler except a super-champion was allowed to wear a sword, and though the sword is now only a symbol, the custom still survives, and the sword of the super-champion must be carried in behind him.

To one accustomed to the sort of wrestling practised in the Western world, many of these champions do not look like athletes, since they are, as a rule, so fat that their paunches bulge like balconies over the tops of their aprons and loin cloths, and their arms and thighs tremble like jelly when they walk. Under the Japanese method of wrestling, however, each match is quickly settled, wherefore endurance is not so important as great weight and power in the first moment of attack. It is for this reason that fat wrestlers are usually the most successful. Some of them have weighed as much as three hundred and fifty pounds. But now and then there comes along a super-champion like Tachiyama, who is not very fat, and who conquers by strength, speed, and reach rather than by mere weight.

When the super-champions have exhibited themselves, the two groups of lesser champions return and occupy their seats around the ring. The four referees—retired wrestlers—take seats on cushions, one at each corner of the kiosk, and the umpire, wearing beautiful flowing silks and a strange little pointed hat like that of a Buddhist priest, enters the ring and, holding up the lacquered wooden fan, which is his badge of office, announces in impressive tones the names of the two men who are about to meet.

The adversaries then enter the ring and go through the same old series of stampings and flexings. Each takes a handful of salt from a box at his side of the ring, puts a little in his mouth and throws the rest upon the ground before him. This is supposed to have a purifying effect, not in the antiseptic sense, but in some occult way. Salt is often used thus in Japan.

Having completed these preliminaries the two men take their positions facing each other, braced upon all fours. But this apparent readiness by no means indicates that the contest is commencing. Instead of immediately attacking, they will often remain thus poised for minutes, sharply watching each other. Then one of them will get up and take a drink, or will go for some more salt and throw it in the ring. Also one or the other will often make a false start, attacking when his adversary is not ready to accept combat; whereafter the two resume their crouching attitudes, toes braced, hands on the ground. This sort of thing may continue for ten or twenty minutes, to the accompaniment of howls from the fans, who shout the names of their favourites and bellow Japanese equivalents for such Americanisms as "Go to it!" and "Atta Boy!"

But whereas the period of preparation may often be measured in fractions of an hour, the actual struggle usually consumes but a few seconds. The men spring at each other like a pair of savage fighting dogs and the contest is settled before you know it. There is none of that straining to get a certain hold, or to break one, which is so characteristic of our style of wrestling, and you never see the contestants writhing in deadly embrace upon the floor. The vanquished need not necessarily be thrown at all, though often he is. If any portion of his body, other than the soles of his feet, touches the ground, or if (whether he be thrown or not) any portion of his body touches the ground outside the ring, that means defeat. In case both men fall, or are forced from the ring together, the one who first makes contact with the ground, or first leaves the ring, is vanquished.

Often a man is beaten by being bent over until he is forced to support himself on one hand, and there have been cases in which decisions were rendered merely because one man's head was bent down until his top-knot touched the floor. A wrestler will sometimes win in one hard push, backing his opponent out of the ring; but in this there is always the danger that the one being pushed will at the last moment step aside, causing the adversary's own momentum to carry him beyond the boundary, thus applying an underlying principle of *jiu-jutsu*,—or *jiudo*, as it is called in its improved form—in which a man's own strength is used to defeat him. Frequently, however, there will be a spectacular throw; and sometimes, when this occurs, the ringside seats, so coveted at wrestling and boxing matches in this country, are not highly desirable. I have seen huge wrestlers hurled through the air to land sprawling on their comrades in their seats.

When a close decision has to be made the umpire confers with the referees, and at such times the audience and the two opposing groups of wrestlers are vociferous in support of the contestant they favour.

To the credit of the Japanese be it said, however, that they do not yell: "Kill the umpire!" when displeased by a decision rendered in connection with their national sport; that they do not throw bottles at the umpire, and that it never becomes necessary to give police protection to an umpire whose judgment has not accorded with that of the crowd. The Japanese, you see, have not adopted every detail of Western civilization.

I must have seen twenty-five or thirty bouts that day. But though I was interested I cannot pretend to find in Japanese wrestling the qualities of a really great sport. Skill their wrestlers have, but there is no call for stamina. Their style of wrestling seems to me to let off where ours begins.

Japanese life runs at lower pressure than our life. There is not the nervous rush about it. Matters move at a more comfortable pace, and people seem to have more patience. An American crowd would become restless over the interminable preliminaries of each Japanese wrestling bout, and would find the bout itself unsatisfactory because of its brevity and the lack of sustained effort. The Japanese, on the other hand, seem always to be willing to wait for something to happen. One notices this in innumerable ways. Motion pictures made in Japan are likely to be, from our point of view, intolerably slow in their action. So also with the all-day plays of the typical Japanese theatre.

The Japanese business man's custom of taking a day off whenever it happens to suit him is doubtless due in part to the fact that until recently Sunday in Japan was just like any other day. There was no regular day of rest. One day a month was usually appointed as a holiday for commercial and industrial workers; later it became two days a month; and at last there developed a custom of making those days the first and third Sundays of the month. For though Sunday has, of course, no religious significance in the eyes of the large body of Japanese, it seemed the most practical day to select for a holiday if only because it was a day on which the offices of American and European residents were closed.

CHAPTER X

It amused me to hear, a little while ago, that a party of our Congressmen, on a junket in Japan, had been implored by certain pious Americans over there, to avoid such sinful things as teahouses and geisha. No doubt the poor devils of Congressmen had fancied they would be able to lead their own lives five thousand miles from home and constituents. And evidently they proposed to do it, for they replied with uncongressmanlike boldness that teahouses and geisha were among the things they most desired to see. That pleased me not only because it showed that a Congressman can be spunky—even though he has to go to another hemisphere to do it—but because it showed a normal human interest in what is assuredly a very curious phase of life.

I, too, was interested in tea houses and geisha, and I made it a point to find out as much about them as I could.

The first geisha I saw were in attendance at a luncheon for some forty persons—about half of them Americans—given by a Tokyo gentleman for the purpose of showing us what a purely Japanese luncheon was like. It was held at the Maple Club, a large, rambling Japanese-style building standing in charming gardens in the midst of one of the Tokyo parks—a Far Eastern equivalent of such Parisian restaurants as the Café d'Armenonville or the Pré Catelan.

As we alighted from our rickshas a flock of smiling serving maids appeared in the doorway to greet us, indicating to us that we were to sit on the high door-step and have our shoes removed by the blue-clad coolies who were in attendance—each with the insignia of the Maple Club in a large design upon the back of his coat. (If you wish the coolie who draws your ricksha or does other work for you to wear your crest you supply his costume and pay him a few cents extra per day.)

When our shoes had been checked and our feet encased in soft woollen slippers like bed-bootees, we were bowed into the building and escorted through a series of rooms with soft straw-matted floors and walls of wood and paper. Emerging upon an outer gallery of highly polished wood, we followed it, looking out over the lovely garden as we moved along, and finally reached a flight of stairs, also of wood having a satiny polish, which led to the banquet hall. Our escorts on this journey were several little Japanese maids in pretty kimonos, who, though they spoke no English, talked to us in soft international smiles. No one without a sweet nature could smile the smile of one of these Japanese serving maids. They are called *nesan*, meaning literally "elder sister." This familiar appellation is generally used in speaking to a maidservant whose name one does not know, and in the term is revealed a hint of the beautiful relationship which exists in Japan between master and servant, whether in a private house or a Japanese inn. In the great cities this old relationship is to some extent breaking down as Japan becomes Westernized, but in Japanese hotels and country inns, and in prosperous homes one sees it still. Service is rendered with a grace and friendliness which make it very charming. Even about the menservants in the houses of the rich there is nothing of the flunkey spirit. The Japanese manservant generally wears silken robes which give him a fine dignity and make it difficult, sometimes, to differentiate him from members of the family. He is extremely polite, but not rigid. You feel that he is a self-respecting *man*. As for maidservants, they are like so many pet butterflies. One of Japan's strongest claims to democracy, it seems to me, is founded on the attitude existing between master and servant.

No one without a sweet nature could smile the smile of one of these tea-house maids. They are called *nesan*—"elder sister"

Those who have visited Japan, yet who do not agree with me as to the exquisite courtesy of the Japanese servant, will be those whose stopping places have been European-style hotels in the large cities. In such hotels the service is often poor and one occasionally encounters a servant who is surly and ill-mannered. I encountered one such in Kobe—said to be the rudest city in Japan. But by the time I ran across him I had seen enough of the real Japan to know what such rudeness signified. It showed merely that in this individual case native courtesy had been worn away by contact with innumerable ill-bred foreigners.

But to return to our luncheon.

As a concession to American custom our host greeted us with a handshake, and his Japanese guests walked in and shook hands instead of dropping to their knees on entering and bowing to the floor according to the old national custom.

The room, which was large, well illustrated the elasticity of the Japanese style of building. Five or six private dining rooms usually occupied this section of the house, but for the requirements of the present occasion the walls forming these rooms had been removed making the entire area into one spacious chamber. It is a simple matter to remove such walls, since they consist only of a series of screens of wood and paper which slide in grooves and can easily be lifted out and put away in closets. And let me add that, though the climate of Japan is very damp, the Japanese use such thoroughly seasoned wood, and work in wood so admirably, that I never once found a sliding screen that stuck in its grooves.

Cocoons—Five thousand silk worms eat 125 lbs. of mulberry leaves and yield eight skeins of silk, which make one kimono

For the meal we knelt upon silk cushions laid two or three feet apart around three walls of the room. As the weather was chilly there stood beside each of us a brazier, or hibachi, consisting of a pot of live charcoal standing in a wooden box. The Japanese love of finish in all things is shown in the careful way they have of banking the ashes in a hibachi, and making neat patterns over the top of them.

In front of each of us was placed a little table of red lacquer about a foot high, with an edge like that of a tray, and on this table were sundry covered bowls of lacquer and of china, and little dishes containing sour pickles and a pungent, watery brown sauce. In front of every one or two guests knelt a nesan, presiding over a covered lacquered tub, containing boiled rice, which is eaten with almost everything, and even mixed with green tea and drunk with it out of the rice-bowl.

Also, in attendance upon each guest, there was a geisha. Some of the geisha were women perhaps twenty years old, wearing handsome dark kimonos which they generally carried with a great deal of style, but others were little *maiko*, dancing girls, in brilliant-coloured kimonos with the yard-long sleeves of youth. The youngest of these was perhaps twelve years of age, while the oldest may have been sixteen.

As I afterward learned, there is a vast difference between various grades of geisha. Those present at this luncheon were among the most popular in Tokyo. They were truly charming creatures, sweet-faced, soft-eyed and gentle, with beautiful manners and much more poise than is shown by the average Japanese lady. For Japanese ladies are not, as a rule, accustomed to our sort of mixed social life, in which husbands and wives take part together, whereas geisha are in the business of entertaining men and presumably understand men as women seldom do.

Since few geisha speak English, and very few Americans speak Japanese, we travellers from abroad are rather outsiders with the geisha, and our appreciation of them must be largely ocular. But a geisha can come as near to carrying on a wordless conversation as any woman can. Mine smiled at me, filled my shallow little cup with warm saké from time to time, and showed me how to use my chop-sticks. I found the lesson most agreeable, and was presently rewarded by being told, through the Japanese friend at my side, that for a beginner I was doing very well.

If you want to know what it is like to eat with chop-sticks try sitting on the floor and eating from a bowl, placed in front of you, with a pair of pencils or thick knitting needles. It is a dangerous business, and the risk is rendered greater by the fact that the Japanese do not wear napkins in their laps, and that to soil the spotless matting is about the greatest sin the barbarian outlander can commit. The Japanese napkin is a small soft towel which is brought to one warm and damp, in a little basket. It is used on the face and hands as a wash-cloth and is then removed.

Family luncheon à la Japonaise. The serving maid is kneeling in the corner at the back. If you would essay eating with chopsticks, try it with a pair of heavy knitting needles

Presently my geisha called one of her sisters in the craft to witness my progress with the chop-sticks. The new arrival was named Jitsuko—otherwise "truthful girl"—and she seemed to be quite the most fashionable of them all. Her kimono, with its dyed-out decorations and its five ceremonial crests, was very handsome and was worn with great *chic*, her obi was a gorgeous thing richly patterned in gold brocade, and I noticed that she wore upon it a pin containing a very fine large diamond—a most unusual sort of trinket in Japan. Also she wore a ring containing a large diamond. Nor was this foreign note purely superficial. For, to my delight, Jitsuko spoke to me in English. She was one of Tokyo's two English-speaking geisha, and as I later learned, had the honour of being nominated as the geisha to entertain the Duke of Connaught at dinners he attended at the time of his visit to the Japanese capital.

Jitsuko and the other geisha talked together about me. Then Jitsuko paid me the compliment of saying that they agreed in thinking that I looked a little bit like a Japanese. I thanked her, and returned the compliment in kind, saying that I thought they also looked like Japanese, and very pretty ones, whereat they both giggled.

By this time we had established an *entente* so cordial that it seemed fitting that we should drink to each other. Aided by the gentleman at my side and by Jitsuko, I learned the proper formalities of this ceremony. First I rinsed my saké cup in a lacquer bowl provided for the purpose, then passed it to Jitsuko. The preliminary rinsing indicated that she was now to fill the cup and drink. Had I passed it to her without rinsing, it would have meant that she was to refill it for me—for a geisha never "plies" one with saké but waits for the cup to be passed. When she had sipped the saké she in turn rinsed the cup, refilled it, and handed it to me to drink. Thus the friendly rite was completed.

I had heard that saké was extremely intoxicating, but that is not so. It is rice wine, almost white in colour, and is served sometimes at normal temperature and sometimes slightly warm. It is rather more like a pale light sherry than any other Occidental beverage, but it lacks the full flavour of sherry, having a mild and not unpleasant flavour all its own. On the whole I rather liked saké, and I found myself able to detect the difference between ordinary saké and saké that was particularly good. While on this subject I may add that liquor of all sorts flows freely in Japan. Saké is the one alcoholic beverage generally served with meals in the Japanese style, but at the European-style luncheons and dinners I attended two or three kinds of wine were usually served, and there were cocktails before and sometimes liqueurs afterward. The Japanese have also taken up whisky-drinking to some extent. They import Scotch whisky and also make a bad imitation Scotch whisky of their own. But saké still reigns supreme as the national alcoholic drink, and when you see a Japanese intoxicated you may be pretty sure that saké—a lot of saké—did it.

In my evening strolls, particularly in the gay, crowded district of Asakusa Park in Tokyo—a Japanese Coney Island, full of theatres, motion-picture houses, animal shows, conjuring exhibitions, teahouses, bazaars and the like, surrounding a great Buddhist temple—I saw many intoxicated men, but I never came upon one who was ugly or troublesome. Whether because of some quality in the Japanese nature, or in the saké, this drink seems only to make gay, talkative and sometimes boisterous those who have taken too much of it. I should not be surprised if the Japanese need alcoholic stimulants rather more than other races need them. For one thing the climate of Japan, except in the mountains, is enervating; and for another, the Japanese nature is generally repressed, and saké tends to liberate it.

I noticed this at another entertainment in Tokyo—a dinner of newspaper editors. Being the only foreigner there, and being enormously interested in the problems connected with relations between the United States and Japan, I launched forth, telling them my views in the hope of learning theirs. But although I sensed that they did not agree with all I said, their responses exhibited only the sort of polite tolerance that a courteous host will show a somewhat obstreperous guest. For some time I felt that I had acted like a bad boy at a party. But after the geisha had filled our cups with saké more than once, I got what I was looking for—an argument. It was a polite argument, but we had become friendly enough to speak frankly. *In saké veritas.*

This was a case of just enough saké, but so far as I was able to observe, even too much saké produces no very objectionable results. I shall never forget the young man, brightly illuminated with this beverage, who came up to me one evening on the street, in a small town. He was full of a desire to practise English on me and to help me. He didn't care what he helped me to do. He would help me to buy whatever I wanted to buy, go wherever I wanted to go, or stay wherever I wanted to stay.

I explained to him that I was only strolling about while waiting for a train and that it was now time for me to return to the station.

"Wait!" he cried. "I like you. I am drawn to you. I have been in America. I can talk to you. We are friends. Wait!" He looked about him hurriedly, then darted into a near-by shop.

In a moment he emerged and came running toward me bearing in his extended hand a curious-looking object, resembling, as nearly as I could see in the dim light, a somewhat soiled popcorn ball. This he pressed into my hand with a generous eagerness which could not fail to convey to me the fact his heart went with the gift.

"It is a present. It is for you. You will remember me. Another kind might be better, but you are in a hurry."

My fingers grasped something heavy but yielding and glutinous. As I thanked my new-found friend I examined it. It was a ball of rice somewhat larger than a baseball. Scattered through it were brown objects the precise nature of which I was unable to determine. I might very accurately have told the donor that I was "stuck on" his present, since the mass in my hand was held in form not merely by the cohesiveness of the rice, but also by some substance of the nature of molasses.

We parted. I moved toward the railroad station where my family and friends were waiting with Yuki, our invaluable maid. As I walked along I studied the object. Obviously it was intended to be eaten. Yet there were other purposes to which it might be put. It was a thing that a Sinn Feiner would like to have in his hand as the British Premier passed by in a silk hat. Charley Chaplin would have known what to do with it. It was heavier than a custard pie and fully as dramatic.

My first impulse was to drop it as soon as I could do so unobserved; but the thought occurred to me that it was probably a Japanese delicacy, and that Yuki might like it; wherefor I carried it to the station.

When I offered it to Yuki she looked surprised. Her refusal was courteous but determined.

"Where Mr. Street get that?" she demanded.

"A man gave it to me. Here, you take it."

Yuki giggled and stepped back.

"But what the man give it to Mr. Street for?"

"A present. What's the matter with it? Isn't it good to eat?"

"Yes—good to eat."

"Why don't you take it, then?"

Giggling, she shook her head.

"But Yuki—I don't understand. What's the joke?"

Shaking with merriment she whispered to my wife. It developed that the saké-inspired Japanese had presented me with a tidbit specially prepared for prospective mothers.

All things considered it seemed advisable to get rid of it at once. I threw it on the railroad track.

CHAPTER XI

A Japanese Meal—Other Meals—Smoking and the Duty on Cigars—Japanese Music—Geisha Dancing—What Is a Geisha?—Their Refinement—Autumn Leaves—Filial Piety and Certain Horrors Thereof

As the luncheon at the Maple Club was my first meal in the Japanese style I had not realized the volume of such a repast. I ate too much of the first few courses, and as a result found myself unable to partake of the last two thirds of the feast. The amount of food was simply stupendous. I might have realized this in advance, and governed myself accordingly, had I looked at the menu. But I failed to do so until driven to it by my surprise as course after course was served. This was the bill of fare:

FIRST TABLE

Hors d'œuvres—Vegetables

Soup—terrapin with quail eggs and onions

Baked fish with sea-hedgehog paste

Raw fish with horseradish and eutrema root

Fried prawns and deep-sea eels

Duck, fish-cake and vegetables in egg soup, steamed

Roast duck with relishes

When this much had been served the nesans took up the little tables from in front of us and went trooping out of the room. As I had already eaten what amounted to about three normal dinners, I concluded that the meal was over, but not so. In they came again bearing other little lacquered tables of the same pattern as the first, but slightly smaller; whereupon, as it seemed to me, an entire second luncheon was served. The menu was as follows:

SECOND TABLE

Hors d'œuvres—Vegetables

Fish consommé

Grilled eels

Rice

Pickled vegetables

Fruits

I am told that indigestion is a prevalent ailment of the Japanese, and as regards prosperous persons who do no hard physical work I can readily believe it. The toiling coolie is the only man in Japan who might reasonably be expected to digest an elaborate Japanese meal, and he, of course, never gets one, but subsists almost entirely upon a diet of rice and fish.

Though some Japanese dishes are found palatable by Americans there are many things we miss in the Japanese cuisine. It lacks variety. Breakfast, luncheon, and dinner are composed of about the same dishes. The divers well-cooked vegetables which form such an important part of our diet are entirely absent from theirs, nor do they have stewed fruits, salads, sweets, or the numerous meats to which we are accustomed.

Of their best-known table delicacies it may be said that grilled eels with rice are very good; that the pink fish, the flesh of which is eaten raw, is pleasing to the eye and by no means unpalatable when dipped in the accompanying *shoyu*, a brown sauce not unlike Worcestershire, made from soy beans; that though they have no cream soups, some of their soups are pleasant to the taste, albeit they have the peculiarity of being either thin and watery on the one hand, or of the consistency of custard on the other; that bamboo shoots are rather tough, lily roots sweet and succulent, and quail eggs delicious. The Japanese, by the way, domesticate the quail for its eggs, regard the cow not as a milch animal but as a beast of burden, and cultivate the cherry tree not for its fruit but for its flower.

The diet of ancient Japan was even less varied than that of to-day, for more than a thousand years ago the Japanese became vegetarians, and for some centuries thereafter adhered scrupulously to the Buddhistic injunction against killing living creatures. For several hundred years they even abjured fish, but by degrees they have fallen away from the strict observance of the vegetarian doctrine, until to-day a Japanese who is at all sophisticated will thoroughly enjoy a dinner in the European style, beef and all. Indeed many of those who have travelled abroad and acquired a taste for foreign cookery make it a point to have at least one of their daily meals prepared in the foreign fashion.

Government officials or wealthy cosmopolitans who entertain on a large scale usually do so in the European manner. A banquet at the Imperial Hotel in Tokyo is much like a banquet in New York, and one at the Bankers' Club is even more so, except that the meal itself is likely to be better than at our banquets. To dine with a large gathering at the Peers' Club is like dining at some great club or official residence in Paris; while as for the cocktail hour at the Tokyo Club, I cannot imagine anything in the world more completely and delightfully international.

An important part of the equipment for a meal in the pure Japanese style is a smoker's outfit, consisting of a tray on which stands a small urn of live charcoal, and a bamboo vase with a little water in it—the former for lighting the tobacco, the latter a receptacle for ashes. The native smoke is a tiny pipe, called a two-and-a-half-puff pipe, with a bowl as small as a child's thimble. Finely shredded Japanese tobacco is smoked in this pipe, which is used by men and women alike, and the constant refilling and relighting of it seem to figure as a part of the pleasure of smoking. The Japanese smoke cigarettes also, and cigars, but the tobacco industry of Japan, like that of France, is a government monopoly, with the result that, as in France, good cigarettes and cigars are difficult to obtain.

A visit to a government tobacco factory left me with the impression that, from the point of view of management, mechanical equipment, and perhaps also labour conditions, the plant would compare not unfavourably with some large tobacco manufactories in our own Southern States; but as to the product of this factory, the best of which I sampled, I can pretend to no enthusiasm. Japanese tobacco goes well enough in the little native pipes, but it does not make good cigarettes or cigars, and even the cigarettes made of blended tobaccos, or from pure Virginia or Egyptian leaves, would hardly satisfy a critical taste. Cigars made in Japan are uniformly poor, like the government-made cigars of France, but whereas in France it is possible to buy a good imported Havana, I found none for sale in Japan. One reason for this is that the duty on cigars is 355 per cent., so that only a millionaire can afford good Havanas.

Whether because the enormous luncheon at the Maple Club left me in a stupor, or because my mind could not adjust itself quickly to appreciation of an unfamiliar and extremely curious art, I did not find myself enchanted by the shrill falsetto singing of the geisha musicians, or the strange sounds they evoked from the samisen, fife and drums, as they accompanied the dancers.

The native Japanese music, with its crude five-tone scale, is demonstrably inferior to that of Western peoples. To the foreign ear it is unmelodious, even barbarous, and yet I must say for it that the more I heard it the more I felt in it a kind of weird appeal—an appeal not to the ear but to the imagination. Even now, when I am far away from Japan, a note or two struck on a guitar, a mandolin, or a ukulele, in imitation of the samisen, conjures up vivid pictures in my mind. I see a narrow geisha street, with a musician seated in an upper window, or I get a vision of a geisha dancer arrayed in brilliant silks, posturing, fan in hand, against a background of gold screens, in the exquisitely chaste simplicity of a Japanese teahouse room. The sound that evokes the picture is not harmonious, but the picture itself is harmonious beyond expression.

One thing that sometimes makes the stranger in Japan slow to appreciate the dancing of geisha, is the very fact that it is called dancing; for the term suggests to us a picture of Pavlowa poised like a swiftly flying bird, or Genée looking like a bisque doll and spinning on one toe. Dancing, to us, means, first of all, rhythm. We look for rhythm in a geisha dance, and failing to find it—at least in the sense in which we understand the meaning of the word—we are baffled. It is only one more case of preconception as a barrier to just appreciation.

Many travellers, and at least one author who has written a book on Japan, have made the mistake of confusing geisha with prostitutes. This is a gigantic error. The error is kept alive by ricksha coolies who, understanding that it is a common mistake of foreigners, often use the term "geisha house" as meaning an establishment of altogether different character. A geisha house is in fact simply a house in which geisha live under the charge of the master or mistress to whom they are bound by contract or indenture. Geisha are booked through exchanges and meet their patrons at restaurants or teahouses. When not on duty they are private citizens, and it would be considered the height of vulgarity for a man to call upon a geisha at the geisha house, however innocent the purpose of his call.

A further reason for the erroneous idea of what a geisha is, lies in the fact that Western civilization has no equivalent class. Geisha correspond more nearly to cabaret entertainers than to any other class we have, yet even here there is no real parallel. It is not customary in Japan—except in foreign-style hotels—to dine in public. If a man be alone in a hotel he dines by himself in his room, save that the little nesans who serve him will try to make themselves agreeable and that the proprietor may do the same. Or if a man gives a luncheon or a dinner party at a restaurant he will have a private room. Therefore, under the Japanese system, there is never a general assemblage of persons, strangers to one another, who may be entertained as a body while they are dining. Thus the geisha is a private entertainer, and in order that the most desirable geisha may be secured it is customary to make arrangements for a luncheon or dinner several days in advance. This is usually done through the proprietor of the restaurant, who is told the names of the geisha the host desires to summon, and who notifies them through the local geisha exchange.

Men who frequently lunch and dine out naturally become acquainted with many geisha, and have their preferences; and if a host knows that one of his guests particularly likes a certain geisha he will generally try to arrange to have her at his party.

There are three classes of geisha. Those of the best class frequently have good incomes. They are often given large presents by their wealthy patrons, and many of them are the mistresses of men of means, who sometimes take them off on week-end outings and spend a great deal of money on them.

However this may be, a geisha of the first class is a creature of exquisite refinement of manner, and there is about her not the faintest suggestion of coarseness. She will be friendly, even pleasantly familiar, but never, in public, is she guilty of the slightest impropriety. I have been to many gay parties in Japan, but I have never seen a geisha or her patron behave in a way that would shock the most fastidious American lady. Naturally the situation is somewhat different among low-class Japanese and the geisha they patronize. There are vulgar geisha to entertain vulgar men. But even a low-class geisha, if sent for in an emergency to entertain a man of taste, will often be sufficiently clever to adjust herself to the situation.

During the meal the geisha will sit before or beside the gentleman she is designated to entertain, chatting with him, amusing him and serving him with saké. Afterward she will join the other geisha in giving an entertainment, the part she takes in this depending upon her special talent, which may be for singing, playing, or dancing. Pretty young geisha are most often dancers, while those who are older are generally musicians. Also there are some geisha who are merely bright and pleasing and who succeed without other accomplishments. The host, making up a party, selects his geisha with these various requirements in mind, so that his whole company of geisha will be well balanced.

Foreigners are generally most taken with the little dancing girls, or maiko, who are mere children, and who with their sweet, bright, happy little faces, and their bewitchingly brilliant flowered-silk costumes, are altogether fascinating. Once at a party in a great house in Tokyo I saw a score of these little creatures scampering down a broad flight of stairs, making a picture that was like nothing so much as a mass of autumn leaves blown by a high wind.

These children are in effect apprentices who are being schooled in the geisha's arts. Often they are in this occupation because their parents have sold them into it as a means of raising money. With the older geisha it is frequently the same. The Japanese teaching of filial piety makes it incumbent upon a daughter to become a geisha, or even a prostitute, to relieve the financial distress of her parents. In either case she goes under contract for a term of years—usually three.

A girl who is refined, pretty, and talented can raise a sum in the neighbourhood of a thousand dollars by becoming a geisha, but if she is not sufficiently talented or attractive to be a geisha, her next resource is the "nightless city." The opening to women of professional and commercial opportunities should tend to improve this situation.

I am told that geisha and the little dancing girls are generally kindly treated by the geisha-masters, and the gaiety they exhibit leads me to conclude that this is true. The little dancers, in particular, want but slight encouragement to become as playful as kittens.

CHAPTER XII

I Entertain at a Teahouse—Folk Dances—The Sense of Form—The Organization of Society—Jitsuko Helps me Give a Party—Pretty Kokinoyou—Geisha Games— Rivalries of Geisha—The Cherry Dance at Kyoto—Theatre Settings—Unmercenary Geisha—Teahouse Romances—Restaurants, Cheap and Costly—Reflections on Reform

"'Tis pleasing to be schooled in a strange tongueBy foreign lips and eyes...."—Byron

The way to see geisha and maiko to the best advantage is at small parties where the guests are well acquainted and formality can be to some extent cast off. I was much pleased when I learned enough of the ways of teahouses and geisha to be able to give such a party.

My first essay as host at a Japanese dinner was not, however, entirely independent, since I had the help of a Japanese friend. It occurred at the charming Maruya teahouse, in the ancient town of Nara.

The theatre street in Kyoto is one of the most interesting highways in the world

It was at the Maruya that I first began to feel some real understanding and appreciation of geisha dancing, and I think the thing that assisted me most was the fact that the little maiko executed several Japanese folk dances, the action of which, unlike that of most geisha dances, was to a large extent self-explanatory. One of these dances represented clam-digging. In it the dancers held small trays which in pantomime they used as shovels, going through the motion of digging the clams out of the sand and throwing them into a basket. The dance was accompanied by a song, as was also another folk dance in which two of the maiko enacted the rôles of lovers who were obliged to part because the mother of the girl was forcing her to marry a rich man. I was interested to notice in this dance that the gesture to indicate weeping—the holding of one hand in front of the eyes at a distance of two or three inches from them—is not taken from life, but is copied from the gesture of dolls in the marionette theatre. That is the gesture for a man. When a woman weeps she holds her sleeve-tab before her eyes, for it is a tradition that women dry their tears with their sleeves. When in Japanese poetry moist sleeves are spoken of, the figure of speech signifies that a woman has been weeping.

Digging clams at low-tide in Tokyo Bay

The girls who executed the last-mentioned folk dance were respectively thirteen and fifteen years old, and they were evidently much amused by the passionate utterances they were obliged to deliver. The one who played the part of the youth—a fetching little creature with a roguish face—was unable at times to restrain her mirth as she recited the tragic and romantic lines, and her rendition of them was punctuated by little explosions of giggling, which though they cannot be said to have heightened the dramatic effect of the sad story, her audience found most contagious. Then with a great effort she would pull herself together and try to live down the mirthful outburst, lowering her voice, to imitate that of a man, and assuming a tragic demeanor which, in a creature so sweet and childish, habited in silken robes that made her like a butterfly, was even more amusing.

People who follow the arts, or have a feeling for them, seldom fail to appreciate geisha dancing after they have seen enough of it to get an understanding of what it is. This, I think, is because they generally have a sense of form, and as geisha dancing is a sort of animated *tableau vivant*, a sense of form is the one thing most essential to an appreciation of it.

Indeed I will go further and proclaim my belief that, to a visitor who would really understand Japan, a sense of form is a vital necessity.

Japan is all form. In Japanese art even colour takes second place. Nor does the Japanese feeling for form by any means stop where art ends. It permeates the entire fabric of Japanese life. The formal courtesy of old French society was as nothing to the formal courtesy of the Japanese. The whole life of the average Japanese is so regulated by form that his existence seems to progress according to a sort of geometrical pattern. The very nation itself is organized in such a way as to suggest a compact artistic composition. Not only every class, but every family and individual has an exact place in the structure. A friend of mine who knows Japan as but few foreigners do, goes so far as to say that the shades of difference between individuals are so finely drawn that no two persons in Japan are of exactly the same social rank, and that the precise position of every man in the country can be established according to the codes of Japanese formalism. Though this may be an exaggeration it expresses what I believe to be essentially a truth. I visualize the social and political structure of Japan as a great pyramid in which the blocks are families. At the bottom are the submerged classes—among them, down in the mud of the foundation, the *eta* or pariah class. Then come layers of families representing the voteless masses, among which the merchant class was in feudal times considered the lowest. Next come the little taxpayers who vote, and these pile up and up to the place where the more exalted classes are superimposed upon them—for in Japan it may be said that there is practically no middle class. I am told that there are now about a million families who are descended from samurai. This is where the aristocracy begins. So the pyramid ascends. Layers of lower officials; layers of higher officials, layers of ex-officials, high and low; layers of those having decorations from the

Government; layers of army and navy families, and so on to where, very near the summit, are placed the *Genro*, or elder statesmen. Above them is a massive block representing the Imperial Family, and at the very peak, is the Emperor, Head of all Heads of Families.

My party in Nara having given me confidence, I gave a luncheon at the delightful Kanetanaka teahouse which overlooks a canal in the Kyobashi district of Tokyo.

I cannot claim much credit for the fact that this party was a success, since Jitsuko, the English speaking geisha I met at my first Japanese luncheon, was there to help me. Jitsuko's English, I must own, was not perfect. Nor would I have had it so, for I enjoyed teaching her, and learning from her.

"Naughty boy!" was one expression that I taught her, and I showed her how to accompany the phrase with an admonitory shake of the finger, with results which altogether charmed the American gentlemen at my luncheon.

One of these gentlemen, a new arrival in Japan and consequently entirely unfamiliar with Japanese fare, asked Jitsuko about a certain dish that was set before him.

"What is this?" he demanded, looking at it doubtfully.

"That fried ears," said Jitsuko.

"Fried ears!" he cried. "Not really?"

"Yes."

But it was not fried ears. Jitsuko had the usual trouble with her *l*'s and *r*'s. She had meant to say "fried eels."

Besides Jitsuko I had at my luncheon six of the lovely little maiko. One of them, an intelligent child called Shinobu—"tiptoes"—was picking up a little English. She sent for ink and a brush and wrote out for me the names of her companions. Later I had the names translated, getting the meaning of them in English—for geisha generally take fanciful names. They were: Kokinoyou—"little alligator" [1] Akika—"scent of autumn"; Komon—"little gate"; Shintama—"new ball"; and Kimi-chiyo, whose name was not translated for me, but who was the prettiest little dancing girl I saw in all Japan.

1 "What a queer name!" a Japanese friend writes me. And he adds: "Your translation cannot be right. A little alligator might be taken for a mascot in America, but it could never be the name of a dainty little geisha."

Though the Japanese idea of female loveliness does not generally accord with ours, I think Kimi-chiyo was an exception and was as lovely in native eyes as in those of an American, for she seemed very popular, and was at almost every Japanese-style party I attended in Tokyo. Moreover, though she could not have been older than sixteen, she carried herself with the placid confidence of an established belle. I have met many a lady twice or three times her age who had not her aplomb.

The little dancing girl at the right, Kimi-chiyo, was at almost every Japanese-style party I attended in Tokyo. She carried herself with the placid confidence of an established belle

After luncheon the maiko danced for us while Jitsuko and another geisha played. Then, as my guest of honour had not yet acquired a taste for geisha dancing, the programme was changed and Jitsuko set the little maiko to playing games. First they showed us how to play their great game of *ken*, but though we learned it we could not compete with them in playing it. They were too quick for us. We pitched quoits with them—and were beaten. We played bottle-and-cup—and were beaten. And finally they introduced us to a Japanese version of "Going to Jerusalem," which they play with cushions instead of chairs, with the samisen for music. Of course they beat us at that. Who can sink down upon a cushion with the agility of a little Japanese girl? All in all, the Americans were beaten at every point—and thoroughly enjoyed the beating.

I could tell a story about the president of one of the greatest corporations in America. He was at my luncheon. He is a very dignified and formidable man, and is considered able. But he can't play ken worth a cent. Kimi-chiyo herself said so. She told Jitsuko and Jitsuko told me.

"In America he is a great man," I said.

"He is very slow at ken," Kimi-chiyo insisted, unimpressed.

"In business he is not slow," I told her.

"Perhaps. But any one who is really clever will be quick at ken."

I decided to avoid the game of ken in future. It shows one up.

Between the geisha of the various great cities there exists a gentle rivalry. Kyoto, for example, concedes a certain vivacity to the geisha of the five or six leading districts of Tokyo, but it insists that the Kyoto geisha have unrivalled complexions, and that the famous Gion geisha of Kyoto are more perfect in their grace and charm than any others in Japan. This they account for by the fact that the Gion geisha have a long and distinguished history, and that there is a geisha school in Kyoto, whereas the Tokyo geisha have no school but are trained by older geisha under the supervision of the master of the individual geisha-house to which they are attached. Similarly the Tokyo geisha consider those of Kyoto rather "slow," and regard the Yokohama geisha as distinctly inferior. Once I asked a Tokyo geisha to give a dance of which I had heard, but she replied with something like a shrug that the dance in question was given by the Yokohama geisha, wherefore, she and her associates did not perform it.

So far as I know there is not to be seen in Tokyo or Yokohama any large geisha show, resembling a theatrical entertainment, such as one may see in Kyoto in cherry-blossom season, or at the Embujo Theatre in Osaka every May. These exhibitions are delightful things to see, the Cherry Dance of Kyoto, in particular, being famous throughout Japan. The buildings in which they are held are impressive. The one in Kyoto was built especially for the Cherry Dance, and the interior of it, while in a general way like a large theatre, is modelled after the style of an old Japanese palace. The geisha dancers and musicians are splendidly trained and the costumes are magnificent.

Rapid changes of scene are made in these theatres by means unfamiliar to American theatre-goers. As in our playhouses, flies and drops are sometimes hoisted upward when a scene is being changed, but quite as frequently they sink down through slots in the stage floor. Also, in the dimness of a "dark change" one sees whole settings going through extraordinary contortions, folding up in ways unknown in our theatres, or turning inside-out, or upside-down. One feels that their stage is generally equipped with less perfect mechanical and lighting devices than ours, but that a great deal of ingenuity is shown in the actual building of scenery. One of the most astonishing things I ever saw in any theatre was the sudden disappearance of a back-drop at the Embujo in Osaka. The bottom of this drop began all at once to contract;

then the whole funnel-shaped mass shot down through a small aperture in the floor, like a silk handkerchief passing swiftly through a ring.

The most perfect illusion of depth and distance I ever saw on a stage was in one scene of the Kyoto Cherry Dance. From the front of the house the scene appeared to go back and back incredibly. Nor could I make out where the back-drop met the stage, so skilfully was the painted picture blended with the built-up scenery. When the performance was over I inspected this setting and found that the scenic artist had achieved his result by a most elaborately complete contraction of the lines of perspective, not only in the painted scenery but in objects on the stage. A row of tables running from the footlights to the rear of the stage had been built in diminishing scale, and rows of Japanese lanterns, apparently exactly alike, became in reality smaller and smaller as they reached back from the proscenium, so that the whole perspective was exaggerated. The stage of this theatre was not in fact so deep as that of the New York Hippodrome or the Century Theatre.

At the geisha dance in Osaka I asked what pay the hundred or more geisha musicians and dancers received, and was told that they are not paid at all. There are two reasons for this. First, it is regarded as the duty of all geisha to celebrate the spring with music and dancing; and second, they consider it an honour to be selected for these festivals, since only the most skilful members of their sisterhood are chosen.

Geisha, you see, are not entirely mercenary. When two or three of them go off for a little outing together, or when they shop, they spend money freely; and there are stories of geisha who pay their own fees in order to meet their impecunious lovers at teahouses.

In Japanese romances the geisha is a favourite figure. A popular theme for stories concerning her is that of her love affair with a student whose family disown him because of his infatuation. The geisha sweetheart then supports him while he completes his education. He graduates brilliantly, securing an important appointment under the government, and rewards the girl's devotion by making her his bride. Or if the story be tragic—and the Japanese have a strong taste for tragedy—the student's family is endeavouring to force him into a brilliant match, wherefore the self-sacrificing geisha, whom he really loves, takes her own life, so that she may not stand in the way of his success.

There was a time a generation or two ago when Japanese aristocrats occasionally took geisha for their wives, much as young English noblemen used to marry chorus girls. But those things have changed in Japan and it is a long time since a man of position has made such a match. The plain truth is that, however justly or unjustly, the geisha class is not respected. They are victims of the curious law which operates the world over to make us always a little bit contemptuous of those whose occupation it is to amuse us. Moreover, geisha are not as a rule highly educated, and it is said that this fact makes it difficult for them to adjust themselves to an elevated place in the social scale.

Thus it comes about that, when geisha marry, their husbands are as a rule business men or merchants on a modest scale.

Yuki our treasured maid, had a friend who became a geisha, but who retired from the profession through the matrimonial portal.

"She smart girl," said Yuki. "She too head to be geisha."

"Why did she become one, then?" I asked.

"Her family have great trouble. Her father need fifteen hundred yen right off. Must have. So she be geisha. But after while she meet rich man in teahouse, and he pay for her, so she don't have to be geisha any more, and they get married."

Some excellent people I met in Japan—Americans imbued with the spirit of reform—objected strongly to the geisha system, contending that it is a barrier to happy domesticity. They felt that so long as there are geisha in Japan the average Japanese husband will have them at his parties, and will continue his present practice of leaving his wife at home when he goes out for a good time. I suppose this is true. Undoubtedly, to the Japanese wife, the geisha is the "other woman." And as is so often the case with the "other woman," in whatever land you find her, the geisha has certain strategic advantages over the wife. Like good wives everywhere, the Japanese wife is concerned with humdrum things—the children, housekeeping, the family finances—the things which often irritate and bore a husband if harped upon. But the circumstances in which a husband meets a geisha are genial and gay. Her business is to make him forget his cares and enjoy himself.

The expense of the geisha system is also urged against it. To dine at a first-class teahouse, with geisha, costs as much as, or more than, to dine elaborately at the most expensive New York hotels. It is well for strangers in Japan to understand this, since they often jump to the conclusion that the Japanese teahouse, which looks so simple—so delightfully simple!—by comparison with the gold and marble grandeur of a great American hotel dining room, must necessarily be cheaper. I remember a case in which some Americans, newly arrived in Tokyo, were entertained in the native manner by a Japanese gentleman, and felt that they were returning the courtesy in royal style when they invited him to dine with them at their hotel. Yet in point of fact their hotel dinner-party cost less than half as much per plate as his Japanese dinner had cost. While one does not value courtesy by what it costs, it is important not to undervalue it on any basis whatsoever.

There is, of course, a great variation in the cost of meals in teahouses and restaurants, and the fact that those which are inexpensive look exactly like those which are expensive helps to confuse the stranger. A great deal may be saved if one does without geisha. Also there are very agreeable restaurants in which the guest may cook his own food in a pan over a brazier which is brought into the dining room.

This chafing-dish style of cooking is said to have been introduced by a missionary who became tired of Japanese food and formed the habit of preparing his own meals as he travelled about. Now, however, it has come to be considered typically Japanese.

There are two names for cooking in this simple fashion. The word *torinabe* is derived from *tori*, a bird, and *nabe*, a pot or kettle; and *gyunabe* from a combination of the word for a pot with *gyu*, which means a cow, or beef. The Suyehiro restaurants, having three branches in Tokyo, are famous for *torinabe*, as well as for an affectation of elegant simplicity and crudity in chinaware. A good place for the *gyunabe* is the Mikawaya restaurant in the Yotsuya section, not far from the palace of the Crown Prince.

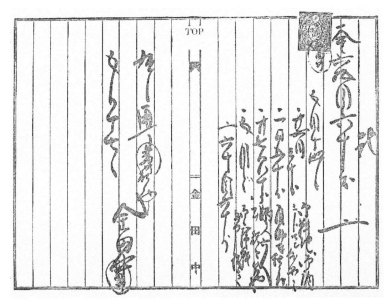

A bill from the Kanetanaka teahouse, with items of ¥ 26.30 for food, saké, etc., and ¥ 27.80 for "six saké-servers (geisha) tips to geisha and their attendants."

To be more specific about prices, I gave an excellent luncheon of this kind for four, at one of the Suyehiro restaurants, at a cost of about four dollars and a half, whereas a luncheon for the same number of persons, with geisha, at a fashionable teahouse, which looked just about like the other restaurant, cost thirty dollars, and a dinner for eight with geisha, came to fifty-three. All tips are however included on the teahouse bill. One does not pay at the time, but receives the bill later, regular patrons of a teahouse usually settling their accounts quarterly.

Adversaries of the geisha system informed me with the air of imparting scandal, that one sixth of all the money spent in Japan goes to geisha and things connected with geisha, presumably meaning restaurants, teahouses, saké and the like.

"A reformer," says Don Marquis, the Sage of Nassau Street, "is a dog in the manger who won't sin himself and won't let any one else sin comfortably." That is a terrible thing to say. I wouldn't say such a thing. It is always better in such cases to quote some one else. But I will say this much: If I were a reformer I should begin work at home—not in Japan. I should join the great movement, already so well started, for making the United States the purest and dullest country in the world. I should work with those who are attempting to accomplish this result entirely by legislation. But instead of trying, as they are now trying, to bring about the desired end by means of quantities of little pious laws covering quantities of little impious subjects, I should work for a blanket law covering everything—one great, sweeping law requiring all American citizens to be absolutely pure and good, not only in action but in thought. I assume that, if such a law were passed, everybody would abide by it, but in order to make it easier for them to do so I should abolish restaurants, theatres, motion pictures, dancing, baseball, talking-machines, art, literature, tobacco, candy, and soda-water. I should put dictographs in every home and have the police listen in on all conversations. Light-heartedness I should make a misdemeanor, and frivolity a crime.

Then, when our whole country had reached a state of perfection that was absolutely morbid, I should consider my work here done, and should move to Japan. But I should not stop being a reformer. Assuredly no! I should start at once to improve things over there. Take for instance this report that one sixth of all the money spent goes to geisha and such things. I should try first of all to remedy that situation. One sixth of the national expenditure represents a vast amount of money. Think of its being spent on good times! Such a lot of money! Still it isn't quite enough. A quarter or a third would be better than a sixth. It would make things perfect. Not being a Japanese wife, I should advocate that.

I see but one serious objection to this plan. Should Japan become any more attractive than it now is, the Japanese might feel forced to pass exclusion laws. If they were to do so I hope they would not discriminate against people of any one race. I hope they would bar out everybody—not Americans alone. Because if they were to bar us out and at the same time allow the riffraff of Europe to come in, that might hurt our feelings. It isn't so hard to hurt our feelings, either. We are a proud and sensitive race, you know. Yes, indeed! It is largely because we are so proud and sensitive that we treat the Japanese with such scant courtesy. That's the way pride and sensitiveness sometimes work. Of course the Japanese are proud and sensitive, too. But we can't be bothered about that. We haven't the time. We are too busy being proud and sensitive ourselves.

CHAPTER XIII

Commercialized Vice—The Yoshiwara—An Establishment Therein—Famous Old Geisha—A "Male Geisha"—The Stately Shogi—They Show Us Courtesy—The Merits of the Shogi—Kyoto's Shimabara—The Shogi in Romance—The Tale of the Fair Yoshino

Some Americans are horrified because commercialized vice is officially recognized in Japan. The thought is unpleasant. But I am by no means sure that, since this form of vice does exist everywhere in the world, the policy of recognizing and regulating it is not the best policy.

The Japanese work, apparently, upon the theory that, as this evil cannot be stamped out of existence, the next best thing is to stamp it as far as possible out of the public consciousness. This is done by segregating the women called *shogi* in certain specified districts, and keeping them off the city streets.

Whatever may be urged for or against this system it enables me to say of Japan what I am not able to say of my own country or any other country I have visited: namely, that in Japan I never saw a street-walker.

The Tokyo district called the Yoshiwara is entered by a wide road spanned by an arch. Within, the streets look much like other Japanese streets, save that they are brightly lighted and that some of the buildings are large and rather ornate. First we went to a teahouse of the Yoshiwara, and I was readily able to perceive that the geisha in this teahouse were of a lower grade than those I had hitherto seen. Their faces were less intelligent, and they lacked the perfect grace and charm of their more successful sisters.

From the sounds about us it was apparent that a Yoshiwara teahouse is a place for drinking and more or less wild merrymaking.

Proceeding down the street from this teahouse we passed through orderly crowds and presently came to the district's most elaborate establishment. It was a large three-story building of white glazed brick, with an inner courtyard containing a pretty garden. To enter this place was like entering a very fine Japanese hotel.

In the corridor hung a row of lacquered sticks each bearing a number in the Chinese character. There were, I think, about thirty of these sticks, and each represented a shogi. The number-one shogi was the most sought-after; number two ranked next, and so on. We were shown by the proprietress and some maids to a large matted room on the second floor, where saké, cakes and fruit were served to us. Then there appeared three geisha of a most unusual kind. They were women fifty-five or sixty years of age, rather large, with faces genial, amusing, and respectable. These I was told were geisha with a great local reputation for boisterous wit. My Japanese friends were thereafter kept in a continual state of mirth, and though I could not understand what the old geisha were saying, their droll manner was so infectious that I, too, was amused. Presently they were joined by a man with the face of a comedian. He was described to me as a "male geisha." That is, he was an entertainer. He sang, told comic stories and showed real ability as a mimic.

This entertainment lasted for the better part of an hour. Then the mistress of the house came in with the air of one having something important to reveal. At a word from her the entertainers drew back and seated themselves on cushions at one side of the room. There was an impressive silence. Slowly, a sliding screen door of black lacquer and gold paper slipped back, moved by an unseen hand. We watched the open doorway.

Presently appeared the figure of a woman. She did not look in our direction, but moved out into the room as if it had been a stage and she an actress. Her step was slow and stately, and she was arrayed in a brilliant robe of red satin, heavily quilted, and embroidered with large elaborate designs. This was the number-one shogi. Her costume and bearing were magnificent, but her face was expressionless and not at all beautiful.

When she was well within the room the number-two shogi, dressed in the same style, moved in behind her, and followed with the same stately tread. In procession they walked across the room, turned slowly, trailed the hems of their wadded kimonos back across the matting, and made an exit by the door at which they had entered. Then the door slipped shut.

The chatter began once more, but after a few minutes we were again silenced. For the second time the door opened and the two women appeared. They were now arrayed in purple kimonos, quilted and embroidered like the first. Again they made a dignified progress across the room and back; again they disappeared.

That was the end of the inspection. By now we should, in theory, have been entranced with one or the other of the shogi we had seen. It was time to go. But as the Japanese gentleman whom I had asked to bring me to this place was a man of consequence, an especial courtesy was shown us ere we departed. In ordinary circumstances we should not have seen the two women again, but now they unbent so far as to come in and kneel upon the floor beside us—for we had checked our shoes at the entrance, and were seated Japanese-fashion upon silk cushions.

My Japanese friends attempted to chat with the shogi, but evidently the latter did not shine in the arts of conversation. The talk was grave and unmistakably perfunctory, and after a little while the two arose, bowed profoundly, with a sort of grandeur, and trailed their wondrous robes out of the room. It was like seeing in the life a pair of courtesans from a colour-print by Utamaro. As they went I wondered whether, in the beginning, they had striven to be geisha instead of shogi, but had been forced to the Yoshiwara by reason of their lack of talent for music and conversation.

Before we left I was shown some of the other rooms of this huge house, including those of several of the women. The woodwork was like light brown satin and the matting glistened almost as though it were lacquered. There were some kakemono and fine painted screens with old-gold backgrounds, and in the women's rooms were cabinets and dressing-stands lacquered red and gold. The dressing-stands were of a height to suit one squatting on the floor. It was as though the top section of one of our dressing tables were set upon the floor—a mirror with small drawers at either side.

The mistress and her maids accompanied us to the street door when we departed. They made profound obeisances, and the mistress declared her appreciation of the great honour we had paid her by visiting her establishment. My Japanese friends replied in kind. The whole affair was conducted with a fine sense of ceremony.

As for the three elderly geisha, they took another way of complimenting us. Instead of making ceremonious speeches they continued to be gay and amusing, but they did something which, when geisha do it, is considered a mark of high respect. They left the place with us, accompanying us as far as the gate of the Yoshiwara. One of them, a jolly old creature, with a fine, strong humorous face, linked arms with me as we walked along, and conversed with me in English. Perhaps the word "conversed" implies too much. Her entire English vocabulary consisted of the words: "All right," but she repeated the expression frequently and with changing intonations which gave a sort of variety.

It was a strange evening, and the strangest part of it was the absence of vulgarity. I had seen nothing that the most fastidious woman could not have seen.

As to what treatment is accorded the shogi themselves I cannot say. Certainly they did not have the air of being happy. Almost all of them are there because of poverty, and it is said that all live in the hope that some man will become fond of them and buy them out of the life of the *joroya*. This I believe occasionally happens. It should be added that, under the Japanese law, contracts by which women sell themselves, or are sold by others into this life, are not valid. It may further be added that all authorities on Japan seem to be in accord with Chamberlain who says that "the fallen women of Japan are, as a class, much less vicious than their representatives in Western lands, being neither drunken nor foul-mouthed." They also have a high reputation for honesty.

The name Yoshiwara is not a generic term, though strangers sometimes use it as if it were, speaking of "a Yoshiwara." Similar districts in other cities are known by other names—as, for example, the historic Shimabara, in Kyoto, which dates back about four centuries.

Like the Yoshiwara, the Shimabara has been moved from time to time, with a view to keeping it away from the heart of the city. History records that Hideyoshi caused the district to be uprooted and transplanted, and Ieyasu, the first Tokugawa shogun, did the same, on the ground that it was too near the palace and the business centre.

I find some odd items in a book giving the history of the Shimabara. It is said that in the old days only ronin—samurai acknowledging no overlord—were given charters to operate resorts in the Shimabara, and that court gentlemen visiting this quarter were required to wear white garments. There is also the story of a city official who used to meet now and then upon the streets of Kyoto a beautiful woman riding in a palanquin. It was his custom to salute her respectfully, for he thought her a court lady. But one day, upon inquiry, he learned that she was a courtesan, whereupon he became indignant, and caused the Shimabara quarter to be again removed, placing it still farther away from the city's heart.

There is some evidence that in feudal Japan the most admired courtesans were persons of more consequence than those of to-day. In olden times, for example, the Shimabara women were considered to rank above geisha, whereas now the situation is decidedly the reverse.

The stories of certain famous women of the ancient Shimabara are still remembered, and are favourites with writers of romances. One quaint tale tells of a beautiful girl named Tokuko, the daughter of a ronin. When her father and her mother died, leaving her penniless, she went into the Shimabara. Here, because of her grace, she became known as *Uki-fune* "floating ship." But she wrote a poem about the cherry blossoms at Mt. Yoshino, in Yamato Province, a place which for more than ten centuries has been noted for these blooms, and her poem was so much admired that she herself came to be called Yoshino.

A rich man's son fell in love with this girl and married her, but when his father learned what had been her occupation he disowned the youth. The young couple were however courageous. In a tiny cottage they lived a happy and romantic life.

One day it happened that the father, caught in a heavy rainstorm, asked shelter in a little house at the roadside. Here he found a beautiful young woman playing exquisitely upon the harp-like musical instrument called the *koto*. She welcomed him charmingly, made him comfortable, served him tea.

When the storm had passed the old man thanked her for her hospitality and departed. But he had been so struck with her beauty and grace that he made inquiries about her.

"Ah," exclaimed the one of whom he asked, "she is none other than Yoshino, wife of your disinherited son!"

Upon hearing this the father relented. He sent for the young couple, took them to live in his own mansion, and directed the daughter-in-law to resume her original name, Tokuko—which means "virtue."

However, I have noticed that in Japan and all other lands, romantic stories making heroines of courtesans have to be dated pretty far back. The living courtesan is but rarely regarded as a romantic figure. She is like a piece of common glass.

But a piece of common glass, buried long enough in certain kinds of soil, acquires iridescence. This iridescence is not actually in the glass, but exists in a patine which gradually adheres to it. Under a little handling it will flake off.

I suspect that it is much the same with famous courtesans the world over. When, after having been buried for a hundred years or so, they are, so to speak, dug up by novelists and playwrights, there adheres to them a beautiful iridescent patine.

It is best, perhaps, to refrain from scratching the patine lest we find out what is really underneath.

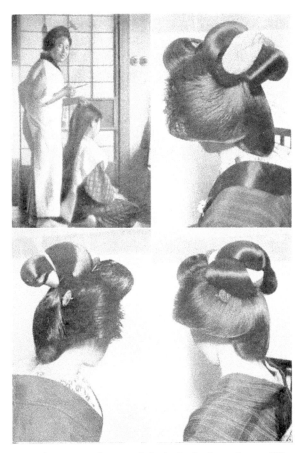

It takes two hours to do a geisha's hair, but the coiffure, once
accomplished, lasts several days

CHAPTER XIV

Japan and Italy—The Sense of Beauty—Poetry—Japanese Poems by an American Woman—A Poem on a Kimono—Garden Ornaments—Garden Parties and Gifts—The Four Periods of Landscape Gardening—The Volcanic Principle in Gardens

It is interesting to observe that the two races in which highly specialized artistic feeling is almost universal have, despite their antipodal positions on the globe, many common problems and one common blessing. Both Japan and Italy are poor and overpopulated, both are handicapped by a shortage of arable land and natural resources, both lack an adequate supply of food and raw materials for manufacturing, both are mountainous, both are afflicted by earthquakes; but both are endowed with the peculiar, passionate beauty of landscape which is nature's compensation to volcanic countries—a beauty suggesting that of some vivid and ungoverned woman, brilliant, erratic, fascinating, dangerous.

Where Nature shows herself a great temperamental artist, her children are likely to be artists, too. As almost all Italians have a highly developed sense of melody, so almost all Japanese possess in a remarkable degree the artist's sense of form.

One day in Tokio I fell to discussing these matters with a venerable art collector, wearing silks and sandals.

"What," he asked me, "are the most striking examples of artistic feeling that you have noticed in Japan?"

I told him of two things that I had seen, each in itself unimportant. One was a well-wheel. The well was in a yard beside a lovely little farmhouse, one story high, with walls of clay and timber, and with a thick thatched roof, upon the ridge of which a row of purple iris grew. There was a dainty bamboo fence around the farmyard, with flowering shrubs behind it, and a cherry tree in blossom. The well-house was thatched, and the pulley-wheel beneath the thatch seemed to focus the entire composition. With us such a wheel would have been a thing of rough cast-iron, merely something for a rope to run over; but this wheel had been fondly imagined before it was created. Its spokes were not straight and ugly, but branched near the rim, curving gracefully into it in such a way as to form the outlines of a cherry-blossom. It was a work of art.

My other item was a little copper kettle. I saw it in a penitentiary. It belonged to a prisoner, and every prisoner in that portion of the institution had one like it. The striking thing about it was that it was an extremely graceful little kettle, embellished in relief with a beautiful design. It, too, was a work of art, and there was to me something pathetic in the evidence it gave that even in this grim place the claims of beauty were not entirely ignored.

These trifling observations seemed to please my friend, the art collector.

"But," said he, "I think our national love of the beautiful is perhaps most strongly exhibited in our feeling for outdoor beauty—our pilgrimages to spots famous for their scenery, our delight in the cherry-blossom season, the wistaria season, the chrysanthemum season, and by no means least in our gardens."

Undoubtedly he was right. The feeling for nature among his countrymen is general, mystical, poetic. Almost all Japanese write poetry. The poems of many emperors, empresses, and statesmen are widely known; and among the most celebrated Japanese poems those to Nature in her various aspects are by far the most numerous.

Let me here digress briefly to mention the interesting custom of *O Uta Hajime*, or Opening of Imperial Poems, a court function dating from the ninth century.

Each December the Imperial Household announces subjects for poems which may be submitted anonymously to the Imperial Bureau of Poems, in connection with the celebration of the New Year. The poems are examined by the bureau's experts, who select the best, to be read to the Imperial Family.

The choice for the year 1921 was made from seventeen thousand poems sent from all parts of the Empire, and when announcement was made of the names of those whose poems were read at the Court, it was discovered that, among them was an American lady, Frances Hawkes Burnett, wife of Col. Charles Burnett, military attaché of the American Embassy at Tokyo. Mrs. Burnett thus attains the unique distinction of being the only foreign woman ever to have won Imperial approval with a poem in the Japanese language.

Mrs. Charles Burnett in a 15th-Century Japanese Court costume. Mrs. Burnett's poems written in Japanese have received Imperial recognition

It is interesting, in this connection, to remark that the lady is a grand-niece of the late Dr. Francis Lister Hawkes, of New York, who accompanied Commodore Perry to Japan, and was Perry's collaborator in the writing of the official record of the voyage, published under the title, "The Narrative of the Expedition of an American Squadron."

But to return to my friend the art collector.

"Speaking of poetry and the love of Nature," said he, "have you noticed the kimono of our host's daughter?"

(We were strolling in a lovely private garden as we talked.)

I had noticed it. It was a beautiful costume of soft black silk, the hem, in front, adorned with a design of cherry-blossoms and an inscription in the always decorative Chinese character.

"Do you know what the inscription is?" he asked.

I did not.

"It is a poem of her own," he explained; and presently, when in our stroll we caught up with the young lady, he made me a literal translation, which might be done over into English verse as follows:

Farewell, O Capital! I grieve
Thy lovely cherry-blooms to leave.
But now to Kioto must I fare
To view the cherry-blossoms there.

We fell to talking of Japanese gardens.

"You must see some of our fine gardens," he said, "before you leave Japan."

I mentioned some I had already seen—the gardens of the Crown Prince, the Prime Minister, Marquis Okuma, Viscount Shibusawa, Baron Furukawa, and others.

"But do you understand our theory of the garden?"

I told him what little I then knew: that flowers are not essential to a garden in Japan; that, where used, they are generally set apart in beds, and removed when they have ceased to bloom; that because of the skill of the Japanese in transplanting large trees a garden of ancient appearance may be made in few years; that boundaries are artfully planted out, so that some houses, standing on a few acres of ground in great cities, appear to be surrounded by forests; that small garden lakes are sometimes so arranged as to suggest that they are only arms of large bodies of water concealed from view by wooded headlands; and that optical illusions are often employed to make gardens seem much larger than they are, this being accomplished by a cunning scaling down in the size of the more remote hillocks, trees, and shrubs, increasing the perspective.

Also, I had seen examples of the *kare sensui* school of landscape gardening—waterless lakes and streams, their beds delineated in sand, gravel, and selected pebbles, and their banks set off by great water-worn stones brought from elsewhere, and by trees and shrubs carefully trained to droop toward the imaginary water—water the more completely suggested by stepping-stones and arched bridges reaching out to little islands, with stone lanterns standing among dwarf pines.

I knew, too, of the fondness of the Japanese for minor buildings in their gardens. Thus in the garden of Viscount Shibusawa, there is an ancient Korean teahouse of very striking architecture; in that of Dr. Takuma Dan, General Manager of the vast Mitsui interests, a farmhouse several centuries old; in that of Baron Okura, a famous museum of Chinese and Japanese antiquities and art works; and in the gardens of Baron Furukawa and Baron Sumitomo, smaller private museums. Tucked away in the corner of one garden near Kobe I had even seen a little factory in which the finest wireless cloisonné was being made, the owner of that garden having a deep interest in this art and using the productions of his artist-workmen to give as presents to his friends. And of course in many gardens I had seen houses built especially for the *cha-no-yu*, or Tea Ceremony.

Moreover, I had been to garden parties at some of which luncheons were served under marquees of bamboo and striped canvas, while at others were offered entertainments consisting of geisha-dancing and juggling. At such parties souvenirs are always given—fans and kakemono painted by artists on the premises, or bits of pottery which, after being painted, are glazed and fired, and still warm from the kiln, presented to the guests.

"Yes, yes," said my venerable friend, "you have seen a good deal; but as to the history and theory of our gardens, what do you know?"

"Very little," I admitted, and asked him to enlighten me.

Japanese landscape gardening began twelve hundred years ago, when the Emperor Shomu, in residence at Nara, sent for a Chinese monk who was famed for his artistry and ordered him to beautify the ancient capital. This the monk accomplished chiefly by cutting out avenues among the lofty trees which to this day make Nara not only a place of supreme loveliness, but one rich in the aroma of antiquity. Thus came the first period of landscape gardening in Nippon, the Tempyo period.

Five and a half centuries ago the second period began when, in the terrain surrounding the Kinkakuji Temple at Kyoto, gardens containing lakes, rocks, and gold-pavilioned islands were constructed in resemblance to the natural scenery near the mouth of the Yangtse River in China.

The third period is best represented by the gardens of the arsenal in Tokyo. These were made three hundred years ago by a Chinese master named Shunsui, who was brought to Japan for the purpose by the Lord of Mito, brother of the shogun who at that time ruled Japan. In order to get water for this park a canal thirty miles long was constructed, and this same canal later supplied water to the city of Yedo, as Tokyo was then called.

The current period is the fourth, and it is the aim of the present-day masters to combine in their work all the fine points of the preceding periods. This development is largely due to the ease of modern transportation, which has enabled the landscape gardeners of our time to travel widely and become familiar with the best work of their distinguished predecessors and the finest natural scenery. For instance, the Shiobara region, in northern Japan, a district famous for its lovely little corners, has been the inspiration for many modern gardens.

"And now," said my learned friend as we paused in a little shelter of bamboo and thatch, overlooking the corner of a lake bordered with curiously formed rocks and flowering shrubs, "I will tell you the great secret of this art; for of course you understand that with us landscape gardening is definitely placed as one of the fine arts." He paused for a moment, then continued: "The one sound principle for making a garden wherever water is used is what may be called the volcanic principle. That is to say, the artist in landscape gardening should go for his themes to places of volcanic origin; for in such places the greatest natural beauty is found.

"And why? First of all, you have hills of interesting contours, made by eruptions. Then you have mountain lakes which form in the beds of extinct volcanoes. Our famous Lake Chuzenji, above Nikko, for example. From these lakes the water overflows, making splendid falls, like those of Kegon, which empty out of Lake Chuzenji. Below the falls you have a torrent rushing down a rocky valley, like the River Daiya, which flows from the Kegon Falls past Nikko, where it is spanned by the famous red-lacquered bridge. There is the basis for your entire garden composition.

"But you must also remember that volcanic outpourings make rich soil. This soil, thrown into the air by volcanic explosions, settles in the crevices of rocks. Pines take root in it. But in some places the pocket of soil is small; wherefore the roots of the pine cannot spread, and the tree becomes a dwarf, gnarled and picturesque. Again, on the hillsides the rich soil makes great trees grow, with rich shrubbery and verdure beneath them. The torrent completes the landscape effect by sculpturing the rocks into fascinating forms. In that combination you have every element required. Reproduce it in miniature, and your garden is made."

CHAPTER XV

The garden theory of my friend the art collector, so Japanese in its completeness, charmed and satisfied me.

"Now," I thought to myself, "I *know*."

Thenceforward I looked at gardens not with the unenlightened enthusiasm of the casual amateur, but with a critic's eye. Here and there I would make a mental reservation, saying to myself that the man who made this garden had missed something in one respect or another; that the one great principle, the volcanic principle, had not been fully carried out.

So time went on until presently I found myself in Kyoto, the cultivated city of Japan, seated at a table (upon which were glasses and a bottle) beside one of the most interesting Japanese I had met, a man of ripe age and experience and of a philosophical turn of mind. He loved the history, the legends and the psychology of his native land, and enjoyed sifting them through the interpretative screen of his own intelligence.

I listened to him with eager interest.

"To boast," said he, "is, according to our point of view, one of the cardinal sins. We so detest boasting that we go to the other extreme, depreciating anything or anybody connected with ourselves. Thus, when some one says to me, 'Your brother has amassed a fortune; he must be a man of great ability,' I will reply: 'He is not so very able. Perhaps he is only lucky.' As a matter of fact, it happens that my brother is a man of exceptional ability. But I must not say so; it is not good form for me to praise his qualities.

"In speaking of our wives and children we do the same. We say, 'my poor wife,' or, 'my insignificant wife,' although she may fulfil our ideal of everything a woman should be.

"Also the reverse of this proposition is true. We sometimes signify our disapproval or dislike of some one by speaking of him in terms of too high praise.

"Among ourselves we fully understand these things. It is merely a code we follow. But I fear that this practice sometimes causes foreigners to misunderstand us. Being themselves accustomed to speak literally, they are inclined to take us so. Also, they are not likely to realize that we are most critical of those for whom we have profound regard. Why should we waste our time or our critical consideration upon persons who mean nothing to us or whom we dislike?

"Yet, after all," he continued, with a little twinkle in his eye, "human nature is much the same the world over. There was an American here in Kyoto once who used to forbid his wife and sister to smoke cigarettes, but I observed that he was quick to pass his cigarette-case to other ladies."

He drifted on to a further discussion of differences between the point of view of Japan and that of the Occident.

"For twenty-five centuries," said he, "our emperors never lived behind a fortification. There was no need of it. The present imperial palace at Tokyo is, to be sure, protected by a moat and great stone walls, but that was originally built for shoguns, and was taken over by the Imperial House only at the time of the Restoration.

"Our old Japanese idea is that the Emperor is the father of his people. There is a certain reverence, yet a certain democracy, too, in our feeling on this subject. We who have the old ideas regret that the Emperor now appears in a military or naval uniform. It is too much like the European way, too much like abandoning the feeling that he is the head of the family. For a uniform seems to make him only a part of the army or the navy.

"But we had to modify our customs to suit those of other nations. Ambassadors began to come from foreign lands. The Emperor did not wish to see them, but was obliged to do so because they represented great powers to whom we could not say no.

"At first, when the Emperor received ambassadors, he wore his ancient imperial robes and was seated upon cushions, Japanese fashion. But the ambassadors were arrayed in brilliant uniforms covered with decorations, and in accordance with their home customs they *stood* in the imperial presence. They would stand before a European king or an American president. Therefore it seemed to them respectful to stand before our Emperor.

"But, according to our customs, that is the worst thing that can happen. We must always be lower than the Emperor; we must not even look from a second-story window when he drives by. The Emperor's audience-room was so constructed that he sat in an elevated place at the head of a flight of steps. But even so, one never entered his presence standing fully erect. The idea of deference was visibly indicated by a stooping position, and as one ascended the steps toward the Imperial Person, one bent over more and more, until, on reaching the plane on which the Emperor was seated, one knelt, with bowed head, so as still to be below him.

"A foreigner, on the other hand, wishing to show proper respect to an exalted personage, would make a bow from the waist and then assume a stiffly erect attitude, almost like a soldier standing at attention. Can you imagine an Occidental admiral or general, with his tight uniform, heavy braid, and sword, approaching any one upon his hands and knees? It would be foreign to his nature and training, not to say ruinous to his costume. [2]

2 An extremely interesting account of the first audience given by the Emperor to a foreign ambassador is contained in "Memories," by the late Lord Redesdale, who was present. Lord Redesdale was then Mr. Mitford, and was engaged in preparing a volume which later became widely known under the title "Tales of Old Japan."

"Moreover, the important foreigners who came to Japan at the beginning of the period of transition were gorgeous with gold lace and jewelled decorations. Up to that time we had no decorations and no modern uniforms and trappings of rank. Even our Emperor, in his magnificent robes, was not adorned with gold braid, and no jewels flashed from his breast.

"Naturally, then, we had to change. We created new orders of nobility; decorations were devised, uniforms were designed, all according to the European plan. In the old days we had shogun, daimyo, and samurai. Now we have princes of the blood, princes not of the blood, marquises, counts, viscounts, and barons. We have decorations to shine with foreign decorations. We have field-marshals and admirals to meet the foreign field-marshals and admirals."

He sighed, and looked through the open window to the garden shimmering in moonlight.

"Sometimes," he said, reflectively, "it seems to me that the only place where the spirit of Old Japan can feel at home is when it wanders through our ancient gardens. They are unchanged."

He paused, still gazing through the open window, then went on:

"That is another thing I must talk to you about. We Japanese have a profound feeling about gardens. The structure of a garden is a matter of the first importance. You must see some of our gardens."

"I have done so already," I replied. "I have taken pains to visit many of them, and I——"

"But," he interrupted, "I am not speaking entirely of vision in the sense of sight. One must have understanding of these things. I am talking of the basic principles upon which every garden should be made."

"That is just what I am talking about," I returned, enthusiastically. "It happens that I have made quite a study of your theory of gardens."

A tea-house garden, Tokyo.—"The artist in landscape gardening should go for his themes to places of volcanic origin."

I must own that I did not speak without a certain complacency. I had the comfortable feeling that always comes to one who hears a subject broached and feels himself well equipped to discuss it.

"That is very gratifying," said the philosopher, politely.

It was indeed very gratifying. My memory was good. I casually mentioned the four periods of Japanese landscape gardening, making easy references to the Emperor Shomu, the scenery near the mouth of the Yangtse River, and the Chinese master Shunsui. Then I began to file my bill of particulars.

"Of course," I said, "the one great secret of the art is to apply the volcanic principle. One should go for themes to places of volcanic origin—places like Lake Chuzenji and Nikko, places where lakes, formed in the beds of extinct volcanoes, overflow, making beautiful waterfalls and torrents which rush through rocky valleys. There, of course, is the basis for your entire garden composition."

He sat staring at me. His eyes shone. Evidently I was making a deep impression on him.

"Of course," I resumed, "volcanic explosions throw rich soil into——"

"Stop!" he cried, half rising from his chair. "Who gave you those theories? Where did you learn all this?"

"In Tokyo," I answered proudly, "I happened to meet——"

"Never mind whom you met," he broke in, his voice trembling with intensity. "These things you have been saying are terrible—terrible! Such ideas are ruining art and beauty in Japan. A garden of that kind is an abomination."

I sat stunned while he stood over me.

"The thing above all others to keep away from," he continued, vehemently, "is anything volcanic. That should be apparent to any one—any one! The very cause of volcanic structure is violence. It is the embodiment of turmoil, unrest." He made a wild gesture with his arms. "A volcano blows up, it explodes—*bang!* It throws everything about helter-skelter. It is horrible. That is a garden for a madhouse or the palace of a *narikin*—a new millionaire."

"But don't you think——"

"If one thing is more essential than another in a garden," he went on, ignoring my effort to interrupt, "it is peace, tranquillity, an atmosphere conducive to meditation. Fancy a cultivated gentleman, a philosopher, trying to meditate among volcanoes, waterfalls, and roaring torrents! A garden should have no waterfalls. Water, if it is there at all, should flow as placidly as philosophic thought. There should be no fish darting about, no noisy splashing fountains, no gaudy peonies, or other striking and distracting things. The purpose of a garden should not be display. Its proper purpose is not to excite the beholder, but to fill him with a rich contentment. A garden should be a bathing-place for the soul. And one no more wishes to plunge the soul than the body into a roaring torrent. No; there is in life already too much stress and turmoil. The soul cries out for repose. One must lave it in a crystal pool, healing and refreshing."

He paused, short of breath.

"But don't you think——"

"Say no more! It is late. I must go home."

I walked with him to the garden gate. A new moon hanging in a sky of blue and silver was reflected in a still pool, its margins soft with the dark, cloud-like forms of shrubbery. Near the gate some calla lilies stood like graceful, silent ghosts. The night air was fragrant with the scent of rich, damp soil and growing things.

"But don't you think," I pleaded as I opened the gate to let him pass, "that there is, after all, something poetic in the volcanic conception of a garden?"

"No, no," he cried. "Poetic? No. Good night. Good night. I do not understand this new Japan. There is no repose any more. It is all volcanoes, all exploding. It is the beauties of calm that we are losing. Calm! Yes, that is it, calm! calm! calm!"

His agitated voice, shouting, "Calm! calm! calm!" came back to me as like a typhoon he whirled off into the darkness, leaving me in the sweet quiet of the garden—to meditate.

PART III

CHAPTER XVI

The "Connecticut Yankee" in Old Japan—Commodore Perry—The Elder Statesmen—Marquis Okuma—Self-made Men—Viscount Shibusawa—The Power of the Daimyo—Samurai Privileges, Including That of Suicide—Education in Old Japan—Jigoro Kano and Jiudo—The Farewell Letter of a Patriot—Kodokwan and Butokukai—The Old Military Virtues—General Nogi—His Death With Countess Nogi

Despite the convulsions, overturnings, and transitions through which so many nations have lately been passing, Japan still holds the world's record for swift and stupendous change. The thing that happened to Japan staggers the imagination. History affords no parallel. The nearest parallel is to be found in the fiction of a great imaginative writer. An American or a European going to Japan at approximately the time of the Imperial Restoration of 1868, found himself, in effect, dropped back through the centuries after the manner of Mark Twain's "Connecticut Yankee"; and the Japanese who lived through the transition which then began, met an experience like that pictured in Mark Twain's fantasy as having befallen the people of King Arthur's Court when modern knowledge was suddenly visited upon them.

The true story of Japan, however, surpasses in its wonder the invention of Mark Twain; for whereas the facts of history compelled the author of "A Connecticut Yankee in King Arthur's Court" to let ancient Britain backslide into her semi-barbarism after the disappearance of the Connecticut Yankee, Japan not only changed completely but held her gains and continued to progress.

The beginning of the period of transition is customarily dated from the year 1853, when Commodore Perry first arrived, or from 1854, when he negotiated his treaty; but though that treaty did open the door through which the spirit of change was soon to enter, the actual modernizing of the nation did not start until 1868, when Yoshinobu Tokugawa, fifteenth of his line, and last shogun to govern Japan, relinquished his power to the Emperor.

Men able to remember the events of the Restoration are about as rare in Japan as are those who, in this country, remember the impeachment of Andrew Johnson, which occurred in the same year; and men who played important parts in the Restoration are of course rarer still—as rare, say, as Americans who played important parts in the Civil War. As for Japanese who can recall Perry's visit, they would correspond in years to those who, with us, can recollect the beginning of the struggle for Free Soil in Kansas. In neither land, alas, is there more than a handful of such old folk left.

It so happens, however, that in Japan several very remarkable men have survived to great age.

The three most powerful figures in politics at the time of my visit were the octogenarian noblemen known as the Genro, or Elder Statesmen: Field Marshal Prince Yamagata, Marquis Matsukata, and Marquis Okuma. Prince Yamagata, as a soldier, took an active part in the civil warfare attending the Restoration. Both he and Marquis Okuma were born in 1838—that is to say seven years before Texas was admitted to the Union as the twenty-eighth state. Marquis Matsukata was born in 1840.

Of these venerable statesmen, Prince Yamagata and Marquis Matsukata figured, I found, as great unseen influences; but Marquis Okuma, while perhaps not actually more active than his colleagues of the Genro, appeared frequently before the public, and was more of a popular idol, being often referred to as Japan's "Grand Old Man." In politics he had long been known as a great fighter and an artful tactician; also he was sympathetically regarded by reason of his having been, many years ago, the victim of a bomb outrage in which he lost a leg.

I knew of his having been thus crippled, but through some trick of memory failed to recall the fact when, one day, I found myself a member of a small party of Americans received by the Marquis at his house. We were with him for something more than an hour; perhaps two hours. During that time he stood and made an address, moved about the room, and even stepped out to the garden, yet I was not once reminded of his physical handicap. I have never seen a person so seriously maimed who, in his movements, revealed it so little. And that at eighty-three years of age!

I should have guessed him twenty years younger. Lean, tall, wiry, alert, with close-cropped white hair and snapping black eyes, he appeared to be at the very apex of his powers.

That he was versatile I knew. All three of the Genro have at various times been Prime Minister, and have held other high offices under the Government, but Marquis Okuma's positions have been extremely varied, calling for the display of a wide range of knowledge and of talents. I was told that he had organized the Nationalist Party, published a magazine, edited a number of important literary and historical works, founded and presided over Waseda University, and had long been famed as a horticulturist.

It was a curious thing to hear him speak in a language I could not understand, yet to feel so strongly his gift for swaying men with oratory.

The experience reminded me of that of a newspaper man I know, who accompanied William Jennings Bryan on one of his political speech-making tours long ago.

"I was a dyed-in-the-wool Republican," he told me, in recounting the experience, "and did not believe in Bryan or his measures, yet I continually found myself carried away by his oratory. While he was speaking he made me believe in things I *didn't* believe in. I would want to applaud and cheer him like the rest of the audience.

"Afterwards I would go back to the train and sober up. I wanted to kick myself for letting him twist me around his finger like that. But the next time I heard him the same thing would happen. It wasn't what he said; it was his voice and phrasing and his magnetism."

I have no doubt that a Japanese unacquainted with English would sense Bryan's elocutionary power precisely as I did that of Marquis Okuma; indeed I am not sure that a foreigner, unfamiliar with the language of the orator, is not in a sense the auditor who can best measure his power.

Marquis Okuma's features indicated extraordinary pugnacity, yet I should say that his pugnacity was under perfect control. He could exhibit both passion and icy coolness, and I believe he could turn on either at will, as one turns on hot or cold water. If he was William Jennings Bryan he was also Henry Cabot Lodge.

It is worth remarking that these Elder Statesmen are without exception self-made men. None of them was born with a title; all were members of modest samurai families; all rose through ability.

In this respect, as in many others, comparisons between the governmental system of Imperial Japan and that of Imperial Germany that was, do not hold. Japan is not governed by a hereditary ruling class. The government service is open to all men, under a system of competitive examinations, and promotion does not go by family or favour, but is in almost all cases a recognition of ability exhibited in minor offices. Young men in the consular service are in line for ambassadorships and may reasonably hope, if they exhibit great talents, ultimately to reach the highest offices.

It would seem, moreover, that in Japan as in some other lands, aristocratic and wealthy families do not, as a rule, produce the strongest men. Thus I was informed that, of the entire cabinet of Prime Minister Hara, but one member was a man of noble family, that one having been Count Oki, Minister of Justice. And even Count Oki was only of the second generation of nobility.

In the business world the same rule applies. The titled business men of Japan have risen, practically without exception, from humble beginnings. I was told that one of them, whom I met, had begun life as a pedlar, and was proud of it. Looking up another business genius in the national "Who's Who," I find the following statement, which may be assumed to have been furnished by the gentleman to whom it refers:

> Arrived in Tokyo in '71, with empty purse; proceeded to Yokohama, supporting himself by hawking cheap viands.

If the honorary title, "Grand Old Man of Japan," had not already been conferred, and I had been invited to make nominations, I should have gone outside the realm of politics and cast my vote for Viscount Eiichi Shibusawa.

Had the Viscount been, at the time of the Restoration, a member of one of the great clans responsible for the return of the reins of government to Imperial hands, his career might have resembled more closely the careers of the three old nobles of the Genro. But whereas Prince Yamagata, Marquis Matsukata, and Marquis Okuma were respectively men of Choshu, Satsuma, and Saga—clans that cast their lot with the coalition that returned the Emperor to power—Viscount Shibusawa was on the other side, having been a retainer of the last shogun.

The spoils went, naturally enough, to the victors. Strong men belonging to the clans which had supported the Imperial House became the strong men of the centralized government. Even to-day, when clans, as such, no longer exist, the old clan sentiment survives, with the result that men of Satsuma and Choshu origin are most influential in politics. The militaristic tendency sometimes noticed in the action of the Japanese Government is said to be largely due to this fact, for the clan of Satsuma was in the old days notorious for its warlike inclinations, and there is evidence to show that those inclinations have, to some extent survived. Naval officers are to-day drawn largely from old Satsuma families, while Choshu furnishes many officers to the army.

At twenty-seven years of age, Viscount Shibusawa had by his ability become vice-minister of the Shogun's treasury. Naturally, then, after the fall of the shogunate, he went in for finance. He founded the First Bank of Japan— literally the first modern bank started there—and, prospering greatly became a man of large affairs. Repeatedly he was offered the portfolio of Finance under the Government, but always refused it. A few years ago he retired from active business, and as has already been mentioned, gave his time thereafter to all manner of good works.

When I met him he was nearing his eighty-second birthday. He distinctly remembered Perry's arrival in Japan and the events that followed. I wished to get the story of a representative man who had seen these things, and therefore asked him to grant me an interview. This he was so kind as to do, allowing me the better part of two days—for interviewing through an interpreter, even though he be the best of interpreters, is slow work.

We talked in a pretty brick bungalow in the Viscount's garden. Outside the door was an English rose-garden, with bushes trained to the shape of trees.

Prior to that time I had always seen the Viscount wearing a frock coat or a dress suit, but here at home, on a day free from formalities, he was clad in the silken robes that Japanese gentlemen put on for comfort—though they might well put them on for elegance, too.

Short, stocky, energetic, with a strong neck and large round head, the face seamed with deep wrinkles, he was one of the most extraordinary-looking men I had ever met. He radiated force, courage, honesty. I knew a Sioux chief, long ago, who had a face like that, even to the colour, and to the deep wrinkles of humour about the mouth and eyes. Nor, in either case, did the promise of those wrinkles fail.

When, having likened Viscount Shibusawa to an Indian chief, I also liken him to a barrel-bodied, square-jawed, weather-beaten old British squire of the perfect John Bull type, I may overtax the reader's imagination; yet there was in him as much of the one as of the other.

He was born in the country, coming of a good but not aristocratic family. The Japan of his youth and early manhood was divided into some two hundred and fifty or three hundred feudal districts, each ruled by a daimyo, or chieftain, having his castles, his court, his concubines, his retainers— among the latter soldiers in armour, equipped with swords, spears or bows and arrows, and wearing hideous masks calculated to terrify the foe.

These chiefs had absolute power over the people and lands in their domains. They could make laws, issue paper money, levy taxes, impose labour and punishment on the people, or arbitrarily take from them property or life itself.

It was a land without railroads, without steam power, without window-glass; a land in which nobles journeyed by the highroads in magnificent processions, surrounded by their soldiers, mounted and afoot, their lacquered palanquins, their coolie bearers; a land in which, when great lords passed, humble citizens fell to their knees and touched their foreheads to the ground; a land of duels, feuds, vendettas, clan wars; a land in which the samurai, or gentry, alone were allowed to wear swords, and in which one of the privileges most highly prized by the samurai was that of dying by his own hand, if condemned to death, instead of by the hand of the executioner. Involved with the privilege of *hara-kiri*, or *seppuku*, was a property right. The property of a man beheaded by the executioner was confiscated, whereas one committing hara-kiri could leave his estate to his family.

The education of young men varied in those times according to rank. Youths of the aristocracy were instructed in the Chinese classics, which in Japan take the place of Latin and Greek with us. Medicine and astronomy were also taught. The sons of lesser samurai received a training calculated to fit them for practical affairs. All those entitled to wear swords studied swordsmanship, and the process by which they learned it was sometimes severe, for it was the custom of masters to attack the pupil suddenly from behind, or even when he was asleep at night, on the theory that he should be ready at all times to defend himself. A samurai found killed with his sword completely sheathed was disgraced. At least two inches of the blade must show in proof that the dead man had attempted a defence. Jiu-jutsu was also taught to many samurai youths, and in this, as in swordsmanship, it was the practice of instructors to make surprise attacks upon their pupils.

Viscount Shibusawa's recollections of old days, as he recounted them to me, will make a separate chapter, but before that chapter is begun, let me mention several points of samurai tradition—among them jiu-jutsu, and the more advanced art or science of jiudo, developed by my friend Mr. Jigoro Kano.

As after the Restoration the craze for all things American and European spread through Japan, the old arts of jiu-jutsu, which for more than three centuries had been practised by samurai, fell into disuse. Before that time there had been many different schools of jiu-jutsu, teaching a variety of systems, but as the old masters of the art became superannuated no followers were arising to take their places.

In 1878, when Mr. Kano took up the study of jiu-jutsu, he saw that, through lack of interest, many of the fine points of the art were likely to be lost. In order to preserve as much of it as he could, he went to great pains to make himself proficient, not merely in one system of jiu-jutsu, but in several systems as taught by the several great masters then alive.

His first interest in jiu-jutsu arose through the fact that he had been a weak child and wished to make himself a strong man. I was reminded of Theodore Roosevelt's sickly childhood when Mr. Kano told me that; and it is interesting to recall that it was President Roosevelt who first caused jiu-jutsu to be widely talked of in the United States, and that he studied it, while in the White House, under one of Mr. Kano's pupils. Also I was interested to hear from Mr. Kano that, as a young man, he gave an exhibition of jiu-jutsu before General Grant, at Viscount Shibusawa's house in Tokyo.

Far from being a professional athlete, Mr. Kano is a gentleman of samurai family, a graduate of the Literary College of the Imperial University, a linguist, a traveller, an educator of high reputation, the holder of several decorations. Among other offices he has been head master of the Peers' School in Tokyo.

As the reader is doubtless aware, the theory of jiu-jutsu was to defeat the adversary, not by pitting force against force, but by yielding before the opponent's onslaughts in such a way as to turn his strength against him.

Jiudo, which means "the way or doctrine of yielding," is a combination, created by Mr. Kano, of all systems of jiu-jutsu interwoven with a plan of mental, moral, and physical training, calculated to elevate the art above any mere consideration of combat alone—although that side is by no means neglected.

Innumerable stories, exciting or amusing, might be told of the heroic adventures of celebrated jiudoists, but I know of nothing which sheds more light upon Mr. Kano's teachings, in their moral aspect, than does a letter written to him by Commander Yuasa of the Japanese Navy, a former pupil of the Kodokwan, the school of jiudo established by Mr. Kano in Tokyo. The letter was written by Commander Yuasa when he was about to take the steamer *Sagami Maru* and sink her at the harbour entrance in the third blockading expedition at Port Arthur. The following are extracts from it:

> We shall do all that human power can, and leave the rest to Heaven. Thus we can calmly ride to certain death. I am happy to say that among the members of this forlorn hope are three of your former pupils: Commander Hirose, Lieutenant Commander Honda, and myself. May this fact redound to the credit of the Kodokwan.
>
> Though I greatly regret that while living I could not do justice to the kindness you have shown me, still please accept as an expression of my gratitude the fact that I lay down my life for the sake of our country, as you have so kindly taught us, in time of peace, to be ready to do.

The writer of this letter was lost, as was also Commander Hirose, one of the brother officers he mentions. The other, Lieutenant Commander Honda, was wounded by a shell, but was rescued and lived to tell the tale.

Foreigners visiting Japan and wishing to see jiudo demonstrated, are welcome at the Kodokwan, where, if notice is given, an interpreter is provided. There are now some twenty thousand practitioners of jiudo who look to the Kodokwan as headquarters and to Mr. Kano as their master.

Another place where jiudo may be witnessed is at the Butokukai—Association for the Inculcation of the Military Virtues—in Kyoto. The latter is a private organization, like an athletic club, with a fine temple-like building, and many branch establishments throughout the country. It has some two hundred thousand members, of which several thousands are active.

The primary idea of this organization is to keep alive certain old Japanese military arts, such as jiudo, archery, fencing, the use of lances and spears, and the employment of the curious lance-like *naginata*, which, with its curved blade and long handle, was used only by women.

Contests between men armed with dummy swords and women using wooden naginata are sometimes to be witnessed at the Butokukai, and are extremely interesting as recalling the days when the women of Old Japan fought beside their men, using the naginata as an offensive weapon, and a short dagger, worn in the fold of the obi, as a defensive weapon corresponding to the shorter of the two swords that men used to wear.

Samurai women were taught to defend themselves with the dagger, and to use it for suicide if in fear of defeat and dishonour. Families in which the samurai tradition is sedulously maintained still make it a custom to present their daughters, at the time of marriage, with daggers of this type, though such weapons are now recognized merely as emblems of a spirit to be preserved.

The great modern samurai hero of Japan was General Count Nogi, the hero of Port Arthur, in memory of whom a shrine was recently dedicated in Tokyo.

This shrine stands in the grounds behind the simple house in Tokyo where Count and Countess Nogi lived, and where they died together by their own hands. Nogi is canonized in Japan, and his house is held a sacred place, and is visited by thousands of persons each year.

The theory upon which self-destruction is practised according to the old samurai tradition, and is widely approved in certain circumstances, is one of the things that baffles the Occidental mind.

I therefore asked Viscount Kentaro Kaneko, who knew General Nogi, to tell me the story of his death, and to explain to me how he came to commit seppuku.

Viscount Kentaro Kaneko (Harvard '78), Privy Councilor to the Emperor, President of the America-Japan Society of Tokyo, and friend of President Roosevelt

"When Nogi was given command at Port Arthur," said the Viscount, "his two sons were officers under him. He told his wife to prepare three coffins, and to hold no funeral services until all three were ready to be buried together.

"In the assault on Port Arthur some thirty thousand Japanese soldiers gave up their lives. This sacrifice of life was at first much criticized in Japan, but public sentiment changed in face of the fact that the General lost both his sons. He returned to Japan a victor, it is true, but a most unhappy man. Always in his mind were thoughts of the families of the thirty thousand brave young men it had been necessary to sacrifice. He did not want to be acclaimed in the streets, but to be let alone. He went about in an old uniform and tried to be as inconspicuous as possible.

"One day at an audience with the Emperor Meiji, Nogi said to him as he was leaving, something to the effect that he should never see him again.

"The Emperor, gathering that Nogi was contemplating seppuku, called him back.

"'Nogi,' he said, 'I still have need of you. I want your life.'

"So the General did not carry out his plan at that time, but lived on, as the Emperor had ordered him to do, becoming president of the school at which the sons of nobles are educated.

"All through the years, however, he was haunted by the memory of the thirty thousand soldiers he had been compelled to send to their death.

"When the Emperor Meiji died, Nogi was one of the guard of honour, made up of peers, who in rotation watched at the Imperial bier for forty days and forty nights.

"Then came the state funeral. On the day of the funeral Nogi wrote a poem which declared in effect, 'I shall follow in the footsteps of Your Majesty.' This poem he showed to Prince Yamagata, who took it to mean merely that Nogi would be in the procession following the Imperial remains to the grave.

"But when the guns announced the departure of the funeral cortège from the palace, Nogi was not there. Like the samurai of old, he desired to follow his dead master into the beyond. At the sound of the guns he took his short sword and committed seppuku, while in the next room Countess Nogi, his devoted wife, dressed all in white, cut the arteries of her neck. Thus the two died together, for the sake of the Emperor and the thirty thousand soldiers who had sacrificed their lives."

At no point is the outlook of the Oriental more completely at odds with that of the Occidental, than in the view it takes of suicide.

Whereas with us suicide is condemned as cowardly, being resorted to as a means of escape from the hardships of life, there will oftentimes be something highly heroic in a Japanese suicide. Unhappiness, it is true, does drive some Japanese to self-destruction, but in many other cases the suicide represents something more in the nature of a self-inflicted punishment for failure of some kind. Thus it is with the schoolboys who sometimes kill themselves because they have failed in their examinations. Likewise, while in Japan I heard of two railroad gatemen who had, by failing to close their gate when a train was coming, been responsible for the death of a man travelling in a ricksha. A few days after this accident both these gatemen suicided by throwing themselves beneath a train. For their neglect they paid voluntarily with their lives.

"And," said the Viscount, "we had in the old days another sort of suicide, examples of which sometimes occur even to this day. When a man believed profoundly in something, and was unable to attract attention to the thing in which he believed, he would sometimes commit seppuku as a means of drawing notice to it. He would leave a paper setting forth his beliefs, and people would give it attention, feeling that if a man was willing to die in order to emphasize a point, his message was worth considering."

The Viscount paused. Then rather reflectively he added: "It is as though he were to underscore his protest—in red."

CHAPTER XVII

The Old-time Anti-Foreign Sentiment—Prince Yoshinobu Tokugawa—Emperor and Shogun—Prince Yoshinobu becomes Shogun—His Highness, Akitaké, Goes to France—Humorous Episodes—The Defeat of Prince Yoshinobu's Army—Various Explanations—The Restoration of the Emperor—Prince Yoshinobu's Retirement—The Viscount's Theory—Prince Keikyu Tokugawa—A Roosevelt Anecdote—Swords and Watchchain

"I was a boy of fourteen," said Viscount Shibusawa "when your Commodore Perry came to Japan. At that time, and for a considerable period afterwards, I was 'anti-foreigner'—that is, I was opposed to the abandonment of our old Japanese isolation, and to the opening of relations with foreign powers.

"The majority of thoughtful men felt as I did. Our trouble with the Jesuits, in the latter part of the sixteenth and early part of the seventeenth century came about through a fear which grew up amongst us that the Jesuits were trying to get political control of Japan. This fear brought about their expulsion from the country, as well as some persecution of themselves and their converts, and it was then that our policy of isolation began. More lately we had seen the Opium War in China, and that had added to our conviction that foreign powers were merely seeking territory, and that they were utterly unscrupulous.

"When I reached the age of twenty-five, I became a retainer of Yoshinobu Tokugawa, a powerful prince, kinsman of Iyemochi Tokugawa, who was then Shogun. Not being of noble family, I did not belong to Prince Yoshinobu's intimate circle, but was a member of what might be termed the middle group at his court.

"He was then acting as intermediary between the Shogun and the Imperial Court at Kyoto—for though the Shogun ruled the land, as shoguns had for centuries, there was maintained a fiction that he did so by imperial consent.

"When Iyemochi died, the powerful daimyos nominated my lord, Prince Yoshinobu, to succeed him. I was opposed to his accepting the office, for the country was then in a very unsettled condition, and I felt sure that the next shogun, whoever he might be, would have serious difficulties to encounter; especially with the important question of foreign relations to the fore, and with such powerful lords as those of Satsuma, Choshu, Tosa, and Hizan becoming increasingly hostile to the shogunate and increasingly favourable to the Imperial House.

"The fact that Prince Yoshinobu had acted as intermediary between his kinsman, the fourteenth Shogun, and the Imperial Court at Kyoto, made it a delicate matter for him later to accept the shogunate. Moreover, though he belonged to the Tokugawa family, his branch of the family, the Mito branch, had continually insisted upon Imperial supremacy in Japan. However, circumstances compelled him to accept the office. I was greatly disappointed when he did so.

"This occurred two years after I became his retainer. I was now vice-minister of his treasury, with the additional duties of keeping track of all modern innovations and supervising the new-style military drill, with rifles, which we were then taking up.

"Shortly after becoming Shogun, Yoshinobu decided to send his brother, Akitaké, to France to be educated, and he appointed me a member of the entourage that was to accompany the young man. I was then twenty-seven years old.

"We sailed in January 1867—a party of twenty-five, among whom were a doctor, an officer who went to study artillery, and various others besides Akitaké's seven personal attendants.

"For international purposes the Shogun was now called Tycoon, for the word 'shogun,' meaning 'generalissimo,' carried with it no connotation of rulership; whereas 'tycoon' means 'great prince'—and of course it seemed proper enough for a great prince to treat with foreign powers. As brother of the Tycoon, Akitaké received, in Europe, the title 'Highness'.

"Matters looked very ominous for the shogunate at the time we left Japan, but I felt that the best thing for me to do was to go abroad and learn all I could, with a view to being better able to serve my country when I should return.

"The members of our party wore the Japanese costume, including topknots and two swords. I, however, devised a special elegance for myself. I heard that the governor of Saigon, where our ship was to stop, intended to welcome our party officially, so I had a dress coat made." The Viscount shook with laughter as he recalled the episode. "It wasn't a dress suit—just the coat. And when we got to Saigon I wore that coat over my Japanese silks, in the daytime.

"Our lack of experience with European ways caused many amusing things to happen. For instance, when we were in the train crossing the Isthmus of Suez—there was no canal then—one member of the party, unaccustomed to window-glass, threw an orange-peel, expecting it to go out of the window. The peel hit the glass and bounced back falling into the lap of an official who had come to escort us across the isthmus. We were much embarrassed.

"Later, in Paris, another absurd thing occurred. You must understand that in Japan it is customary for guests, leaving a house where they have been entertained, to wrap up cakes and such things and take them home. One member of our party, who had never seen ice-cream before, attempted this, wrapping the ice-cream in paper and tucking it in the front of his kimono. Needless to say, the ice-cream was no longer ice-cream when he got back to the hotel, and he himself was not very comfortable.

"The Paris Exposition of 1867 was in progress when we arrived. When it was over we travelled through Switzerland, Holland, Belgium, Italy, and England. Originally it was planned that after our official tour we should settle down to study, and I was eager for this time to come. However, it was not long before we received news that the shogunate had fallen.

"The news was puzzling. I could not gather what was happening in Japan. First I heard that Yoshinobu, as shogun, had publicly returned full authority of the Emperor, but later came word of the battle of Toba-Fushimi, in which troops of the Imperial Party defeated troops of the Shogun. This made it appear that Yoshinobu had played false, first publicly relinquishing the shogun's power and then fighting to maintain it. These seemingly conflicting acts puzzled me, for I knew that Yoshinobu was a man of the highest honour.

"Presently came a messenger from Japan saying that Akitaké had become head of the Mito branch of the Tokugawa family, which made it necessary for us to abandon our plans and return. We sailed from England in December 1867, reaching Japan in November 1868, eleven months later.

"I was dumbfounded by the changes I found. Though I knew that the Shogun Government had fallen I had not visualized what that would mean. My lord, Yoshinobu, was held prisoner in a house in Suruga. Learning that he was allowed to see his intimate friends and retainers, I journeyed to Suruga, where I had audience with him several times. I found him reticent, and was able to get from him little information as to the mysterious course he had pursued.

"After having been held prisoner for a year he was released, but he continued for thirty years to reside in the neighbourhood of Suruga, leading a secluded life. Not until thirty-one years after his resignation of the shogunate did he come to Tokyo. Four years later the Emperor created him a prince of the new régime. This showed pretty clearly that the Emperor had not mistrusted him.

"For twenty years after my return to Japan I was unable to get at the bottom of this matter. I tried to get some explanation from Yoshinobu himself, but he evaded my inquiries. Meanwhile the question was constantly discussed in Japan. Those hostile to Yoshinobu contended that he had not acted with sincerity, having been led by the burdens connected with the opening of foreign relations, to lay down the shogunate, and having later changed his mind and fought to retain it. On the face of it, this seemed true. Yoshinobu was called a coward and a traitor, and was severely criticized for having escaped after the battle of Toba-Fushimi.

"On the other hand, those who supported Yoshinobu asserted that he had acted logically and wisely: that he had seen that his government was going to fall, and had been entirely honest in surrendering the shogunate prior to the battle. These adherents insisted that he had not wanted a battle, but had set out for Kyoto to see the Emperor with a view to arranging details, especially with regard to the future welfare of his retainers. "But when a great lord, travelled, in those times, he travelled with an army, and Yoshinobu's defenders maintained that this was what had brought on the battle—that when the men of Choshu and Satsuma learned that Yoshinobu was moving toward Kyoto with his soldiers, they came out and attacked him, believing, or pretending to believe, that he was on a hostile errand.

"At this time the Emperor was but seventeen years of age, and the Government was in the hands of elder statesmen of the Imperial Party. The Emperor himself probably had no idea on what errand Yoshinobu was approaching Kyoto; and whether the elder statesmen knew or not, they belonged to clans hostile to the shogunate, and preferred to fight.

"Many years passed before the truth began to become clear. At last, when the old wounds were pretty well healed, I undertook the compilation of a history of Yoshinobu's life and times. Finally I asked him point-blank about the events connected with his resignation and the subsequent battle. He told me that he had indeed started to Kyoto on a peaceful errand, but that when the forces sent out by the great clansmen appeared, he could not control his own men. He had neither sought nor desired battle. Feeling that his highest duty was to the Emperor, he withdrew from the battle, taking no part in it, and returned whence he had come, going into retirement. He knew, of course, that the battle would put him in a false light, and he decided that the wisest and most honourable course for him to pursue was to show, by his life in retirement, his absolute submission to the Emperor.

"In order fully to appreciate why Yoshinobu was so ready to lay down his power, the old Japanese doctrine of loyalty to the throne must be fully grasped. This loyalty amounts to a religion, and permeates the whole life of Japan. That is why the shoguns who for so many centuries ruled Japan, never attempted to usurp imperial rank, but were satisfied, while usurping the power, to preserve the form of governing always as vice-regents.

"It is my personal belief that when Yoshinobu Tokugawa accepted the shogunate despite the opposition of his trusted retainers, he did so with the full intention of restoring to the Imperial House its rightful power. I used to ask him about this, and while he never admitted it, he never denied it. That was characteristic of him. He was the most modest and self-effacing of men—the last man who would have claimed for himself the credit for performing a self-sacrificing and heroic act of patriotism. For him the performance of the act was sufficient."

Throughout my talk with Viscount Shibusawa I felt in him the passionate loyalty of the retainer to his lord. Where I had wished for reminiscences of a more personal nature, the Viscount, I could see, thought of himself first of all in his relation to the family of Prince Yoshinobu, the last shogun, whose retainer he was. He was not interested in telling me of his own career, but he was profoundly interested in seeing that I, being a writer, should understand the relationship of Prince Yoshinobu to the Imperial Restoration. His attitude reminded me of that of a noble old Southern gentleman, now dead and gone, who had been the adjutant of Robert E. Lee, and who loved Lee and loved to talk about him. When I talked with him it was the same. I had great difficulty in getting him to tell me about his own experiences.

The loyalty of the retainer to the family of his lord is also to be seen in the relationship between the Viscount and young Prince Keikyu Tokugawa, son of Yoshinobu. After the death of the father the Viscount continued to act as advisor to the son. He became his chief counsellor, and when, a few years since, he resigned from the board of directors of the First Bank of Japan— the bank which he founded five years after the Restoration—it was young Prince Tokugawa who succeeded to his empty chair.

The Prince, who is a member of the House of Peers, is known in the United States, having come here during the war as representative of the Japanese Red Cross.

Viscount Shibusawa is also a figure not unfamiliar to Americans, having visited this country several times. I am indebted to him for an anecdote illustrative of the prodigious memory of President Roosevelt.

"Eighteen years ago," he said, "when Mr. Roosevelt was president, I called upon him at the White House. We had a pleasant talk. He complimented the behaviour of the Japanese troops in the Boxer trouble, saying that they were not only brave but orderly and well disciplined. Then he spoke with admiration of the art of Japan.

"I said to him, 'Mr. President, I am only a banker, and I regret to say that in my country banking is not yet so highly developed as is art.'

"'Perhaps it will be,' he replied, 'by the time we meet again.'

"Thirteen years later, when I called upon him at his home at Oyster Bay, he took up the conversation where we had left off.

"'The last time I saw you,' he said, 'I did not ask you about banking in Japan. Now I want you to tell me all about it.'"

As I was leaving the bungalow in the garden late in the afternoon of the second day spent in interviewing the Viscount, the thought came to me that probably I should never again talk with a man who had lived through such transitions. I wanted a souvenir, and I wished it to be something emblematic of the changes witnessed by those shrewd, humorous old eyes.

Therefore, not without some hesitation, I asked the Viscount if he would be so kind as to put on his two samurai swords and let me take his photograph.

He dispatched a servant who presently returned from the house bearing the weapons. The Viscount tucked them through his sash, and I snapped the shutter, hoping fervently that the late afternoon light would prove to have been adequate.

Viscount Shibusawa, one of the Grand Old Men of Japan, consented to pose for me, wearing his samurai swords

As the reader may see for himself, the picture turned out well. Indeed it turned out better than I myself had anticipated, for besides the swords and silken robes of Old Japan, there may be seen in it a very modern note.

It was the Viscount's grandson who, when I showed him the photograph, called attention to that.

"Yes," he said, with a smile, "you have there the swords of Old Japan. But the watch-chain—that is an anachronism."

CHAPTER XVIII

Viscount Kaneko's Home—Some Souvenirs—A Rooseveltian Memory—Doctor Bigelow's Prophecy—A First Meeting with Roosevelt—The Russo-Japanese War—Luncheons at the White House—Roosevelt's Interest in the Samurai Tradition—Sagamore Hill—Mrs. Roosevelt and Quentin—A Simple Home—The President Brings Blankets—A Bear Hunt—The Peace of Portsmouth and a Bearskin for the Emperor—A Letter of Roosevelt's on Relations with Japan—A Letter from Mid-Africa—"American Samurai"

Never while in Japan did I feel quite so close to home as on the several occasions when I sat in the study of Viscount Kentaro Kaneko, in Tokyo, listening to his reminiscences and looking at his souvenirs of Theodore Roosevelt.

No Japanese has been more widely known in the United States, or more familiar with our ways, than Viscount Kaneko (Harvard '78), Privy Councilor to the Emperor, chairman of the commission which is engaged in preparing the history of the reign of the late Emperor Meiji, and president of the America-Japan Society of Tokyo.

I found him living in a good-sized but not ostentatious house, purely Japanese in architecture. But it was not purely Japanese in its equipment. Like the houses of other Tokyo gentlemen accustomed to see much of foreigners, it had carpet over the hall matting, rendering the removal of shoes unnecessary, and certain of its rooms were furnished in the Occidental style.

Such rooms, in Japan, usually are stiff reception-rooms which look as if they were used only when visitors from abroad put in an appearance; but Viscount Kaneko's study held a homelike feeling which made me think the room was frequented by the master of the house when no guests were present.

On the walls were framed photographs of notables, European and American, with the Roosevelt family very much to the fore, and I noticed beneath the photograph of President Roosevelt a cordial inscription in the familiar handwriting, so honest and boyish—writing as unlike that of any other great man as Roosevelt himself was unlike any other great man.

When I had crossed and read the inscription, Viscount Kaneko called my attention to the frame.

"That frame," he said, "is made from a piece of Oregon pine which was brought among other presents to the Shogun by Commodore Perry. The Emperor presented me with a piece of the wood, and I had made from it that frame and a writing box on which the scene of Perry's arrival is depicted in gold lacquer."

There was also a photograph of Mrs. Roosevelt with two of her sons, and one of Quentin Roosevelt as a child, astride a pony, with an inscription to the Viscount's son Takemaro, dated August seventh, 1905. In the corner of the frame was inserted a photograph which the Viscount had caused to be taken of Quentin's grave in France.

Viscount Kaneko was a student at Harvard when Roosevelt entered the university, but they were two years apart and did not know each other there. Their first meeting occurred in Washington in 1889, when Roosevelt was Civil Service Commissioner and Viscount Kaneko was returning to Japan after having visited the principal countries of Europe for the purpose of studying parliamentary forms. The first Japanese Parliament met in the year following, 1890, when Japan adopted a Constitution.

In looking back upon my interviews with the Viscount I find myself marvelling to-day, as I did then, at the detailed accuracy of his memory. He recounted events of fifteen and more years before with a vividness and an attention to trifles that was extraordinary. It was as if he had refreshed his memory by reading from a diary.

"I had two letters of introduction to Roosevelt," he told me, "when I went to Washington in 1889. One had been given to me by James Bryce, later Viscount Bryce, who was then in Gladstone's Cabinet. The other I received from my friend Dr. William Sturges Bigelow.

"When Doctor Bigelow gave me the letter, he said: 'This will introduce you to a man who will some day be President of the United States.' I always remembered that and watched Roosevelt's career with the more interest for that reason.

"On reaching Washington I called on Roosevelt at a private boarding house where he was living, and he returned my call next day. Naturally I perceived at once that he was a man of extraordinarily vigorous mind. I enjoyed him greatly, and was pleased and interested, after my return to Japan, to see him steadily ascending. He became Assistant Secretary of the Navy, Colonel of the Rough Riders, Governor of New York. 'Now,' I said to myself on reading that he had been elected Governor, 'he is on the way to fulfilling Doctor Bigelow's prophecy.' Then he became Vice-President, and I thought: 'That is too bad. They have shelved him. He won't be President after all.' But McKinley was assassinated and Roosevelt came to the White House.

"Early in 1904, at the time of our war with Russia, I was sent to the United States on an unofficial embassy. I went first to New York, where I remained for a week; then to Washington. There I called on my old friend Mr. Justice Holmes of the Supreme Court—'Brother Kaneko' he used to call me—requesting him to take me to the White House to meet the President, who I thought would not remember me. But Justice Holmes had disagreed with Roosevelt over the Northern Securities case, and did not feel that he was persona grata at the White House just then. Therefore I arranged through our Minister, Mr. Takahira, for a meeting.

"One morning in May, 1904, the Minister took me to call upon the President. Our appointment was for half past ten. We were not kept waiting long. I will never forget the picture of Roosevelt as he quickly thrust open the door and rushed into the room. The Minister had no chance to present me. 'I am delighted to see you again Baron!' the President exclaimed in that wonderfully hearty way of his. And as we shook hands he threw his arm over my shoulder, demanding: 'Why did you stay for a week in New York? Why didn't you come and see me right away?'

"During our talk, which lasted an hour, he let me see that he was absolutely neutral in his official attitude toward our war with Russia, but nevertheless made me feel that he had much personal sympathy for Japan. He declared frankly that popular sentiment in the United States was favourable to Japan, and added that the Russian Government had complained that American army and navy officers were openly pro-Japanese. This had made it necessary for him to issue a proclamation of neutrality. But though, as President, he was particular to be scrupulously just to both sides, I was in no doubt as to the friendliness of his private sentiments.

"He advised me not to stay in Washington, but to make my headquarters in New York, coming over to Washington to see him when it was necessary. This I did, and as time went on, and we became closer friends, he often did me the honour of inviting me to luncheon *en famille* at the White House.

"At one of these luncheons I told him of Doctor Bigelow's prophecy, and of how I had watched him mounting step by step to its fulfilment. That seemed to please him.

"'Edith,' he called across the table to Mrs. Roosevelt, 'do you hear that? Here is a man who has kept a friendly eye on me from away off in Japan.'

"Once at one of these intimate White House luncheons he remarked that as President it was necessary to preserve a certain style. 'Coming to see us here,' he said, 'you don't get an accurate idea of what our family life really is. You must come and pay us a visit at Oyster Bay this summer when we get home. Then you will know more about us.'

"He did not forget the invitation, but early in July 1905, repeated it by telegraph. I went to Oyster Bay and stayed over night. It was in many ways a memorable experience.

"He was always greatly interested in our samurai tradition and in the doctrine we call bushido. I remember his asking me how much money was required for the keeping up of a samurai's position. I explained that there were different classes of samurai—that the shoguns had themselves been samurai, with others of various grades below them.

"'Middle-class samurai,' I said, 'do not need a great deal of money. They require only enough for dress to be worn on social occasions, for the education of their families, and the maintenance of their political position, whatever it may be. They need no money for pleasures or extravagances.'

"'Just the same,' the President replied, 'a man doesn't want to fall behind his ancestors, materially or otherwise. Take my own case: I want to keep my place as my forbears kept theirs. I desire neither more nor less than what my father had. I want my children to be able to grow up in this old home at Oyster Bay just as the children of my generation did.' Then he began to ask me more about the details of samurai life.

"'What about doctor's bills?' he asked. 'You didn't mention that item in estimating the expense of living.'

"I told him of a curious custom we used to have. In each samurai class there were families of doctors who were endowed by the Government, the profession being passed down from father to son. These doctors took care of samurai families of the rank corresponding to their own, and charged nothing for so doing. Twice a year, in January and July, when it is customary to give presents, presents were given to the doctors. They also took care of the poor as a matter of charity.

"That interested him, too. He was always intensely interested in the samurai, because our samurai virtues were virtues of a kind he particularly admired—courage, stoicism, love of duty and of country.

"We sat on the wide verandah, overlooking the lawn sloping down toward Long Island Sound. Mrs. Roosevelt sat with us, knitting. It was July, but she was knitting mittens. Presently a maid came and spoke to her, and she left us.

"When she came back she said to me, 'Baron, I want to ask a favour of you. Quentin has been crying. He took great pains to clean his pony to-day, to show it to you, and we promised that he should be allowed to do so. He has been riding around the lawn hoping you would notice him.'

"Of course I sent for Quentin, and he appeared proudly upon his pony. I asked him to ride around the lawn, which he did.

"'You ride splendidly!' I said, when he drew up again before the porch.

"'Do you think so?' he asked, evidently much pleased.

"'Indeed I do!' I said, and asked him to go around the lawn again.

"When he came back I told him about my son, who was just his age. 'I shall have him learn to ride,' I said, 'and when he can ride as well as you can I shall have his picture taken on a pony and send it to you.'

"That," continued the Viscount, "is how we happen to have this picture of Quentin on his pony. He sent it to my son, and my son sent him a picture. I always like to think of the good-will there was between those two boys—an American boy and a Japanese boy who had never seen each other.

"That night we sat talking in the drawing room which is to the left of the hall as you go into the house. Mrs. Roosevelt was still knitting mittens for the children. It was all wonderfully simple and homelike. I could hardly believe that I was in the home of the head of a great nation. At that time the house was lighted with kerosene lamps, yet in Japan I had been using electric light for fifteen years.

"At about ten o'clock Mrs. Roosevelt said good night to us and retired. Before she went upstairs she moved about, fastening windows and putting out lamps in parts of the house in which they would not be needed any more. Then she brought candles and matches so that we should have them when we were ready to go to bed.

"After an hour's talk about the war, which was still raging, the President rose and lit the candles. Then he put out the remaining lamps, and conducted me upstairs to my room. It was a cool night. He felt of the coverings on my bed, and decided that I might need another blanket. 'I'll get you one,' he said, leaving the room. And in a minute or two he reappeared with a blanket over his shoulder.

"'Come,' he said, as he put it on the bed, 'and I'll show you the bathroom.' I went with him. 'Here's soap,' said he, 'and here are clean towels.' Then he took me back to my room and wished me a good night.

"As for me, I was fascinated, almost dazed. I kept saying to myself, 'This man who has lighted me upstairs with a candle, and carried me a blanket, and shown me where to find soap and towels, is the President of the United States! The President of the United States has done all these things for me. It is the greatest honour a man could have.'

"Earlier in the same year, before the President moved from the White House to Oyster Bay, he went bear hunting. That was just before Admiral Togo's victory over the Russian fleet, in the Sea of Japan.

"Before leaving, the President sent for me and told me, in the presence of Mr. Taft, who was Secretary of War, that if anything of importance should come up during his absence, I was to see Mr. Taft about it, and that in the event of its being anything absolutely vital, Mr. Taft would know how to reach him.

"Mr. Taft showed me a photograph hanging on the wall of the President's office, showing the wild country to which the President was going on his hunting trip.

"I remarked playfully to him that I thought it advisable, at that time, that the President refrain from killing bears, whatever other animals he might see fit to slay.

"Roosevelt, sitting at his desk, overheard me.

"'What's that you are saying?' he asked.

"I repeated what I had said to Mr. Taft.

"'Why do you think I should not kill bears?' demanded the President.

"'Well, Mr. President,' I replied, 'you know that the various nations have their special symbols in the animal kingdom. America has the eagle, Britain the lion, France the cock, and Russia, well——'

"He got up, laughing and came over to me.

"'Nevertheless,' he said, 'I shall go right ahead and kill bears!'

"Before he left on that hunting trip I went to see him and asked as a special favour that he give me the skin of one of the bears he should kill.

"He refused, saying that if he were to start presenting trophies to his friends they would all be after him.

"At that I said to him, 'If I were asking this for myself, Mr. President, I would not pursue the matter further, but I am not asking it for myself. I want that bear skin for our Emperor.'

"'Very well, then,' he said. 'You shall have it.'

"He went off on his hunting trip, and came back. Then followed the negotiations for a cessation of hostilities between Japan and Russia, and the Portsmouth Peace Conference, through which Roosevelt brought about the end of the war.

"In August of the same year, 1905, I received this letter from him."

The Viscount handed me the letter to read. It was as follows:

Oyster Bay, N, Y,.
August 30, 1905.

Personal

MY DEAR BARON KANEKO:

I cannot too highly state my appreciation of the wisdom and magnanimity of Japan, which make a fit crown to the prowess of her soldiers. Will you tell the Emperor that I shall take the liberty of sending him by you a bear skin? I want you soon to come out here and take lunch.

Sincerely yours,
THEODORE ROOSEVELT.

"Later," the Viscount went on, "I was asked by the President to come to Oyster Bay and select one of the skins. I however did not wish to make the selection, so the President did that, picking out the largest skin of all and giving it to me for the Emperor Meiji.

"His Majesty was greatly pleased with the skin, not only because it was a trophy from the President himself, but because of the emblematic nature of the gift. That bearskin was in his library at the Imperial Palace in Tokyo as long as he lived."

———————————

One of the most important Roosevelt letters shown me by Viscount Kaneko was on the subject of Japanese-American relations. As this letter is not included in the two-volume collection of Roosevelt correspondence compiled in such masterly fashion by Joseph Bucklin Bishop, Roosevelt's literary executor, I have asked the permission of Mrs. Roosevelt and of Mr. Bishop to quote it here.

It was as follows:

THE WHITE HOUSE

WASHINGTON

May 23, 1907.

Confidentia
MY DEAR BARON KANEKO:

I much appreciate your thought of Archie. The little fellow was very sick but is now all right. His mother and I have just had him on a short trip in the country.

I was delighted to meet General Kuroki and Admiral Ijuin with their staffs. General Kuroki is, of course, one of the most illustrious men living. Through his interpreter, a very able young staff officer, I spoke to him a little about our troubles on the Pacific Slope.

Nothing during my Presidency has given me more concern than these troubles. History often teaches by example, and I think we can best understand just what the situation is, and how it ought to be met, by taking into account the change in general international relations during the last two or three centuries.

During this period all the civilized nations have made great progress. During the first part of it Japan did not appear in the general progress, but for the last half century she has gone ahead so much faster than any other nation that I think we can fairly say that, taking the last three centuries together, her advance has been on the whole greater than that of any other nation. But all have advanced, and especially in the way in which the people of each treat people of other nationalities. Two centuries ago there was the greatest suspicion and malevolence exhibited by all the people, high and low, of each European country, for all the people, high and low, of every other European country, with but few exceptions. The cultivated people of the different countries, however, had already begun to treat with one another on good terms. But when, for instance, the Huguenots were exiled from France, and great numbers of Huguenot workmen went to England, their presence excited the most violent hostility, manifesting itself even in mob violence, among the English workmen. The men were closely allied by race and religion, they had practically the same type of ancestral culture, and yet they were unable to get on together. Two centuries have passed, the world has moved forward, and now there could be no repetition of such hostilities. In the same way a marvellous progress has been made in the relations of Japan with the Occidental nations. Fifty years ago you and I and those like us could not have travelled in one another's countries. We should have had very unpleasant and possibly very dangerous experiences. But the same progress that has been going on as between nations in Europe and their descendants in America and Australia, has also been going on as between

Japan and the Occidental nations. In these times, then, gentlemen, all educated people, members of professions and the like, get on so well together that they not only travel each in the other's country, but associate on the most intimate terms. Among the friends whom I especially value I include a number of Japanese gentlemen. But the half century has been too short a time for the advance to include the labouring classes of the two countries, as between themselves.

Exactly as the educated classes in Europe, among the several nations, grew to be able to associate together generations before it was possible for such association to take place among the men who had no such advantages of education, so it is evident we must not press too fast in bringing the labouring classes of Japan and America together. Already in these fifty years we have completely attained the goal as between the educated and the intellectual classes of the two countries. We must be content to wait another generation before we shall have made progress enough to permit the same close intimacy between the classes who have had less opportunity for cultivation, and whose lives are less easy, so that each has to feel, in earning its daily bread, the pressure of the competition of the other. I have become convinced that to try to move too far forward all at once is to incur jeopardy of trouble. This is just as true of one nation as of the other. If scores of thousands of American miners went to Saghalin, or of American mechanics to Japan or Formosa, trouble would almost certainly ensue. Just in the same way scores of thousands of Japanese labourers, whether agricultural or industrial, are certain, chiefly because of the pressure caused thereby, to be a sources of trouble if they should come here or to Australia. I mention Australia because it is a part of the British Empire, because the Australians have discriminated against continental immigration in favour of immigration from the British Isles, and have in effect discriminated to a certain degree in favour of immigration from England and Scotland as against immigration from Ireland.

My dear Baron, the business of statesmen is to try constantly to keep international relations better, to do away with causes of friction, and secure as nearly ideal justice as actual conditions will permit. I think that with this object in view and facing conditions not as I would like them to be, but as they are, the best thing to do is to prevent the labouring classes of either country from going in any numbers to the other. In a generation I believe all need of such prevention will have passed away; and at any rate this leaves free the opportunity for all those fit to profit by intercourse, to go each to the other's country. I have just appointed a commission on general immigration which will very possibly urge restrictive measures as regards European immigration, and which I am in hopes will be able to bring about a method by which the result we have in view will be obtained with the minimum friction.

With warm regards to the Baroness, believe me,

Sincerely yours,
THEODORE ROOSEVELT.

Baron Kentaro Kaneko,

Tokyo, Japan.

The foregoing letter may well be studied at this time when, through lack of the kind of statesmanship shown by Roosevelt, the Californian situation has become worse instead of better.

Another letter shown me by Viscount Kaneko was written in pencil on a large sheet of yellow paper torn from a pad. It came from the African jungle, and ran as follows:

Mid-Africa Sept. 10th, 1909.

MY DEAR BARON, [3]

I have no facilities for writing here; but I must just send you a line of thanks for your welcome note. I have had a most interesting trip; my son Kermit has done particularly well. He has the spirit of a samurai! I greatly hope to visit Japan; but when it may be possible I can not say.

With warm regards to the Viscountess, [3] believe me,

Sincerely yours,
THEODORE ROOSEVELT.

[3] Despite the fact that Roosevelt knew that Kaneko had been made a Viscount he addressed him in this letter by his old title.

The last letter of the series was written on the stationery of the Kansas City *Star*, of which Roosevelt was an associate editor with an office in New York. The letter read:

New York, Aug. 21, 1918.

MY DEAR VISCOUNT KANEKO:

I thank you for your letter; and Mrs. Roosevelt was as much touched by it as I was. Remember to give your son a letter to us when he comes here to go to Harvard. One of our newspapers, the Chicago *Tribune*, when the news was brought that Quentin was dead and two of his brothers wounded, spoke of my four sons as "American samurai." I was proud of the reference! As you say, all of us who are born are doomed to die. No man is fit to live who is afraid to die for a great cause. My sorrow for Quentin is outweighed by my pride in him.

Faithfully your friend,
THEODORE ROOSEVELT.

The foregoing, written less than five months before Colonel Roosevelt's death, was the last letter of the series shown me by Viscount Kaneko.

Reading it I was reminded of what Colonel Roosevelt said to me as he lay on his bed in the hospital the last time I saw him.

Speaking of his four sons in the war he said:

"We have been an exceptionally united family. Come what may, we have many absolutely satisfying years together to look back upon."

CHAPTER XIX

Placidity and Sodans—*Talk and Tea*—*American Business Methods* versus *Japanese*—*The American Housekeeper in Nippon*—*Japan's Problem*—*Population and Food*—*The Militarists*—*Land-Grabbing*—*Liberalism*—*Emigration*—*Industrialism*—*Examples of Inefficiency*—"*Public Futilities*"—*Comedies of the Telephone*—*The Cables*

Elsewhere I have said that the Japanese are generally hard workers; wherefore it may seem paradoxical to add that they are also leisurely workers. But the paradox is not so great as it would seem. The hours of work are longer in Japan than in most other countries, but work is not so vigorously pressed.

Without being in the least lazy, the Japanese take their time to everything. With masters and servants, employers and workmen, it is much the same. They appear placid. They hold *sodans*, conferring and arranging matters with terrible precision. If you attempt to use the telephone you are prepared for a long struggle and a long wait. The clerks in the cable office act as if the cable had just been laid—as if your cablegram were the first one they had ever been called upon to send, and they didn't quite know how to handle it, or how much to charge. Often they are unable to make change. Sometimes even the railway ticket agents have no change. Business conferences are conducted over successive cups of pale green tea, and I am told that it is customary to begin them with talk on any topic other than the main one. In the lexicon of Japanese trade and commerce there is no such word as "snappy."

The hustling American business man who tries to rush things through often arouses the Japanese business man's suspicion. What is he after? Why is he in such a hurry? There must be something behind it all. It is necessary to be particularly careful in dealing with such a man. Negotiations drag and drag until the American, if he be of nervous disposition, is driven nearly wild. And sometimes this results in his making a bad bargain merely for the sake of getting through.

"I'm sorry I ever came to the Far East!" he will declare bitterly. "I feel that I am getting nothing accomplished over here—nothing!" Then he will tell you what is the trouble with the Japanese:

"They are used to playing only with white chips!"

The American housekeeper in Japan, if she knows what nerves are, may have similar difficulties. Her Japanese servants will conduct her ménage well enough if she lets them do it in their Japanese way, but if she attempts to run her home as she would run it in the United States, she is lost. It can't be done. I know of an American woman who could not get a cook because her efforts to Americanize her household had given her a bad reputation with the

Cook's Guild. Another could get no sewing done, for a like reason. For all the servants and working people have their guilds, and news travels. Thus many an American housekeeper in Japan has became a nervous wreck.

Yet on the other hand, numbers of American business men and their wives enjoy Japanese life, and only come home when it is necessary to give their children an American education. The men are successful and their homes are comfortable and well run. But always you will find that they are people of calm disposition: people having sufficient balance to adjust themselves to the customs of the country.

The essential point seems to be that the Japanese view life in longer perspective than we do. Where we see ourselves as individuals having certain things to accomplish in a rather short life, they see themselves as mere links in an endless family chain. We are conscious of our parents and our children but they are conscious of ancestors, reaching back to the mists of antiquity, and of a posterity destined to people the nebulous vaults of the far-distant future.

But while, from a philosophical standpoint, this way of looking at life may be quite as good as ours, or even better, still I believe it tends to handicap the Japanese in meeting the urgent material problems by which they are confronted. And though these problems are not so terrible as those of war-racked Europe, they are, if measured by any other standard, terrible enough.

Japan's fundamental problem—the one out of which grow all other Japanese problems in which the world is interested—is, as I have said before, that of great density of population coupled with an inadequate supply of food and raw materials. Fifty years ago the population of Japan proper was less than 33,000,000. To-day it is more than 57,000,000. There has been an increase in five decades of more than 75 per cent., but there has been no corresponding increase in the country's arable land.

The film was not large enough to hold the family of this youngish fisherman at Nabuto. Nine children! Fifty years ago Japan had a population of 33,000,000. To-day it is nearing 60,000,000.

In Japan itself there have been various theories as to how this problem should be met. The militarists, who are still very powerful, have in the past undoubtedly favoured what we have come lately to call the Prussian system, the grabbing system: the system which has been followed in the Far East not by Japan alone but by England, Russia, France, and Germany—and by the United States (if in a form somewhat more moderate) in the Hawaiian Islands, and the Philippines.

"If the others do it," the Japanese militarists have argued, "why shouldn't we? Why shouldn't we, who need additional territory so much more than they do, grab on the continent of Asia for land to which our surplus population may be sent, and from which we may get food and raw materials?"

To which the other nations answer: "Unfortunately for you, you came along too late. The good old grabbing days are gone. The world is radiant with a new international morality, and woe be unto those who offend against it! Germany tried it—see what happened to her!"

Japan did see what happened to Germany and the lesson was not wasted on her. Nor was the least striking part of the lesson contained in America's exhibition of military might. And truth to tell, Japan needed such a lesson; for her victories over China and Russia had put her militarists in the ascendant, and had made them, and perhaps the bulk of their countrymen also, over-confident, with the result that Japan occasionally rattled the sabre in the Far East somewhat as Germany was wont to do in Europe.

But although it cannot be denied that the Japanese militarists exhibited undue aggressiveness in China and Siberia during the late war, and although their actions since have not been altogether satisfactory to the rest of the world, there is good reason to suppose that their old-time dream of vast territorial aggrandizement has diminished, even though it may not have entirely faded from the minds of some of them.

This new tendency toward moderation is due to the war's lesson and to the marked growth of liberal and anti-militarist sentiment among the Japanese people. The militarists, though they still control the Government, are less aggressive than they used to be, both because the Japanese public protests when too much aggressiveness is shown, and because the more intelligent members of the militaristic group now realize that if Japan were to bring on a great war she would inevitably be ruined. So, while the power and aggressiveness of this dangerous element slowly wane, the liberal element, led by some of the sanest and ablest men in Japan, steadily gains strength.

The outcome of this struggle between the advocates of force and those of fair dealing will, in my judgment, be determined largely by the course pursued by other nations. If, as we all hope, a new order of things is to grow out of the late war, then within a few years I believe we shall see the liberal group running Japan. But if, on the contrary, the world backslides, and the old selfish system is resumed, then the Japanese militarists will say to the people: "Well, you see that we were right after all!"

But however these matters may turn out, I do not believe that Japan will ever fully settle her surplus population problem by means of emigration, whether to annexed territory, or to other countries. The Japanese do not like to leave home. There are only about 300,000 Japanese in China, for example, and they have not colonized to nearly the extent they might have in Siberia. If they do leave home they seek mild climates, but they are now barred from colonizing in the United States, Canada, and Australia and even when they settle in Mexico or South America one sees protests in our press. Yet if Japan's population is to remain static hundreds of thousands of her people must leave the islands every year. All considered, it seems more than improbable that they will ever emigrate in such a wholesale way.

By what means, then, is the problem to be solved?

Apparently the leaders of the small group that governs Japan came, some years ago, to the conclusion that the best means for solving their difficulties lay in turning Japan into an industrial country. They determined to manufacture goods, export them, and with the proceeds pay for imports of raw materials and food—in short, to adopt the plan which England began to follow nearly a century ago, and which Belgium has also followed. England's situation was in many respects like that of Japan, for there were certain essential raw materials which she did not have either at home or in her possessions; and like Japan she is unable to feed herself. With Belgium the situation was even worse than with England. Yet through industrializing themselves both countries have prospered greatly. Is it not then logical to suppose that by following a similar course Japan will likewise prosper? Recent statistics seem, moreover, to indicate that with industrialization the birth-rate tends to decline.

In attempting a great industrial programme Japan has two advantages: she has abundant cheap labour and a short haul to the great markets of Asia. Geographically we are her nearest competitor for Asiatic trade, yet we have at the very least, four thousand miles farther to carry our goods. Obviously this is an immense disadvantage to us, and we are further handicapped by the high cost of our labour.

Having us at so great a disadvantage in the matter of commerce with Asia, it would seem that Japan should have little difficulty in securing for herself the lion's share of the Asiatic trade.

But it must not be supposed that Japan has as yet become sufficiently industrialized to solve her problem. She must become a much greater manufacturing and exporting nation than she now is. And in order to accomplish that she must greatly improve in one particular: she must master much more thoroughly than she has so far mastered them, the horrid arts of "efficiency."

I do not mean to imply that the Japanese are never efficient, but only that they are not always so efficient as they ought to be, and as they must become. I am aware, now, that I expected too much of them in this particular. Reports of their astonishing military efficiency at the time of their war with Russia, caused me to think of them almost as supermen. And they are not that. Nor is any other race.

It may be true that in military matters they are highly efficient. Probably they are. My own observation as a traveller on their ships convinces me that they are efficient on the sea, and this opinion is supported by what American naval officers have told me of their navy and their naval men. I visited a huge cotton mill near Tokyo which was clearly a first-class institution of the kind; also I was much struck, in going through a penitentiary, by the evidences of their understanding of modern and enlightened practice in the conduct of penal establishments; and I might go on with a list of other institutions which impressed me favourably.

But that is not the side I wish here to bring out. On the contrary, I wish to call attention to the fact that the high degree of efficiency shown by the

Japanese in certain instances serves but to emphasize their widespread inefficiency in others.

In an earlier chapter I spoke of the fact that in Japan one sees three men instead of two in the cab of a locomotive, that hand-carts are used for watering city streets, and that more servants are required there than here in a house of given size. These are but minor items in the wholesale waste of labour. It is as if Japan said to herself: "I have all these people to look after and I must put as many of them as possible on every job." And that, in my judgment, is not the way Japan should look at it. Instead of putting on every job more people than are actually needed, she should endeavour to develop her industries to such a point that there will be a full, honest day's work for everyone. For, of course, her labour wastage keeps up her manufacturing and operating costs.

An example of the way time is wasted may be seen wherever railroad gangs are at work. They swing their picks to the accompaniment of a song, and the rhythm is taken from the slowest man. Wastage is also exhibited in the way a house is built. They build the framework of the roof upon the ground. Then they take it apart. Then they go up and put it together all over again, in place. A whole house is constructed in this way. The parts are not fashioned on the premises as the building goes up, but are made elsewhere and brought to the actual scene of building to be fitted together. The tiles are fastened to the roof with mud, but instead of carrying this mud up in bulk they toss it up from hand to hand, six men forming a chain for the purpose.

Or again, to cite a very simple example of domestic inefficiency, consider their method of washing a kimono. Instead of laundering the garment all at once, they rip it apart, wash the pieces separately, dry them on a board, and sew them together again.

In factory management also one sometimes finds the most surprising inefficiency. I know of a great manufacturing plant in Japan which, if you were to go through it, you would call thoroughly modern. The buildings are modern, the machinery is modern. But there is one thing missing, and it is a vital thing. The plant stands a good half mile from the railway line; coal and raw materials are transported from car to factory in carts, or in baskets carried on the backs of coolies, and the finished product is removed in like manner.

Though the cost of labour in Japan was trebled after the war, wages are still low as compared with other countries. But this fact, which should be taken advantage of in the struggle for world trade, is too often used only as an excuse for such waste of labour as I have pointed out. And it is because of this and similar inefficiencies that the Japanese now find themselves unable to compete in costs, in certain lines, with other nations, even though the labour of those other nations is much better paid.

Among the things most criticized by visitors are the bad roads, both in the country and in the cities; the hotels, which except in a few places are poor (I am speaking only of the foreign-style hotels); and the miserable conditions of what the *Japan Advertiser* humorously refers to as "public futilities."

Tokyo, with a transportation problem which ought easily to be solved, has utterly inadequate street-car service. The rush hour there is only saved from being as terrible as the rush hour in New York by the lack of subterranean features.

But it is in all matters having to do with communications that Japanese inefficiency is most strikingly brought to the notice of strangers. The postal service is poor, the cable service is expensive and absurdly slow (when I was in Japan it took about ten days to cable to America and get an answer back), and the telephone service is unbelievably awful. All these, like the railroads, are owned and operated by the Government.

I began to suspect their telephones when I saw the old full-bosomed wall instruments they use, with bell-cranks to be rung; but little did I then guess the full measure of their telephonic backwardness.

It is like opera bouffe. Though the demand for new telephones far exceeds the supply, the Government makes no appreciable effort to remedy the situation. Every year an absurdly small number of lines is added to the existing system. These are assigned by lot among those who have applied for them. Thus, if a man be lucky in the draw, he may get a telephone within two or three years. But I know one gentleman in Tokyo who was not lucky in the draw. At the ripe age of sixty-seven he applied to the Government for an additional office telephone. The instrument was installed shortly after he had celebrated his eightieth birthday. Long may he live to use it!

If one be in a hurry to have a telephone put in, one does not apply to the authorities, but attacks the problem in a manner more direct—either through a telephone broker or through advertising. Thus one can get in contact with a person wishing to sell an installation and a number. The number must, however, be in the exchange serving the district in which the telephone is to be placed.

Though this is a very expensive method, it is the one usually employed in Tokyo and other large cities. A telephone for the business district of the capital may cost as much as twelve hundred dollars, but in a residential district it will be considerably cheaper—five hundred dollars or less.

A curious detail of this business is that low numbers bring the highest price in the open market. This, I was informed, is because green operators, in process of being broken-in, sit at that end of the central switchboard at which the high numbers invariably occur, thus guaranteeing the owners of high numbers a grade of service calculated to drive them to the madhouse.

It must not be imagined that the Japanese are content with their telephone service. They are not. For some time prior to my arrival in Japan the press had been demanding a reform, and at last it was announced that action was about to be taken to improve matters.

But all that happened was this: Instead of increasing the service, the government functionaries started a campaign to discourage the use of telephones. Up to that time, unlimited service had been given. Now, however, a flat charge of two sen (about one cent) per call was announced, the theory being that many persons would think twice before spending two sen on an idle telephonic conversation.

After watching the new plan in operation for a few days the telephone authorities jubilantly announced that it was a great success—the number of calls had appreciably diminished. Apparently it never occurred to them that the result of such a policy, carried to its logical conclusion, would be to eliminate the telephone entirely.

With the Japanese cables the trouble has been largely due to congestion. The use of two important lines was cut off by the war, and as service on these lines has not up to the time of writing been resumed, owing to the disorganization of Russia and Germany, a heavy strain has been placed upon the transpacific cables. I am assured, however, that conditions would not be so bad as they are if the Japanese were entirely efficient in their handling of cable business, and my own experiences with cable messages, while there, would seem to indicate that this is true.

Moreover, at the time when cable congestion was at its worst, the Japanese refused to operate their transpacific wireless for more than seven hours a day; and even then they would take business only for San Francisco and vicinity, for the reason, it was explained, that they did not wish to be bothered with the details of figuring the rates to various parts of the United States. Lately they have increased their service to cover the states of California, Oregon and Washington; but that, at the time of writing, is as far as they have consented to extend it.

CHAPTER XX

The Average American and International Affairs—The Vagueness of the Orient—A Definition by Former Ambassador Morris—"They say"—The "Yellow Peril"—International Insults—Physiognomy—What the Japanese Should Learn About Us—Our Race Problems—Racial Integrity—Assimilation—Californian Methods—The Two Sound Arguments Against Oriental Immigration

> If public opinion is fed with distorted facts, unworthy suspicions, or alarming rumours; if every careless utterance by thoughtless and insignificant men is to be given prominence in print; if every casual difference of view is to be magnified into a crisis, sober judgment and deliberate action become impossible.—JOHN W. DAVIS, *former Ambassador to the Court of St. James's.*

Concerned with making a living, the Average American has as a rule neither the time nor the inclination to study international affairs. He expects his government to see to such things for him. He has no interest in what his government is doing with regard to other nations unless his personal feelings are in some way involved. Thus if he be a German-American he may take cognizance of our relations with Germany; or if he be a Russian-American he may desire that we recognize the so-called government of Lenine and Trotzky; or again, if he be an Irish-American he may wish the President of the United States to go personally to London and knock the British premier's hat off. But if he be simply an average unhyphenated American the chances are that he is disgusted with the clatter of the hyphenates and bored with the whole business of foreign relations and race problems. His main interest in governmental affairs at the present time has nothing to do with foreign relations but comes much closer to home. He is tired of paying heavy taxes, tired of paying exorbitantly for the necessities of life. He wants his government to remedy those two things. Then, because he is sick of hyphenated citizens and internal race problems, he wants immigration stopped.

The Orient is all vague to him. If he does not live on the Pacific Coast or in some large city where Japanese have settled, he may never have laid eyes upon a Japanese. Or if he has seen Japanese over here he may have seen them in the farming districts of the Pacific slope. Whether he has seen them or not, he has gathered some impression of them through newspaper accounts of the trouble there has been about them in California. He understands that their customs, religion, and food are unlike his—which may be taken as implying a certain lack of merit in them. He understands that Japanese women and children work in the fields. His own women and children do not work in the fields, but wear silk stockings, chew gum, and go to the movies— all of which, of course, counts against the Japanese, since to work in the fields is in these times almost un-American. And of course it is still more un-American to do what the Japanese labourers did in California until the patriotic Californians stopped them; namely to save money and buy farms.

Then there is this business about "picture-brides"—my Average American may have heard vaguely about that, though probably he does not know that the Japanese Government, in deference to our wishes, no longer allows picture-brides to come here. He would not think of such a thing as picking out a wife by photograph. None of his friends would do it, either.

It may be well here to state the actual nature of the issue in California. This can be done briefly in no better way than by quoting an editorial published not long since in the New York *World*, a newspaper remarkable for the intelligence with which it has generally treated the Japanese question.

The *World's* editorial was published apropos an address made by Mr. Roland S. Morris, who served under the Wilson Administration as ambassador to Tokyo, and whose admirable work in Tokyo might have borne good fruit but for our unfortunate habit of relieving ambassadors, however able, when the political party to which they belong goes out of power.

Said the *World*:

> In his address at the University Club on the Japanese issue in California, Roland S. Morris, American Ambassador to Tokyo, refrained from discussing the merits of the case and merely defined the question in accordance with the facts. It is only in the light of the facts that a sound decision can be reached where argument and judgment run along the line of fixed prejudices.
>
> As Mr. Morris explained, Japan does not question the right of the United States, subject to its treaty obligations, to legislate on the admission of foreigners. While under the treaty of 1911 Japanese were granted full rights of residence and admission, the Tokyo Government accepted the condition that it would continue limiting emigration from Japan to the United States in compliance with the "Gentleman's Agreement" of 1908. [4]

4 The "limiting" here referred to includes the stoppage of labour emigration, not by us, but by the Japanese Government, which took this amiable and dignified means of avoiding a direct issue on the subject of racial equality.

The Japanese Government and people are not seeking the removal of restrictions on immigration. The Japanese are not eligible to American citizenship, but they have enjoyed in this country the same personal and property rights as other aliens. It is here that the friction has been created by the action of California.

In 1913 California deprived those aliens who were ineligible to citizenship of certain property rights. In 1920, in Mr. Morris's words, "this legislation was amplified by an initiative and referendum act." What he does not state is that this measure was intended to discriminate against the Japanese in buying and leasing land.

Hence the protests of the Government at Tokyo. The Japanese object to what they regard as the injustice of being set apart as a separate class, suffering political disabilities and deprived of rights other aliens enjoy.

Mr. Morris leaves the issue open when he says: "The Japanese protest presents to all our people this very definite question: In the larger view of our relations with the Orient, is it wise thus to classify aliens on the basis of their eligibility to citizenship?"

In pursuance of its local ends, California has adopted a provocative position and played into the hands of Japanese jingoes and militarists.

Lamentably, these simple facts have been cast adrift upon a stormy sea of Californian prejudice. That sea, I fear, so fills the eye of the Average American that oftentimes he fails entirely to descry the shipwrecked waifs of Truth out there upon their little raft. Were he to attempt to state his views upon the California question he would in all probability quote as the source of his information that favourite authority, "They say."

"They say Japanese immigrants are flooding into California and buying up the farming land; they say the Japanese have large families; they say they don't make desirable neighbours; they say that if things keep on this way they will ultimately control the state. Certainly we don't want any part of our country dominated by foreigners." The less familiar he is with certain Californian traits the more he is likely to conclude: "I guess it must be true or the Californians wouldn't be making such a row about it."

His tendency to reason thus may be enhanced by the recollection of a phrase he has heard: the "Yellow Peril"—one of the most poisonous phrases ever coined. He does not know that the term was Made in Germany for the very purpose of exciting international suspicion and ill-will. He may not be alive to our real Yellow Peril—that of the yellow press—but may, upon the contrary, actually acquire his views on international affairs from such inflammatory sheets as those published by William Randolph Hearst, himself a son of California and a leader in the anti-Japanese chorus.

My Average American knows little of Californian politics, and nothing of politics in Japan. He does not realize that Californian politicians are largely responsible for the stirring up of anti-Japanese sentiment, precisely as earlier politicians of the state were responsible for anti-Chinese sentiment, and that in both cases vote-getting was a chief motive. It is sometimes very convenient for a demagogue to have a voteless alien race at hand to bully.

My Average American is probably unaware that more than two hundred thousand Californian voters cast their ballots against the discriminatory laws passed in November, 1920, even though the press of California was generally closed to spokesmen representing sentiment opposed to undue harshness toward the Japanese. Still less is he likely to be aware that politicians in Japan know all the tricks familiar to their Californian counterparts; that they, too, know how to gather votes by stirring up race feeling. So, when he sees in his newspaper-headlines that a Japanese whose name he has never before heard, but who, the paper says, is high in politics, has been talking of war with the United States, he begins to wonder whether those people over there are not, perhaps, looking for trouble. And when he reads of Japan's great naval building programme the notion becomes a little more concrete in his mind.

Of course he does not understand that, meanwhile, in Japan there has been going on a process precisely similar: that hostile and insulting things said by American politicians are cabled to Japan and published there, where they carry undue weight; and that while we are reading of Japan's naval programme and wondering what it signifies, Japan is reading of ours, and likewise wondering.

That any one could suspect the United States of aggressive purpose is inconceivable to my Average American. Though the United States has lately shown that she can fight, she has also shown she is loath to do it. The Average American has no feeling of hostility toward Japan, and the idea of war with Japan seems to him absurd to the point of being fantastic. There is, as he conceives it, but one way in which such a war could be started, and that is by Japanese aggression.

Assure him that the exact reverse of this view represents Japanese sentiment and you will stupefy him. "You must be wrong about that," he will tell you. "The Japanese must know that we hate war and that we have no more desire to fight them than to select our wives out of a photograph album." And he may add something about Japanese "inscrutability."

That is another point:

When my Average American meets a stranger of his own race, or of almost any European nationality, he can form, from the stranger's physiognomy, some estimate of his character. It is a type of face he understands. But the Oriented physiognomy baffles him. He cannot read it. To him it is as a book in an unknown tongue—a very symbol for mystery.

That it may be equally difficult for the Japanese to judge of us would not occur to him. Our faces are—well, they are regular *faces*; there is nothing queer about them. *We* aren't queer in any way. It is other people who are queer.

If certain simple facts about Japan were understood in the United States, and certain simple facts about the United States were understood in Japan, it might not follow that the two nations would thereafter cordially approve of all each other's policies and acts, but it ought certainly to follow that they could view such policies and acts with eyes more tolerant.

You and I, for instance, might not approve the aggressive methods of some canvasser we had encountered, but if we knew that his wife and family were crowded into a single room wondering where to-morrow's breakfast would come from, we could forgive the man a good deal. Similarly, if he were to see you or me bulldozing a helpless guest in our own house, his disapproval of our action might be mitigated if he understood that the entire neighbourhood had fallen into the habit of using our house as a common camping ground for undesirable members of their families, and that we had been goaded by these unwelcome visitors into a state of desperation.

What are the essential things for the Japanese to learn about us?

They must get a better understanding of our various race problems. They must realize that, important as the problem involving their settlers on the Pacific Coast appears to them, it is to us a minor problem—being one of the least of a number of race-problems with which we are confronted.

They must know that our population is derived from all the countries of Europe. And they must be made aware that though we have in the past viewed this situation with fatuous complacency, we no longer do so. Our old beautiful theory that the United States was properly a refuge for the oppressed of all other lands has lost a wheel and gone into the ditch. Some of us have even begun to suspect that the oppressed of other lands were in certain instances oppressed for what may have been good and sufficient cause. We have found that some of these individuals, on arriving in the United States, become so exhilarated by our free air that from oppressed they turn into oppressors who would fain take our government out of our hands and run it in the interest of the Kaiser, the Soviets, or of Mr. De Valera's interesting Republic.

With these and other hyphenated racial problems we are continually contending. We no sooner meet one than another arises. Now we must needs create an Alien Property Custodian to take a hand. Now we deport a band of the more violent Bolsheviks. Now we summon glaziers to put new windows in the Union Club in New York, where the British flag (flying in commemoration of the landing of the Pilgrim Fathers, three hundred years ago) was hailed with bricks by members of a congregation emerging from St. Patrick's Cathedral, across the way.

We used to speak with loving confidence of something called the "Melting Pot," which was supposed to make newly arrived immigrants into good American citizens. Sometimes it did so, but we have lately learned that its by-product consisted too often of bricks and bombs.

We do not boast about the Melting Pot any more. Having overloaded it and found it could not do the work we put upon it, we want time in which to catch up with back orders, as it were. Meanwhile no new ones must be taken.

But while the problems growing out of European immigration have of recent years troubled us most, they do not constitute our greatest race problem. Always in the background of our consciousness, like a volcano quiescent but very much alive, looms our gigantic negro problem—the problem which for the sins of our slave-importing and slave-holding forefathers we inherit, and from which, according to our characteristic way of "meeting" great quiescent problems, we are always endeavouring to hide. For it is not our way to advance upon a bull and take him by the horns. If a bull seeks to be taken by the horns he must do the advancing. We Americans all know this about ourselves, but it is our way to excuse the failing by boasting of the tussle we will give the bull if he ever gets us in a corner.

There is no need here even to outline the tragedies of the negro problem, but there is one aspect of the matter which should be spoken of. Experience has shown that whereas immigrants from Europe can ultimately be absorbed into what we may term the American race, the negro, wearing the badge of his race in the pigment of his skin, is not to be absorbed. Even the octoroon is clearly distinguishable from the white. The negro race must, so far as the future can be read, remain a race apart.

The case of the Indian affords another example of the failure of two races, separated by colour and other physical markings, to fuse. In the early days of this country's settlement, when the Indians strongly predominated, they did not absorb the then few whites. When the time came that there was an equal number of Indians and whites, still they did not fuse. And now, when but a handful remains of the once mighty Indian nations, that remnant still retains its racial integrity.

Here, however, is involved no question of racial inferiority. Whites and Indians have to some small extent intermarried, and when both parties represent the best of their respective races, not only is there no sense of degradation to either, but the white descendants of such alliances are often proud of their Indian blood.

In this whole matter of the fusibility of races there is, then, no basic principle of inferiority or superiority. Such questions are here as extraneous as in the case of oil and water, which though they will not mix are not therefore designated as a superior and an inferior fluid.

The fact is that some inner consciousness tells us that the characteristic physical markings of the chief races of the world were not given them for nothing; that Nature intended the broad lines of race to be maintained; and we are told that crosses which disregard these natural race divisions are usually penalized by deterioration.

To find in this truth the faintest implication of insult would be absurd. It would be as ridiculous to resent the statement that "like seeks like," as to resent the statement that "honesty is the best policy."

No people insists more firmly than the Japanese upon racial integrity. The most fanatical English horseman could hardly be more finicky about the maintenance of pure thoroughbred stock. Marriages between native Japanese and foreigners are not encouraged and seldom occur. Among the upper classes they almost never occur. A citizen of Japan cannot enter into a legal marriage with a Korean or a Formosan, although Korea and Formosa are Japanese colonies. (I am informed that steps were taken in 1918 to make such marriages legal, but up to the time of writing this has not been accomplished.)

The law regulating the acts of the Japanese Imperial Family does not permit the marriage of members of that family with persons other than those of Japanese Imperial or noble stock. This law had to be amended in order to make possible the marriage, several years ago, of a Japanese Imperial princess, the daughter of Prince Nashimoto, with the heir to the Korean Royal Family—which family, by the way, now ranks as a sort of Japanese nobility. The marriage, it may be added, was unpopular with the Japanese masses, because of their strong feeling that Japanese blood, and especially Japanese Imperial blood, should not be diluted. Had the prince been a European it is not improbable that a louder protest would have been heard, for the Japanese does not, as a rule, look with favour upon Eurasians. There are exceptions, but in the main the man or woman of mixed Oriental and

Occidental blood lives socially upon an international boundary line, on neither side of which is exuberant cordiality displayed.

The intelligent and patriotic sentiment of the United States is at present overwhelmingly in favour of the stoppage of all immigration; and even if there comes a time when it is felt that the floodgates may again be opened, they will not, if wisdom prevails, be opened wide, but will admit only such aliens as are susceptible to assimilation.

What does assimilation mean?

It means that the immigrant shall lose his racial identity in ours. It means that he shall be susceptible to absorption into the body of our race through marriage, or at the very least that his children shall be susceptible to such absorption. And this in turn means, among other things, that he shall have no ineradicable physical characteristics which strongly differentiate him from our national physical type.

This is one chief reason why, in my opinion, Orientals should never settle in the United States. Broadly speaking, they are no more suited to become citizens of the United States than are we to become citizens of Japan or China.

Another chief reason why Japanese labour immigration is not acceptable to us is that the Japanese can live on less than we can. They are willing to work longer hours for less pay. Also they are thrifty. These are virtues; but the fact that they are virtues does not make Japanese competition the more welcome to white labour.

This point also should readily be appreciated by the people of Japan, who find it generally necessary to exclude Chinese labour on precisely the same ground—that is, because a Chinaman can live on less than a Japanese, and can consequently work for lower wages.

Had California, in her desire to prevent the further acquirement of land by Japanese settlers, rested her case on these two clean-cut issues: namely, unassimilability and economic necessity; had she refrained from vituperation, taking up the matter purely on its merits; had she recognized her duty as a state to the Nation and coöperated with the Washington Government, instead of ignoring the international bearing of the question and embarrassing the Government by radical and independent state action; and had she, above all, shown any disposition to deal as justly with the Japanese as the circumstances would permit; then, without a doubt, the entire Nation would have been behind California. And what is perhaps as important, the whole matter could then have been presented to Japan in a reasonable and temperate manner, without offence, yet with arguments the force of which Japan could hardly escape.

But it is not apparently in the nature of the average Californian to go at things in a moderate way. Moderation is not one of his traits. His father, or grandfather, was a sturdy pioneer whose habit it was to express resentment with a bowie-knife and answer antagonism with a Colt .45. In the descendant these family traits are modified but not extinguished. If he does not approve of the manner in which an amiable alien wears his eyebrows he is likely to call him something—without a smile.

Antagonism? Why should he mind antagonism? He likes it. He feels the need of it. He must have something to combat—something to neutralize the everlasting sunshine and the cloying sweetness of the orange-blossom and the rose.

And alas, there is Senator Hiram Johnson, of whom the New York *Times* recently remarked that, "he would lose his proprietary political issue if the differences with Japan were peacefully composed. And we know," the *Times* continued, "that it is better to meet a bear robbed of her whelps than a politician deprived of his issue." And again, alas, there is ex-Senator Phelan— though the ex-, which has recently been added to his title, may tend, to some extent, to moderate his effectiveness as a baiter of the Japanese. And thrice alas, there is Mr. V. S. McClatchy, the Sacramento apiarist, whose "Bee" is trained to sting the Japanese wherever it will hurt most.

That the difficulties between the two countries must be harmonized, all thoughtful citizens of both will agree. For myself, I do not see how this can be fully accomplished without some modification of the present discriminatory alien land law of California—a law which, aimed at one alien group alone, is not in consonance with the American sense of justice.

The Japanese labourers who are already legally here—many of them originally brought here, by the way, at the instance of Californian employers—should be treated with absolute fairness. They should not be deprived of the just rewards of their industry and thrift. Their racial virtues should be appreciated and might well be emulated.

It should be clear, however, that for our good and the good of the Japanese, no further immigrants of their labouring class should ever enter the United States. And it should be equally clear that in such a statement there is no cause for offence.

The United States does not invariably act wisely. Neither does Japan. But the American heart is in the right place, and so is the Japanese heart.

Let us try, then, on both sides, to look at these problems with honest and disinterested eyes. Let us try to get each other's point of view. Let us even go so far as to make due allowance for the frailty of human nature, as exhibited on both sides of the Pacific.

But let us have no thought of straining good will by attempting to become on any larger scale inmates of the same house, dwellers under the same national roof.

CHAPTER XXI

Some Reflections on New York Hospitality—And on the Hospitality of Japan—Letters of Introduction—Bowing—How Japanese Politeness is Sometimes Misunderstood—Entertaining Foreigners—Showing the Country at its Best—What is the Mysterious "Truth" About Japan?—Japanese versus *Chinese—Leadership in the Far East—Will Japan Become a Moral Leader?—A "First-Class Power"—The New "Long Pants"—How to Treat Japan—The Wisdom of Roosevelt and Root.*

A vigorous and sustained display of hospitality must always be astonishing to one who calls New York his home; for New York is without doubt the most inhospitable city in the world. In the jaded hotel-clerk, the bored box-office man, and the fish-eyed head waiter, the spirit of its welcome is personified.

There is no dissimulation. The stranger is as welcome in New York as he feels. If there be a hotel room, a theatre seat, or a restaurant table disengaged, he may have it, at a price. If all are occupied he may, so far as New York cares, step outside and, with due regard to the season and the traffic regulations, die of sunstroke or perish in a snowdrift—whereupon his case comes automatically under the supervision of the Street-Cleaning Department—and whatever else that Department may leave lying around the New York streets, it does not leave them littered with defunct strangers. Space in our city is too valuable.

The visitor arriving in New York with a letter of introduction to some gentleman who is important, or who believes he is, may expect a few minutes' talk with the gentleman in his office, and may regard it as a delicate attention if his host refrains from fidgeting.

Should the stranger have some information which the New Yorker desires to possess, he may find himself invited out to lunch. They will lunch at a club in the top of a down-town skyscraper. Or if the letter of introduction has a social flavour, the outlander will presently receive by mail, at his hotel, a guest's card to a club up-town.

Let him make bold to visit this club and he will find there no one to speak to save a rigid doorman and some waiters. The doorman will tell him coldly where to check his hat and coat. He will see a few members in the club, but will not know them, nor will they desire to know him. All New Yorkers know more people than they want to, anyway. The stranger with a guest's card to a New York club is as comfortable there as a cat in a cathedral.

In the West it is different.

And again it is different in Japan.

Those who go well introduced to Japan meet there an experience such as is hardly to be encountered in any other land. Japanese courtesy and hospitality are fairly stupefying to the average Anglo-Saxon. The Occidental mind is staggered by the mere externals.

You see two Japanese meet—two gentlemen, two ladies, or a lady and a gentleman. They face each other at fairly close range. Then, as though at some signal unperceived by the foreigner, they bow deeply from the waist, their heads passing with so small a space between that one half expects them to bump. Three times in succession they bow in this way, simultaneously, their hands slipping up and down their thighs, in front, like pistons attached to the walking-beam of a side-wheeler.

In conjunction with this profound and protracted bowing, especially when the bowers are Japanese of the old school, or are unaccustomed to associate with foreigners, the bystander will oftentimes hear a sibilant sound made by the drawing in of air through the lips. According to the Japanese idea, such sounds denote appreciation as of some delicious spiritual flavour. This ancient form of politeness is, however, being discarded by sophisticated young Japan for the reason that foreigners find it peculiar; and the practice of audibly sucking in food as an expression of gustatory ecstasy is also going out of fashion for the same reason. The old ways are, nevertheless, held to by many an aristocrat of middle age, or older.

The American, accustomed to regard hissing as a sign of disapproval, and noisy eating as ill-bred, is naturally startled on first encountering these manifestations. Japanese bowing, when directed at him, he finds disconcerting. He may wish to be as polite as the politest, but he has in his repertory nothing adequate to offer in return for such an obeisance.

In this country we have never taken to bowing as practised in some other lands. Our men look askance at Latin males when they lift their hats to one another in salutation, and it may be observed that some of us tend to slight the lifting of the hat a little bit even when saluting ladies, clutching furtively at the brim and perhaps loosening the hat upon the head, then hastily jamming it back in place.

The fact is that very few American men have polished manners. We rebel at anything resembling courtliness. It makes us feel "silly." The dancing school bow we were compelled to practise in the days of our otherwise happy youth was a nightmare to us, and now in our maturity we have a sense of doing something utterly inane when, at a formal dinner party, it devolves upon us to present an arm to a lady, as if to assure her of protection through the perils of the voyage from drawing room to table. We much prefer to amble helter-skelter to the dining room.

In these matters, then, as in so many others, we find ourselves at the opposite pole from the Japanese; and though Americans of the class willing to appreciate merits of kinds they themselves do not possess feel nothing but admiration for Japanese courtesy in its perfection, it sometimes happens, lamentably enough, that others, less intelligent, going to the Orient, utterly misread the meaning of Japanese politeness, mistaking it for servility, which it most emphatically is not. Far from being servile it is a proud politeness— a politeness grounded upon custom, sensitiveness of nature, delicacy of feeling, which cause the possessor to expect in others a like sensitiveness and delicacy and to make him wish to outdo them in tact and consideration.

Nor does the failure of certain Americans to appreciate Japanese courtesy and hospitality for what it is, stop here. Our yellow press and organized Japanese-haters, aware that the higher hospitality of Japan has oftentimes an official or semi-official character, are not satisfied to seek a simple explanation for the fact, but prefer to discern in it something artful and sinister.

It is perfectly true that the stranger going to Japan with good letters of introduction meets a group composed almost entirely of government officials, big business men, and their families. It is also true that he is likely to meet a selected group of such men. The reason for this is simple. While English is the second language taught in Japanese schools, and while many Japanese can speak some broken English, there are still relatively few men, and still fewer women, who have been educated abroad and are sufficiently familiar with foreign languages, customs, and ideas to feel easy when entertaining foreigners. This class is, moreover, still further limited by the financial burden of extensive entertaining.

Thus it happens that there exists in Japan a social group which may be likened to a loosely organized entertainment committee, with the result that most Americans who are entertained in that country meet, broadly speaking, the same set of people.

The Japanese are entirely frank in their desire to interest the world in Japan. The Government maintains a bureau for the purpose of encouraging tourists to visit the country and making travel easy for them. The great Japanese steamship companies, the Toyo Kisen Kaisha and Nippon Yusen Kaisha, are energetic in seeking passenger business. Journalists, authors, men of affairs and others likely to have influence at home, are especially encouraged to visit Japan. The feeling of the Japanese is that there exists in the United States a prejudice against them, and that the best way to overcome this is to show Japan to Americans and let them form their own conclusions. They are proud of their country and they believe that those who become acquainted with it will think well of it.

Some Americans charge them with endeavouring to show things at their best, as if to do that were a sly sin.

The attitude of the Japanese in this matter may be likened to that of a man who owns a home in some not very accessible region, the advantages of which are doubted by his friends. Being proud of his place the owner is hospitable. He urges those he knows to come and see it.

When his guests arrive he does not begin by taking them to look at the sick cow, or the corner behind the barn where refuse is dumped, but marches them to the west verandah—the verandah with the wonderful view.

To the average person such a procedure would seem entirely normal. Yet there are critics of Japan who do not see it in that light. Their attitude might be likened to that of someone who, when taken to the verandah to see the view, declares that the view is being shown not on its own merits, but because the host has cut the butler's throat and does not wish his guests to notice the body lying under the parlour table.

Let an American of any influence go to Japan, be cordially received there, form his impressions, and return with a good word to say for the islands and the people, and the professional Japanese-haters have their answer ready. The man has been victimized by "propaganda." He has been flattered by social attentions, fuddled with food and drink, reduced to a state of idiocy, and in that state "personally conducted" through Japan in a manner so crafty as to prevent his stumbling upon the "Truth."

The precise nature of this "Truth" is never revealed. It is merely indicated as some vague awfulness behind a curtain carefully kept drawn.

Having so often heard these rumours I went to Japan in a suspicious frame of mind. Arriving there, I made it my business to dive behind whatever looked like a veil of mystery. As the reader who has followed me thus far will be aware, I found a number of mysteries—the fascinating mysteries of an old and peculiar civilization, out of which an interesting modernism had rapidly grown.

I was considerably entertained in Japan; my sightseeing was oftentimes facilitated by Japanese friends; but the significant fact is that no one ever tried to prevent my seeing anything I wished to. And I wished to see everything, good and bad. I visited the lowest slums, a penitentiary, a poorhouse, a hospital, and some factories. I asked questions. Sometimes they were embarrassing questions—about militarism in Japan, about Shantung, about Korea and Formosa, about Manchuria and Siberia. And though I do not expect any Japanese-hater to believe me, I wish to declare here, in justice to the Japanese, that they gave me the information I asked, even though to do so sometimes pained them.

I saw and learned things creditable to Japan and things discreditable, just as in other lands one sees and learns things in both categories. I found the Japanese neither angels nor devils. They are human beings like the rest of us, having their virtues and their defects.

I came away liking and respecting them as a people. This fact I proclaim with the full knowledge that those who do not like them will accept it, not as a sign of any merit in the Japanese, but as proof of my incompetence, or worse.

"But you have not been to China," some of my friends say. "You would like the Chinese better than the Japanese."

That may be true or it may not. I am inclined to believe that there is, on the surface, more natural sympathy and understanding between Americans and Chinamen than between Americans and Japanese. The Chinaman is more easily comprehensible to us. Also he is meek. We can talk down to him. He will do as we tell him to. He is not a contender—as the Japanese very definitely is—and is therefore easier to get along with. As an individual he has many qualities to recommend him, though neither patriotism nor cleanliness seems to be among them.

If I ever go to China I shall hope and expect not to fall into the mental grooves which lead travellers in the Orient generally to feel that if they like a Chinaman they cannot like a Japanese, and vice versa. I hereby reserve the right to like both.

China appears to be an amiable, flaccid, sleepy giant who has long allowed himself to be bullied, victimized, and robbed. Japan, on the other hand, is a small, well-knit, pugnacious individual, well able to look after himself, and profoundly engaged in doing so. Naturally the two do not get on well together, and equally naturally the impotent giant comes off the worse. One is, to that extent, sorry for him, but one can hardly respect him as one would were he to rise up and assert himself. One may, on the other hand, wish the little Japanese less obstreperous, but one is bound to respect him for his prowess. Physically and materially he has earned for himself the undisputed leadership of the Far East. There remains, however, the question whether he is spiritually great enough to become, as well, a moral leader. In that question is bound up the future of the Orient. Some signs are hopeful, some are not. The answer is locked in the vaults of time to come.

It is not surprising that the Japanese are proud of the leadership they have already attained. Being relatively new members of the hair-pulling, hobnailed family we call the Family of Nations, and having rapidly become important members, they are inclined to harp more than necessary upon this importance, so novel and so gratifying to them. They like to talk about it. They delight in proclaiming themselves a "first-class power." They rejoice exceedingly in their alliance with Great Britain, not because the alliance itself has any very real importance (in view of the attitude of Australia and Canada toward Japan, and of Britain's regard for American sentiment, it cannot have), but because of the flattering association. Japan likes to be seen walking with the big fellows. In this she reminds one somewhat of a youth in all the pride and self-consciousness of his first pair of "long pants."

Now there is this to be remembered about a youth in his first "long pants": he requires careful handling. If you treat him like a child, either patronizing or ignoring him, you will offend him mortally, and not impossibly drive him to some furious action in assertion of his manhood. But if, on the other hand, you are misled by his appearance of maturity, and expect of him all that you would expect of a thoroughly ripened man, then you are very likely to find yourself disappointed.

There is but one course to be pursued with a youth in this intermediate stage. He must be managed with tact, firmness, and patience. In dealing with the young, many adults fail to understand this, and in dealing with a nation in a corresponding state of evolution, other nations are as a rule even stupider than adult individuals.

Britain, wisest of all the world in international affairs, has not made this mistake in her relations with Japan. The alliance is one proof of it. The visit of the Crown Prince of Japan to England in the spring of 1921, is another. Nor was the tact of Britain in this situation ever better displayed than in King George's speech, when, toasting the Imperial guest, he said:

"Because he is our friend we are not afraid for him to see our troubles. We know his sympathy is with us and that he will understand."

Would that the United States might draw the simple lesson from these two short sentences spoken by England's king. Would that we might learn to take that amiable tone. Would that Americans might understand how instantly the Japanese—yes, and all other nations—respond to such approaches.

The problem of maintaining friendly relations with this neighbour on the other side of the Pacific is not, in truth, nearly so difficult as many of our other problems. It has been rendered difficult chiefly by our own incredible bungling.

Among men a bungler is oftentimes feared and disliked exactly as if he were malevolent, and among nations the situation is the same. No nation, however strong, can afford to give offence unnecessarily to other great powers; and the United States can least of all afford to irritate needlessly those powers with which her front yard and her back yard are shared: namely, Britain and Japan. Yet we are constantly annoying these two nations without accomplishing any counterbalancing good purpose.

Britain, feeling, as we do, the tie of consanguinity, and having, moreover, a shrewd eye to her own interest, forgives us, or at least appears to. But in the case of Japan we are dealing with a very different situation. There is no blood relationship to ease the strain; nor is there always in Tokyo the calm, phlegmatic, self-interested statesmanship of London. Tokyo is sometimes temperamental.

If we continue to bungle we shall ultimately gain the lasting ill-will of Japan, and if we do that we shall almost certainly find ourselves looking out of our back window not merely at a frowning Nippon, but at a coalition between Japan, Russia, and Germany—a coalition into which we ourselves, by our attitude, shall have driven Japan.

It is for us to decide whether we wish to encourage such an alliance.

With Mr. Hughes in the State Department we have, it appears, good reason to be hopeful, but Mr. Hughes has not as yet had time to accomplish much of an improvement in American-Japanese relations. If he does so he will be the first American statesman to have made headway in the matter since Roosevelt was in the White House and Elihu Root in the State Department; for not since their time has there been evident in our dealings with Japan a definite and understanding policy. The failure of our diplomacy is all too plainly reflected in the steady diminution of the good feeling which then existed.

Though he never visited Japan, Roosevelt, with his amazing understanding of people, managed to sense the Japanese perfectly. He knew their virtues and their failings. He realized precisely the state they had attained in their evolution from mediævalism to modernity. He knew their samurai loyalty and pride, their sensitiveness, their love of courtesy.

"Speak softly and carry a big stick," he used to say. In those words is summed up a large part of his foreign policy. He knew when to send a bearskin to the Emperor, and when to send a fleet.

Even when he sent that fleet of sixteen battleships, the visit paid was one of courtesy. And courtesy, as I have tried to show, is never, never lost upon Japan.

PART IV

CHAPTER XXII

The Missing Lunch—The Japanese Chauffeur—The Little Train—Japanese Railroads—The Railway Lunch—The Railway Teapot—Reflections on Some American Ways—Are the Japanese Honest?—A Story of Viscount Shibusawa—Travelling Customs—An Eavesdropping Episode

Neither the box of lunch nor the automobile to take us to the station was ready, though both had been ordered the previous night. We waited until twenty minutes before train time; then made a dash for the station in a taxi which happened along providentially—something taxis seldom do in Tokyo.

The drive took us several miles across the city. Through a picturesque and incoherent jumble of street traffic, over canals, past the huge concrete amphitheatre in which wrestling bouts are held, across a steel bridge spanning the Sumida River, through a maze of muddy streets lined with open-fronted shops partially protected from the hot sun by curtains of indigo cotton bearing advertisements in large white Chinese characters, we flew precariously, facing collisions half a dozen times yet magically escaping them as one always does behind a Japanese chauffeur. It is said that the Japanese chauffeur is not, as a rule, a good mechanic. As to that I cannot say, but I assure you he can drive. At an incredible speed he will whirl you through the dense slow-moving crowds of a street festival or around the hairpin curves of a muddy mountain pass with one wheel following the slippery margin of a precipice, but he will never hurt so much as a hair of your head, unless, perchance, it hurts your hair to stand on end.

The Ryogoku Station, where we found our friends awaiting us, is a modest frame structure, terminus of an unimportant railway line serving the farming and fishing villages of the Boso Peninsula—which depends from the mainland in such a way as to form the barrier between Tokyo Bay and the Pacific.

The train seemed to have been awaiting us. It started as soon as we had boarded it, and was presently rocking along through open country at twenty-five or thirty miles an hour. There was something of solemn playfulness about that little train. The cars were no heavier than street cars and the locomotive would have made hard work of drawing a pair of Pullmans, yet in its present rôle it gave a pompous performance, hissing, whistling, and snorting as importantly as if it had been the engine of a great express. The little guards, too, joined gravely in the game, calling out the names of country stations as majestically as if each were a metropolis. And the very landscape took its place in the whimsy, for our toy train ran over it as over a flat rug patterned with little green rice fields.

The Japanese Government, which so woefully mishandles its telephones and cables, does better with its railroads. They are fairly well run. Trains are almost invariably on time, and the cars are not uncomfortable, although the narrower gauge of the Japanese roads makes them necessarily smaller than our cars.

The ordinary Japanese sleeping-car is divided into halves. One half is like an American Pullman sleeper, very much scaled down in size, while the other half resembles a European *wagon-lit* in miniature, with a narrow aisle at one side and compartments in which the berths are arranged transversely to the train.

As in Europe, there are three classes of day coaches. Except where trains are overcrowded, as they often are, one may travel quite as comfortably second-class as first. Coaches of all three classes are like street cars with long seats running from end to end at either side. Usually the car is divided in the middle by a partition, the theory being that one end is for smokers; but in practice the Japanese, who are inveterate users of tobacco, seem to smoke when and where they please while travelling.

Express trains carry dining cars which are like small reproductions of ours. Some of these diners serve Japanese-style meals, some European, and some both.

Much thought has evidently been given to making travel easy for English-speaking people. Each car of every train carries a sign giving, in English, the train's destination; time-tables printed in English are easily obtained, railroad tickets are printed in both languages, and the name of each town is trebly set forth on railroad station signs, being displayed in English, in Chinese characters, and in kana.

As in the United States, station porters wear red caps but they have the European trick of passing baggage in and out of the car windows, so that the doorways are not blocked with it when passengers wish to get on and off. Also at stations of any consequence there are boys wearing green caps, who peddle newspapers, tea, and lunches.

The Japanese railway lunch is an institution as highly organized as the English railway lunch. On the platforms of all large stations you can purchase almost any sort of lunch you desire, neatly wrapped in paper napkins and packed in an immaculate wooden box. On each box the date is stamped, so that the traveller may be sure that everything is fresh. You may get a box containing liberal portions of roast chicken and Kamakura ham, with salad and hard-boiled eggs and a dainty bamboo knife and fork; or if you wish a light repast, a box of assorted sandwiches, thin and moist as sandwiches should always be but so seldom are. Or, again, you may get a variety of Japanese dishes, similarly packed.

On this trip I selected a box of that delicacy known as *tai-meshi*, and was not sorry that my order for lunch had been overlooked at the hotel. Tai-meshi consists of a palatable combination of rice and shredded sea-bream cooked in a sauce containing saké which obliterates the fishy taste of the sea-bream. The box cost me the equivalent of seventeen cents, chop-sticks included. From the green-cap boy who sold it to me I also purchased, for five cents, an earthenware pot containing tea, and a small cup, and when I had drunk the tea I learned that I could have the pot refilled with hot water at practically any station, for a couple of cents more.

Just as your English traveller leaves the railway lunch basket in the train when he is done with it, your Japanese traveller leaves the teapot and cup. Drinking the philosopher's beverage I found myself wondering whether such a system would be successful in the United States. I concluded that it would not. Some of the lunch-baskets and teapots would get back to their rightful owners, but many would disappear. There is a certain type of American, and he is numerous, who has a constitutional aversion to conforming to a nice, orderly custom of this kind. He has too much—let us call it initiative—for that. If he thought the lunch-basket and teapot worth taking home he would take them home; nor would he be deterred by the mere fact that they were not his, having only been rented to him. His subconscious sense of the importance of his own "personality" would lift him over any little obstacle of that kind. Without thinking matters out he would feel that because he had used them they were his. What he had used no one else should use—even though its usefulness to him was past. Wherefore, if he thought the basket and the teapot not worth taking, he would stamp his "personality" upon them. He might take the basket apart to see how it was made, or he might draw out his penknife and cut holes in it. Then he would consider what to do with the teapot. Finding that it fitted nicely in the palm of his hand, and sensing by touch its brittleness, he would want to use it as a missile. If he prided himself on the accuracy of his pitching he would throw it at a telegraph pole, but if he felt quite certain that he could not hit a pole he would wait for a large rock pile or a factory wall, and would hurl it against that with all his might, to make the largest possible explosion.

People often ask me whether the Japanese are honest. Doubt on this subject is, I believe, largely due to the old story that Chinese tellers are employed in Japanese banks—all Chinamen being trustworthy and all Japanese the reverse. I know of no better example of the vitality of a lie than is afforded by the survival of this one. It is a triple lie. Japanese banks do not have

Chinese tellers. The Japanese as a race are no more dishonest than other people. The leading bankers of Japan, many of whom I have met, are men of the highest character and the greatest enlightenment, and would be so recognized in any land. Nor is this merely my opinion. It is the opinion I have heard expressed by several of the greatest bankers and manufacturers in the United States—men who have done business with Japanese bankers and who know them thoroughly.

It is true that trademarks and patented articles manufactured in other countries have been stolen by some Japanese manufacturers and merchants, and that this abominable practice is to some extent kept up even to-day. But conditions in this respect are improving as business morality grows. Nor should it be forgotten that the present standard of international commercial ethics, which so strongly reprehends such thefts, is comparatively a new thing throughout the entire world. It must, however, be admitted that Japan is not, in this particular, fully abreast of the other great nations.

As for the average of probity among the people at large I can say this—that if I were obliged to risk leaving a valuable possession in a public place, on the chance of its being found by an honest person and returned to me, I should prefer to take the risk in Japan, than in most other countries. Certainly, I should prefer to take it there than in the United States—unless I could specify certain rural sections of the United States, where I should feel that my chances were better than in the neighbourhood of New York.

The Japanese are respecters of property, private and public. One may visit the historic buildings of Japan without seeing a single evidence of vandalism. I was immensely struck by this. It was so unlike home! More than once, over there, I thought of a visit I paid, some years ago, to Monticello, the beautiful old mansion built near Charlottesville, Virginia, by Thomas Jefferson, and of what the caretaker told me. All visitors, he said, had to be watched. Otherwise vines would be torn from the walls of the house, bricks chipped, and marble statuary broken. They had even found it necessary to build an iron fence around Jefferson's grave to protect the monument from American patriots who would like to take home little pieces of it.

The custom of visiting historic places and the graves of historic figures is much more common in Japan than in America. Many of Japan's most famous monuments are entirely unprotected, but instead of knocking them to pieces to get souvenirs the pilgrim will burn a little incense before them, and perhaps leave his visiting card on the spirit of the departed. Or he may write a poem.

Dr. John H. Finley has told me a story which well illustrates the delicate and reverential attitude of the Japanese in such matters.

When Baron—now Viscount—Shibusawa came to the United States several years ago, a banquet was given in his honour in New York by the Japan Society, of which Doctor Finley was then president.

At the banquet Doctor Finley remarked to the guest of honour that he heard he had sent an emissary with a wreath to be laid upon the grave of Townsend Harris, first American Minister to Japan, who is buried in Brooklyn.

"No," said Baron Shibusawa, "that is not exactly what occurred. I did not send the wreath. I took it myself and laid it on the grave. And I wrote two poems in memory of Townsend Harris and hung them in the branches of a Japanese maple tree overhanging his resting-place."

But let us get back to our little railroad train.

The men among our Japanese fellow travellers were sitting on the seats with their feet on the floor, as we do, but the women and children had slipped off their clogs and were squatting in the seats with their backs to the aisle, looking out of the windows or dozing with their heads resting upon their hands, or against the window-frame. One elderly lady was lying at full length on the seat, asleep, with her bare feet resting on the cushions.

The Japanese are much less fearful than we of the interest of fellow passengers, and indeed, so far as concerns strangers of their own race, they are justified in this, for Japanese travellers pay little or no attention to one another. In foreigners they are more interested. A Japanese who can speak English will frequently start a conversation with the traveller from abroad, and will almost invariably endeavour to be helpful. Rustics stare at the stranger with a sort of dumb interest, just as American rustics might stare at a Japanese; and young Japanese louts sometimes snicker when they see a foreigner, and comment upon him, just as young American louts might do on seeing a Japanese passing by—especially if he was wearing his national costume.

"Pipe the Jap," a New York street-corner loafer might exclaim; while similarly an ill-bred youth of Tokyo, Kobe or Yokohama might remark: "*Keto*," which means "hairy foreigner." The term *keto* is not intended to be complimentary, yet no more real harm is meant by its user them would be meant by an American smart-aleck who should speak of "chinks," "kykes" or "micks." Such terms merely exemplify the instinctive hostility of small-minded men the world over, for all who are not exactly like themselves.

Some Japanese country folk who sat opposite us on our journey to the Boso Peninsula were clearly much interested in us—particularly in the ladies of our party, and as so few foreigners understand the Japanese language, they felt safe in talking us over amongst themselves.

"What a strange little thing to wear on one's head!" said the husband, to the wife referring to a neat little turban worn by one of our ladies.

"Yes," said the wife, "and I don't see how she can walk in those shoes with their tall, thin little heels. Aren't they funny!"

These remarks and others revealing their interested speculations as to which women of our party were married to which men, were translated to us by the friend who had organized the excursion. Being a good deal of a wag, he let them talk about us until the subject seemed to be exhausted. Then he addressed a casual question, in Japanese, to the husband across the way. I have seldom seen a man look more disconcerted than that one did just then. He answered the question, but that was the last word we heard him speak. Though an hour passed before he and his wife got off the train, and though they had until then talked volubly together, the complete silence which came over them was not broken by so much as a monosyllable until they reached the station platform. There, however, we saw that they had begun to talk again, and with gestures showing not a little agitation. I had a feeling that each was blaming the other for the whole affair. Relations between husband and wife are, in some respects at least, a good deal more alike in all countries than is commonly supposed.

CHAPTER XXIII

Katsuura and the Basha—A Noble Coast—Scenes on a Country Road—The Fishers—A Temple and Tame Fish—We Arrive at an Inn—I See a Bath—I Take One—Bathing Customs—The Attentive Nesan—In the Tub

A journey of about three and a half hours brought us to the seacoast town of Katsuura, the terminus of the little railway line. The industry of Katsuura is fishing, and there is a kind of dried fish put up there which has quite a reputation. Almost every town in Japan has some specialty of its own, whether an edible or something else—something for the traveller to purchase and take home as a souvenir. Many of the best Japanese colour-prints were originally made for this purpose—souvenirs of cities and towns, celebrated inns, famous actors, and notorious courtesans.

Leaving the train we got into a *basha*—a primitive one-horse bus with tiny wheels—and took a highway leading south along the shore. The day was brilliant and our road, skirting the edge of the lofty coastal hills half way between their green serried peaks and the yellow beach on which the surf played below, was white and dusty in the hot sun. On level stretches and down-grades we rode in the basha, but we always got out and walked up hills to spare the venerable horse. Nor will travellers who have ever followed such a system be surprised that, of the twenty miles we covered on our way to Kamogawa, fully fifteen seemed to be up-hill miles.

This shore continually reminded me of other shores—Brittany, in the region of Dinard and Cancale, and the cliffs between Sorrento and Amalfi. But here the contours were more tender. Many a beach I saw, with tiny houses strewn along the margin of the sand, fishing boats drawn up in rows, and swarthy men and women bustling about among the nets and baskets, which made me think of the Marina at Capri. Even the air was that of Capri in the springtime. But here there was no song.

**Tai-no-ura—Tiny houses strewn about the margin of the sand,
fishing boats drawn up in rows, and swarthy men and women
bustling about among the nets and baskets**

A succession of lofty promontories jutting aggressively toward the sea gave
interest to the road. Sometimes they turned its course, forcing it to swing out
around them; in other cases tunnels penetrated the barrier hills, and we would
find ourselves trudging along beside the basha, through damp echoing

darkness, with our eyes fixed on a distant point of light, marking the exit, ahead.

It was a much-travelled road. We were continually meeting other bashas creaking slowly through the white dust, or drawn up before inns and teahouses where passengers were pausing for refreshment. During the entire afternoon we met not a single automobile, and when, after an hour or two, a Japanese lady, beautifully dressed and sheltered from the sun by a large parasol, flashed past in a shining ricksha propelled by two coolies, she made a picture strangely sophisticated, elegantly exotic, against the background of that dusty country highway so full of humble folk.

All the women of this region were hard at work. Some were labouring beside their husbands in the mud and water of the paddy fields, others were occupied upon the beach, piling up kelp and carrying it back to huge wooden tubs in which it was being boiled to get the juice from which iodine is extracted, still others were transporting baskets of fresh shiny fish from the newly landed boats to the village markets, or were drawing heavy carts laden with fish-baskets from one village to another. For this coast is the greatest fishing district of all Japan.

On the streets of every village we saw fish being handled—large, brilliant fish laid out in rows on straw mats, preparatory to shipment, huge tubs of smaller fish, and great baskets of silver sardines. Nor was our awareness of piscatorial activities due only to the organs of sight. Now and then a gust of information reached the olfactory organs disclosing with a frankness that was unmistakable, the proximity of a pile of rotted herring, which is used to fertilize the fields.

Winding down a hill through a grove of ancient trees, with the sea glistening between the trunks on one side of the way, we came upon a weathered temple, and, rounding it from the rear, found a tiny village clustered at its base, in as sweet a little cove as one could wish to see—low, brown houses nestling among rocks and gnarled pines, a crescent of yellow beach with fishing boats drawn up beyond the reach of the tide, and children playing among them looking like nude bronzes come to life.

This place, known as Tai-no-ura—Sea-bream Coast—small and remote as it is, has a fame which extends throughout Japan. For it was the abiding place of the thirteenth-century fisherman-priest Nichiren, who, though he antedated Martin Luther by about two and a half centuries, is sometimes called the Martin Luther of Japanese Buddhism. The Nichiren sect is to this day powerful, having more than five thousand temples and a million and a half adherents. Its scriptures are known as the *Hokkekyo*, and I find a certain quaint interest in the fact that, because this word suggests the call of the

Japanese nightingale, the feathered songster is known by a name which means "scripture-reading bird."

The old weathered temple, which we visited, is known as the *Tanjo-ji*, or Nativity Temple, and is said to have been established in 1286, but to me the most appealing thing about this district is the respect which to this day is accorded Nichiren's prohibition against the catching of fish along this sacred shore. The fishermen of Tai-no-ura go far out before casting their nets, and this has been the case for so long that the fish have come to understand that they are safe inshore, and will rise to the surface if one knocks upon the gunwale of a boat.

The gates of the Tanjo-ji temple, dedicated to Nichiren, "the Martin Luther of Japan"

I should have liked to linger at this place, but the afternoon was waning and we had still half a dozen miles or more to go.

Sunset was suspended like a rosy fluid in the air when our basha drove down the main street of Kamogawa and stopped before the door of the inn.

To an American, accustomed to the casual reception accorded hotel guests in his native land, the experience of arriving at a well-conducted Japanese inn is almost sensational. The wheels of our vehicle had hardly ceased to turn when a flock of servitors came running out to welcome and to aid us. A pair of coolies whisked our bags into the portico, and as we followed we were escorted by the gray-haired proprietress and a bevy of nesans, all of them beaming at us and bowing profoundly from the waist.

While I sat on the doorstep removing my shoes, two coolies came from the rear of the building bearing between them a pole from which two huge buckets of hot water were suspended. Pushing back a sliding paper door they entered an adjoining room. A moment later I heard a great splashing, as of water being poured, and looking after them saw that they were emptying their buckets into a large stationary tub built of wood. Nor was I the only witness to the preparation of the bath. Two Japanese women and three children stood by, waiting to use it. And they were all ready to get in.

There was something superbly matter-of-fact about this whole performance which gave me a sudden flash of understanding. All the explaining in the world could not have told me so much about the Japanese point of view on matters of this kind as came through witnessing this picture.

Adam and Eve were not progenitors of these people nor was the apple a fruit indigenous to Japan.

The other members of our party were preparing to bathe in the sea before dinner, but I desired a hot bath and had asked for it as soon as I arrived. While in my room preparing I found myself wondering whether I was about to have an experience in mixed bathing, and if so how well my philosophy would stand the strain.

But the peculiar notions of foreigners concerning privacy in the bath were, it appeared, not unknown to the proprietress of the inn. When I descended the stairs arrayed in the short cotton kimono provided by the establishment, I was not shown to the large bathroom near the entrance, but was taken in tow by a little nesan, who indicated to me that I was to put on wooden clogs—a row of which stood by the door—and follow her across the street to the annex.

The bath was ready. Entering the room with me the nesan slipped the door shut and in a businesslike manner which could be interpreted in but one way, began looping back her sleeve-ends with cord.

"She intends to scrub you!" shrieked all that was conventional within me. "Put her out!"

"But don't you like to be scrubbed?" demanded the inner philosopher.

"Her being a woman makes me self-conscious," I replied to my other self.

"It shouldn't. Your being a man doesn't make her self-conscious. What was it we were saying a little while ago about false modesty?"

"As nearly as I can remember," replied Convention, evasively, "we agreed that Americans are full of false modesty."

Whereupon I turned to the little nesan and with a gesture in the direction of the door exclaimed, "Scat!"

Understanding the meaning of the motion if not the word, she obediently scatted, closing the door behind her. She did not go far, however. Through the paper I could hear her whispering with another nesan in the corridor. I went to the door with the purpose of fastening it, but there was no catch with which to do so. This left me with a certain feeling of insecurity as I bathed.

A well-ordered Japanese bathroom, such as this one was, has a false floor of wood with drains beneath it, so that one may splatter about with the utmost abandon. One does one's actual washing outside the tub, rinsing off with warm water dipped in a pail from a covered tank at one end of the tub. Not until the cleansing process has been completed does one enter the water to soak and get warm. Bathtubs in hotels and prosperous homes are large, and the size of them makes the preparation of a bath a laborious business; for running hot water is a luxury as yet practically unknown in Japan, the water for a bath being heated either in the kitchen, or by means of a little charcoal stove attached to the outside of the tub. To heat the bath by the latter system, which is the one generally used, takes an hour or two; wherefore it is obviously impracticable to prepare a separate bath for each member of the household. In a private house one tub of water generally does for all.

Foreigners newly arrived in Japan are unpleasantly impressed by this system of bathing, and in a Japanese inn they generally make a great point of having first chance at the bath.

Though I do not expect to convince the reader that what I say is so, I must bear testimony to the truth that it is the idea rather than the fact of the Japanese bath which is at first unpleasant. You must understand that the

Japanese are physically the cleanest race of people in the world; that, as I have already said, they bathe fully before entering the tub; that the tubbing is less a part of the cleansing process than a means for getting warm; and finally that the water in a tub which has been used by several persons looks as fresh as when first drawn.

I once asked a cosmopolitan Japanese whether he did not prefer our system of bathing. He replied that he did not. "I don't think your way is quite so clean as ours," he explained. "Not unless you take two baths, one after the other, as I always do when I am in Europe or America. I wash in the first bath. Then I draw a fresh tub to rinse off in."

Just as this gentleman prefers his native style of bathing I prefer mine; yet I should not object to succeeding him in the bath. Nor am I alone in liking the deep spaciousness of the large-size Japanese bathtub. An American gentleman who was in Japan when I was is having a Japanese bathroom built into his house near New York.

With the bath of the proletariat the system is the same, but the tub is smaller and less convenient. It consists of what is practically nothing more nor less than a large barrel with a small charcoal stove attached to one side. Often it stands out-of-doors.

On emerging from the hot water I found myself without a towel. I went to the door, opened it sufficiently to put my head out through the aperture and summoned the nesan who stood near by.

"Towel," I said.

She smiled and shook her head, uncomprehending.

I opened the door a little wider, thrust out one arm and made rubbing motions on it.

"*Hai!*" she exclaimed, brightly, and went scampering off.

As it was chilly in the room I returned to the hot tub to wait. There I remained for some minutes. Then it occurred to me that, understanding my desire for privacy in the bath, the nesan might be waiting outside with my towel, so I got out again with the intention of looking into the hall.

Just as I emerged, however, the door opened and in she came.

"Scat!" I cried. Whereupon she handed me two towels and fled.

It was well that she did bring two, for the native towel consists of a strip of thin cotton cloth hardly larger than a table napkin. The Japanese do not pretend to dry themselves thoroughly with these towels, but, as I have elsewhere mentioned, wring them out in hot water and use them as a mop, after which they go out and let the air finish the work.

I dried myself as best I could, slipped into the cotton kimono, and returned to the main building of the inn.

In the corridor I encountered my friend the linguist.

"I want to take a photograph of that bathtub," I told him.

"It won't explain itself in a photograph," he returned, "unless there's somebody in it."

I knew what he meant. An American or European, accustomed to the style of bathtub that stands upon the floor, would naturally assume from a picture of this one that it was similarly set. But that was not so. It extended perhaps two feet below the level of the floor; there was a step half-way down the inside to aid one in getting in or out; it was so deep that a short person standing in it would be immersed almost to the shoulders.

"You get in it, then, will you?"

"You ought to have a Japanese."

"But that's out of the question."

"No, it isn't."

Nor was it. By the time I got my kodak and put in a roll of film he had a subject for me.

It was the little nesan to whom I had said "scat!" Nor could a *grande dame* in an opera box have exhibited more aplomb than she did when I photographed her.

Nor could a *grande dame* in an opera box have exhibited more aplomb than she did when I photographed her

CHAPTER XXIV

A Walk in a Kimono—Dinner at the Inn—Sweet Servitors—An Evening's Enchantment—The Disadvantages of Ramma—My Neighbours Retire—A Japanese Bed—Breakfast—"Bear's Milk"—The Village of Nabuto—An Island and a Cave— The Abelone Divers—A Sail with Fishermen

"Let's take a walk before dinner," said the linguist when our photographic enterprise had been accomplished.

"All right. I'll go and dress."

"Come as you are."

"After a hot bath I might take cold in this thin kimono."

"No. That's a curious thing about hot baths in Japan. The reaction from them is much like that we get at home from cold ones."

"But, dressed this way, won't we look queer?" I surveyed the lower hem of my kimono which hung only a little below my knees.

"It's the costume of the country."

"But it's awfully short on us. It seems to me we ought to put on underwear at least."

"Nonsense. A man doesn't know what comfort is until he has strolled out in a kimono after a bath."

Our costumes were identical. We looked equally absurd. I consented.

My one difficulty on that stroll was with my clogs. I could not walk as fast as my companion, nor did I dare to lift my feet from the ground lest the clogs should fall off. And yet I can see that if one is brought up on clogs there is much to be said in their favour. They are durable and cheap. They neither suffocate nor cramp the foot.

Once I spoke to a Japanese friend of the merits of the clog, but though he admitted that his clog-wearing countrymen had no trouble with their feet, he thought clogs, on the whole, a bad thing. "The movement for good roads in Japan," he said, "started when people began to wear shoes. Those who wear clogs do not object to bad pavements, and we shall never get good ones until clogs are discarded by the majority."

We had not walked a block before I perceived that my companion had not overstated the case for the kimono as a costume for a stroll on a balmy evening. It does not bind one anywhere, but leaves one's arms and legs delightfully free. Moreover the air penetrates to the body, and the feeling of it after a very hot bath is as refreshing as an alcohol rub.

The streets were full of people many of them fishermen dressed much as we were. But though reason told me that in our kimonos we were less conspicuous than we should have been in our customary attire, I could not rid myself of the feeling that we were masqueraders, and that if people were to recognize us through the darkness for foreigners, we should have a crowd following us. Wherefore, though our promenade proved absolutely uneventful, I was upon the whole relieved when, after having gone the length of the main street and back, we re-entered the hotel.

Our dinner that night was purely Japanese; the nesans brought the usual little foot-high lacquer tables laden with covered bowls of porcelain and lacquer; we sat upon silken cushions on the matting in the linguist's room and struggled bravely with our chop-sticks.

The room was on the second floor. Through the open shoji we could look across a tiny garden into other rooms, open like ours to the soft evening air, and we could see the nesans gliding back and forth between these rooms and the kitchen, moving along the polished wooden floor of the gallery with their characteristic pigeon-toed shuffle.

In an American hotel our little party would have been served by one waiter; here we were attended by three nesans, one of whom squatted on the matting beside the rice bucket, ready to help us when we held out our bowls for more (for we had rice with our soup, our fish, and our tea), while the other two brought things from the kitchen, below stairs. And no matter how many times they had been in the room before, they always dropped to their knees, on entering, and bent their foreheads nearly to the floor in respectful salutation, ere they served the new course.

This courtesy, so natural to them, made me feel very, very far from home, for in it seemed to be crystallized the romantic charm of the antipodes. The whole environment, moreover, enhanced my feeling. The exquisite simplicity of our room, and of the other rooms across the garden; the soft lights shining through the rice paper of shoji here and there; the silhouettes, so Japanese, which passed across them; the shimmering of the dark green leaves of small trees whose upper branches reached a little bit above the floor level; the tinkling note of a samisen played in some remote part of the building; the almond eyes and massed ebony hair of our gentle little servitors, their butterfly costumes, the strange, soft rattle of their language, the curious unfamiliar flavours of the viands; all these combined to make me feel as one transported into an enchantment, vivid and fantastic as a painting by Rackham or Dulac.

And yet, fascinated as I was with all this magic loveliness, I felt a gentle melancholy. For the shoji at the rear of the room were pushed back like the others, and from the beach on which they opened there came to me through the darkness an insistent note of definite and almost terrible reality: the murmur of that ocean, black, restless, turbulent, ominous, unimaginably vast, by which I was cut off from home.

My own room was next to that of the linguist, but the room beyond mine was occupied by a Japanese couple. The rooms were divided by walls consisting of opaque paper screens, sliding in grooves, and even these frail partitions were incomplete, for, as in all Japanese houses, there were *ramma*, or grills, over the tops of the screens. The purpose of these ramma is to give ventilation at night, when the building is solidly encased in wooden shutters; but though it is true that they do permit some air to circulate, it is equally true that they permit the circulation of sound and light. Herein lies the foreigner's chief objection to the Japanese style of house—it is utterly without privacy.

I endeavoured to be quiet as I made ready for bed, and I am sure my Japanese neighbours likewise tried, but their whisperings and the little rustling sounds they made as they moved about, enhanced rather than diminished my consciousness of their proximity.

After I had put out my light my room continued for some time to be illuminated by the glow which came through the ramma on both sides. Presently the linguist's light went out, but that from the room of my other neighbours persisted, keeping me awake. This was the first time that I acutely missed chairs as an adjunct to Japanese life; if I had a chair I could hang a kimono over it to make a screen for my eyes. At last, however, I heard a little click, which was immediately followed by darkness. Then a sound of soft steps. Then a comfortable sigh. Then silence.

It was my first night in a Japanese bed. The bed consisted of two thin floss-silk mattresses, laid one above the other on the matting, and partly covered with what seemed to be a towel. It was all very clean. The pillow was a cylinder of cotton about six inches in diameter, stuffed with some substance as heavy and as crackling as pine needles, but odourless. I think the stuffing was of rice-husks. My nightgown was a cotton kimono like the one in which I had gone walking, and my coverlet was the usual bed-covering of Japan— a quilted satin robe, very long, with armholes and spacious sleeves: a cross between a comforter and a kimono. I did not use the sleeves, but pulled it over as one would if sleeping under an overcoat.

In all but one respect it was a comfortable bed. The thing that troubled me was the hard round pillow. I moved it about; I tried to flatten it; I tried my hand under it, and over it, between it and my face.

"I shall never be able to sleep on such a pillow!" I thought, irritably. And the next thing I knew it was morning and time to get up.

This inn, being exceptionally well appointed, provided separate wash-rooms for men and women. We trooped down and bathed. Then we breakfasted. The breakfast was much like the dinner of the night before—rice, soup, fish, and tea.

"If any one feels the need of coffee," said the linguist, "we may be able to get it, but the chances are it won't be very good. I've got a can of condensed milk here, too." He held up the can. I noticed that it was called "Bear Brand" Milk, and that the label bore the picture of a bear.

"Don't they have fresh milk at these inns?" someone asked.

"A few of them have it now," he replied, "but it is only in the last few years that the people of this locality have learned to use milk at all."

This reminded him of a story which he told us.

On one of his walking trips he had stopped at an inn which boasted of having been patronized by an Imperial Prince. The friend who accompanied the linguist on that trip wanted coffee for breakfast, and the innkeeper managed to supply it. The linguist had a can of "Bear Brand" Milk in his haversack, but he did not wish to open it if milk could be produced at the inn.

"Can you get me some milk?" he asked the nesan.

"What kind of milk?" she inquired.

Perceiving that she knew nothing of our custom of using milk in tea and coffee, he amused himself by replying:

"Whale's milk."

The nesan went downstairs and presently returned to say that there was no whale's milk to be had.

"This inn has been patronized by an Imperial Prince," exclaimed the linguist, affecting astonishment, "yet you have no whale's milk?"

The nesan admitted that such was the case.

"Then," said he, "bring me elephant's milk. I'll try to make it do."

Again she departed.

"The proprietor is very sorry," she reported when she came back, "but he has just run out of elephant's milk."

"Let me see the proprietor."

When the latter appeared he was most apologetic. There had been an unprecedented demand for elephant's milk in the last few days, he explained, and his supply had been exhausted. He expected to have some more shortly, but the express was slow.

"Very well," said the linguist, "I suppose I'll have to get along as best I can on bear's milk." Whereupon he opened the "Bear Brand" can and poured some of its contents into his coffee, while the hotel proprietor and the nesan looked on with bulging eyes.

"You ought to be ashamed of yourself," I told him when he had finished the story.

"The joke rebounded on me," he said. "After that I became a personage in the inn, and I had to tip correspondingly when I left—for according to the old custom of the country the size of the tip in a hotel is not in proportion to the service received, but in proportion to the rank of the tipper. And besides, the proprietor was very curious to know how they milked the bears. I had a devil of a time explaining that."

After breakfast we set out on foot for the village of Nabuto, several miles farther along the shore. The road, winding around the rampart hills, was as beautiful as that we had travelled the day before, and as full of interesting figures and intimate glimpses of the life of these amiable industrious fisher-folk.

Nabuto proved to be a tiny settlement at the tip of a rocky promontory, sheltered from direct assaults of the sea by a small, pinnacled island known as Niemon Island because it belongs, and has for eight centuries belonged, to a family of that name, residing there.

An old sea-wife, looking like a figure from one of Winslow Homer's paintings, summoned the ferryman with a blast upon a conch shell, and a few minutes later we stepped from his skiff to a natural platform of granite at the island's edge. As we landed we were assimilated by a guide who began by indicating certain circular holes in the granite which, he declared, had been made by the hoofs of Yoritomo's horse. For legend has it that, when pursued, this mediæval military hero used Niemon Island as a hiding place. Nor are the horse's hoof-prints the only evidence supporting this tale. One may see the cave in which the great Yoritomo concealed himself.

Thither, by a rough, ascending path, the guide led us. It was a small, damp cave. If Yoritomo lived there long he must have feared his enemies more than he feared rheumatism. Within was a small shrine dedicated to the ancient warrior, and hanging near it was a cord by which a bell could be rung to notify the spirit of the departed that callers had arrived. The guide signified to us that Yoritomo's spirit would be profoundly gratified if we put a few coppers into the box in front of his shrine. Having contributed we were allowed to ring the bell.

The ledge outside commanded a view of leagues and leagues of amethyst sea into which jutted a succession of green bastioned promontories. Below us, at the base of the cliff, where the long swells were crashing in rhythmic succession, several small skiffs were tossing dangerously near the margin of the foam. These, said the guide, were the boats of abalone fishers—for the Niemon family, besides receiving tourists, and selling them trinkets, picture postcards, and flasks of Osaka whiskey, is in the business of canning abalone meat. I have attempted to eat abalone. Considering that it is a mollusc leading an absolutely sedentary life, it has astounding muscular development. A man who can masticate it ought to be able also to masticate the can in which it comes.

Each skiff contained two men; an oarsman and a diver. The former would nurse his light craft close to where the seas were breaking on the island's rocky wall, while the latter, standing and swaying with the rise and fall of the boat, peered eagerly into the blue depths. Then, suddenly, with the swiftness of a thrown knife, the brown body would cut the water and disappear. One waited. One waited long enough to become a little anxious. But when it seemed that human lungs could not have held a breath for such a length of time, a head of wet black hair would pop out of the water and the glistening body of the diver would slip over the gunwale with the sinuous ease of a swimming seal. A moment later he would be standing again in the bow of the boat, a figure beautifully poised, gazing with the rapt eyes of a seer into the swaying, streaky mysteries of the under-water world.

Out here the fresh sea breeze wove like a cool woof across the warp of rays from a hot noonday sun. Ashore there was no breeze. I was beginning to dread the baking dusty miles of highway leading back to Kamogawa. Then someone suggested that we sail there, and the linguist sent the guide to see about a boat.

The vessel he secured was a two-masted fishing boat with a brave viking prow and long sleek lines. It was a piratical-looking craft and the appearance of the crew was even more so. They were like the Malay pirates in boys' books of adventure: almost naked, and tanned and weathered to a dark copper colour. Two of them wore short white shirts, open in front and terminating at the waist, but the others were innocent of such sophisticated haberdashery, the entire costume of each consisting of a pair of towels—one at the loins, the other wound around the head.

All too soon they landed us upon the beach at the back of the hotel.

"Now," said the linguist, as we waded up through the deep sand, "we'll pack our bags, get lunch, and be off."

And precisely that we did.

The whole staff of the inn assembled to see us depart. The proprietress gave us little presents. There was much bowing. Then the basha creaked away.

CHAPTER XXV

I Take Gen's Photograph—The Pay of Fisher-Folk—Where All the World Works—We Help Gen Pull Her Cart—And Surprise Some Wayfarers—The Road Grows Long—Fairy Débutantes

In an exceptionally picturesque fishing village a few miles on, I paused to take some photographs. On a platform outside an old house overhanging the gray sea-wall at the margin of the beach, three women were unloading baskets of fish from a heavy handcart. One of them was fully sixty years of age, another I judged to be thirty, but the third was a girl not over twenty, a sturdy brown lass with eyes like those of a wild deer, and a ready smile which showed a set of glorious white teeth. She was as pretty a peasant girl as I had seen in Japan, wherefore through my bi-lingual friend, I asked permission to take her picture.

From the amount of talking my friend did, and the laughter with which, on both sides, it was accompanied, I judged that the request, as it reached her, was festooned with gallantries. At all events she readily consented to be photographed—as a pretty girl generally will—and when the shutter had snapped she asked that I send her a print. This I agreed to do if she would write her name and address in my notebook. She did so in kana, which, being translated by my invaluable companion, revealed her name as Gen Tajima.

Pretty Gen was between the shafts, the other girl was pulling at a rope, and the grandmother was at the rear, pushing

Asked if all three of them were of the same family, the women replied that they were merely neighbours. They resided in the village of Amatsu-machi, several miles farther along the road that we were travelling, and it was their daily business to draw the cart from Amatsu-machi to this place, laden with baskets of fish to be salted and shipped. Their pay for this labour amounted to the equivalent of twenty-five cents a day in our money.

"I suppose you are all of you married?" asked my friend.

The old woman replied that she was; the other two laughed and declared that they were not. But they soon betrayed each other. "Don't you believe what *she* says!" they warned us gaily. "She *is* married. *I'm* the one who is looking for a match." Then, having had their little joke, each owned to a husband and children. Their husbands were fishermen, and earned, they said, two yen a day—about a dollar.

"You work hard?" asked my friend.

"Of course."

"Why 'of course'?"

"Everybody down here works hard."

"Even those who don't have to?"

"Yes. Even people with a lot of money work hard. Here any one who did not work would be laughed at."

They were typical Japanese women of the fisher class, happy, innocent, industrious. They interested me profoundly. But there was a long trip ahead of us and it was necessary to push on. We bade them farewell, got into the basha, and drove away.

But we had not seen the last of them. When we had driven a quarter of a mile or so, they came running up behind us with their cart. Pretty Gen was between the shafts, the other girl was pulling at a rope tied to one side, and the grandmother was at the rear, pushing. They ran pigeon-toed, like Indians, and what with the commotion caused by their rope sandals and the wheels, left a cloud of dust behind them.

Full of merriment they closed in upon us. One of them called to us in Japanese.

"What did she say?" I asked.

My friend translated:

"She says that because we are strangers they will escort us."

"Come on," I said, jumping out of the basha. "Let's help them pull the cart."

He joined me at once. We took up our places, naturally, at either side of Gen.

She was full of questions. Where were we from? How long did it take to come all the way from America? What was America like? Didn't the American people like the Japanese people? Her brother was a sailor. He had made a voyage to America and said it was a very fine place, and that everyone was rich. It wasn't like that in Japan. Here almost everyone was poor. It was hard to earn enough to live on, now that food cost so much.

Finding that there were now too many willing hands at the cart, we discharged the grandmother and the other woman, placing them in our seats in the basha.

"It is a pity you can't ride, too," my friend said to Gen, "but it is better for you to stay here and see that we don't steal the cart."

To which the old woman leaning out of the back seat of the basha remarked that she thought us much more likely to steal the cart if Gen went with it.

This caused much hilarity. Gen, I think, was a little embarrassed, but she enjoyed it all the same.

"As things are," she said, smiling and looking at the road, "I am well satisfied to walk."

The chatter was so lively that I had a good deal of difficulty in finding out all that was being said; it was no small task for my companion to keep up his end of the conversation against all three of them, and at the same time translate for me. I began to find myself left out.

Moreover, I had not anticipated that we should attract so much attention. The mere fact that we were aliens made us conspicuous in this part of the country, and the sight of two foreign men helping a peasant girl pull a cart, while the girl's usual companions rode ahead in the comparative magnificence of a basha, caused people in the villages through which we passed not only to stare in amazement, but to call their friends to come and witness the unheard-of spectacle.

I remember an old woman bent under a great load of straw which she was carrying on her back, who, when she glanced up and saw us, looked as if she were going to fall over, and I shall never forget the quizzical, puzzled, fixed gaze of a middle-aged coolie, with a load of wood on his back and a little pipe in his mouth, who, on sight of us, hurriedly seated himself on the bank at the roadside to pass us in review. He was a fine type. I dropped my hold upon the shaft, unslung my kodak, and embalmed his features on a film.

The middle-aged coolie hurriedly seated himself on the bank to pass us in review

"Come on back here!" called my companion. "Gen and I need you with our cart."

Gen and I!... *Our* cart, indeed! Who first thought of helping Gen with her cart, I should like to know!

Without enthusiasm I returned and took hold of the shaft again. The cart was getting heavier. He and Gen weren't pulling as they should. They were too busy talking—that was the trouble with them!

"Say, how far is it to this town where these people live?" I demanded of him.

"I guess it's not very much farther," my friend interrupted his conversation with Gen to reply.

"I should hope not! We've pulled this infernal cart about five miles already."

"If you don't like it," he answered, "why don't you get back in the basha?"

"How am I going to do that, when that old woman is in my place?"

"Tell her you want to ride. Tell her to come back here and get on the job again."

I looked up at her. It was quite out of the question to do such a thing. Much as I should have enjoyed my seat in the basha, she was enjoying it more. She and the younger woman were having a magnificent time, chattering, giggling, hailing every acquaintance they passed. And when other peasants who knew them gazed, astonished, they would burst into roars of mirth. All of which gave our progress more than ever the aspect of a circus parade in which, it began to seem to me, I figured as the clown.

Left to my own thoughts I endeavoured to meet the situation philosophically. If I had been foolish to get myself into this cart-pulling adventure my folly was of a kind common to my sex. Other men without number had made even greater fools of themselves. And, whereas in a little while this incident would be ended, some men got into scrapes that lasted all their lives. It was pleasant to reflect on that.

I began to see an allegory in the episode. In miniature it was like the story of a hasty marriage.... A man travelling the road of life in the comfortable basha of bachelorhood sees a pretty girl. Bright eyes, white teeth shown in a smile, and out he jumps.

"Let me help you pull the cart!" he cries, without giving a thought to the future. So he takes hold, and as likely as not she eases off and lets him do most of the pulling.

He wants companionship, but when he begins to look for it, what does he discover? He discovers that she doesn't know a word of his language, nor he a word of hers. He has sold his birthright for a mess of pulchritude.

The road is long, the hills steep, the cart heavy. Presently appears another man and offers to help—some smart-aleck who *can* talk her kind of talk. And, of course, this linguistic ass begins prattling a lot of nonsense to her and turns her head. The more she listens to him the more inflated he becomes. That's what happens to some men if a pretty girl shows them a little attention! Does he stop for a minute to consider that his advantage is purely one of language? Not at all! The idiot thinks himself fascinating.

So much for that.

But now imagine another picture. Take those two men out of a situation in which one has manifestly an unfair advantage, and place them on an equal footing in a totally different environment. Take them, let us say, to an

American city, place them in a ballroom, bring in a lot of beautiful débutantes—hundreds of them, all in pretty little evening gowns and satin slippers—start up the band. *Then* see what happens!

One of these men is a bookworm. He knows a lot about languages. He can speak Japanese. (You see I am being perfectly fair to him.) But the other, though he cannot speak Japanese, is—you understand this is purely an imaginary case—a handsome, dashing, debonair fellow. While one has been learning Japanese the other has learned a few effective steps. In the intricate mazes of the dance he seems to float godlike through the air.

All right! Now I ask you, which one of these two men is going to be a success with all those débutantes? Is Japanese going to advance a man very far with an American débutante? In all fairness I say No! A débutante is too clever— too clever with her feet—to be misled by mere linguistic talent. True worth is the thing that counts with her. She looks for solid merit in a man. In other words: *What kind of a dancer is he?*

Is not the conclusion obvious? In the environment I have pictured one of those two men will be left practically alone, while the other will find himself constantly surrounded by a bevy of dainty, beautiful——

"This is Amatsu-machi," I heard my companion say.

With a start I came back to Japan.

"They're leaving us at the crossroads," said he.

The basha drew up. The two women got out. They thanked us prettily. Then amid many "*Sayonaras*" we drove off, while they stood and watched us, smiling and waving until we passed from their sight around a bend in the road.

"They have lovely natures, these Japanese women," the linguist presently remarked.

"If you'll look over a lot of American débutantes," I replied, "you'll find that they are just about as——"

"You don't understand," he interrupted. "I'm not talking about mere prettiness—though you'd hardly say that girl Gen wasn't pretty. I'm talking about spiritual quality. Couldn't you tell, just by looking at her, that she was sweet right straight through?"

"I guess she's all right," I answered in an off-hand tone.

That did not half satisfy him. But though he kept at me for a long time, trying to make me say something more enthusiastic, I would not be coerced. He was too much puffed up as it was.

I had another reason, too, for withholding from that pretty peasant girl the fullest praise. I must be faithful to the débutantes who, from far away, had come floating like a swarm of fairies to console me as I tugged Gen Tajima's lumbering cart along a dusty road upon the seacoast of Japan.

CHAPTER XXVI

The Handkerchief as a Travelling Bag—Bags and Bottles—Computing Time—The Mystic Animals of the Zodiac—Superstitions Regarding Them—Temple Fortune-Telling—An Ekisha—The Ema—Yuki Tells of a Wonderful Cure

The national travelling bag of the Japanese is a large, strong handkerchief of silk or cotton, in which the articles carried on a journey are tied up. The elasticity of this container, which is called a *furoshiki*, is its great advantage. It is as large or as small as its contents require, and when it is empty you do not have to lug it about by hand, like an empty suitcase, but merely put it in your pocket.

The trouble with our style of suitcases and bags is that they are heavy, bulky, and not adaptable. On one occasion they are overcrowded, on another we carry them half empty. My own bags remind me of the way I used to feel about wine bottles in the cheery days when one could afford to regard such things with a somewhat critical eye. I always felt that wine bottles were either too large or too small. Pints held a little too much for one, yet not enough for two; and quarts held rather more than was required by three, yet left four dissatisfied. Let us, however, drop this subject. *De mortuis....*

I was often struck with the fact that though the Japanese woman seems to be more heavily dressed than the foreign woman, and though her coiffure is generally more elaborate, she carries so much less baggage when she travels. In our Yuki's furoshiki there was always room for my cigars, cigarettes, books, and kodak films. Her own things seemed to take no space at all.

There are several reasons for this. A Japanese woman carries no hair-brush and wears her comb in her hair. Nor do the Japanese generally take nightclothes with them on a journey, for a clean cotton kimono, in which to sleep, is supplied by all Japanese hotels. More than once, when I saw Yuki starting off with us for a two- or three-days' trip with baggage consisting of a furoshiki tied to about the size of two ordinary novels, I thought of Johnnie Poe's famous "fifty-three pieces of baggage—a deck of cards and a tooth-brush."

A favourite theme for the decoration of the furoshiki embodies the signs of the Chinese zodiac, consisting of twelve animals. The Chinese calendar was adopted centuries ago by the Japanese, and they still take account of it, though they now generally use our Gregorian calendar for computing time. But even so, their era is not the Christian Era, but dates from the beginning of the reign of Jimmu Tenno the Divine, whom the Japanese count as the first of their Imperial line, and who is said to have ascended the throne, 660 B.C. Thus our current year, 1921, is the year 2581 in Japan. Time is also measured arbitrarily by the reigns of emperors, the present year being Taisho 10, or the tenth year of the reign of the present Emperor.

The Chinese zodiac, however, figures largely in Japanese superstition. As there are twelve animals, the years are counted off in cycles of twelve; and the same animals are also associated with days and hours, in cycles of twelve. The attributes of the astrological animal governing the year of one's birth are supposed to attach to one.

"My mother is a cow," a Japanese lady explained to me. "My husband is a snake and I am a rabbit."

The lore of these animals is complicated. I have only a smattering of it, but what I know will suffice to show the general tendency of such superstition.

It is considered good fortune to be born in the year of the horse because the horse is strong and energetic. 1920 was the year of the monkey. It is unlucky to marry in monkey year because the word *saru*, which means "monkey," also means "to go back," the suggestion being that the bride will go back to her former home, or in other words be divorced. A woman born in the year of the rabbit will be prolific. (The lady who said, "I'm a rabbit," though very young, was the mother of four.)

Similarly the animals, in their cycle, bring good luck or ill luck in connection with events occurring on certain days. It is unlucky to take to one's bed with a sickness on the day of the cow, because the cow is slow to get up. It is lucky to begin a journey on the day of the tiger, because the tiger, though he travels a thousand miles, always returns to the point from which he started; but for the same reason it is unlucky for a girl to marry on this day, because she, like the tiger, may return to the place from which she started: her father's house. And the day of the tiger is a bad one for funerals, because the tiger drags its prey with it, suggesting that another funeral will soon follow. The significance attaching to each animal according to the Japanese idea is not always apparent, without explanation, to the stranger. For instance, though I know it is considered lucky for a bride to cut her kimonos on the day of the rooster, I do not know why. Nor do I know why it is considered particularly lucky to have, in one family, three persons born under the same sign.

Superstition of all kinds plays a large part in the daily life of the Japanese masses, and persons of intelligence often patronize fortune tellers, among whom are the Buddhist priests in certain temples.

**At Asakusa, the great popular temple of Tokyo, the fortune-telling
business is so brisk that two or three priests are busy at it all the time**

At Asakusa, the great popular temple of Tokyo, the fortune-telling business
is so brisk that two or three priests are busy at it all the time. The system is
simple. The diviner shakes a lot of numbered sticks in a box, draws one out,
and takes a paper from a little drawer which bears a number corresponding
with that on the stick. Your fortune is written on the paper, in multigraph. I
paid two cents for mine, and when it was translated to me I felt that I had
paid too much.

Yuki, when she saw that I was disposed to take the matter lightly, seemed a
little disappointed, and when later several of us decided to give the
necromancers one more fling, she herself escorted us to the establishment
called Hokokudo, at number 3 Chome, the Ginza, where father, son, and
grandson successively have told fortunes for the past hundred and twenty
years. Here we paid one yen each for our fortunes, but though the *ekisha* took
more time to the job, examining our hands and faces, rattling his divining
rods and making patterns with his Chinese wooden blocks, he didn't do
much better than the priest had done for two cents. Yuki was impressed
when he predicted a sea voyage for me, but the prophecy did not seem to me
to constitute a remarkable example of divination.

The visit to the ekisha was however, an experience. The little house was
picturesque, and it was interesting to see the stream of Japanese coming in,
one after another, intent on learning what the future held in store for them.
Also, while Yuki's fortune was being told I got a good photograph of the
ekisha examining her hand through his magnifying glass.

While Yuki's fortune was being told I photographed her

Another superstition is exampled in the *ema*, votive offerings in the form of little paintings on wood, which are put up at Shinto shrines by those in need of help of one kind or another. For almost any sort of affliction an ema of suitable design may be found, though the meaning of the grotesque design is seldom apparent to the foreigner.

While in Japan I collected a number of these curious little objects and investigated their significance. Among them was one which Yuki recognized as an appeal for relief from eye trouble.

"That very good ema," she told me. "I use one like that once when I have sore eyes."

"Did it cure you, Yuki?"

"Yes—in two weeks. I put it up at shrine and I promise the god I no drink tea for two weeks. In two weeks my eyes all right again."

"And you are sure the ema did it?"

"Yes, sir, I sure."

"You didn't do anything else for your eyes?"

"No, it just like I say. I put up ema for god and not drink tea. Then I wait two weeks."

"Did your eyes hurt you during the two weeks?"

"Oh, yes. They hurt so much I have to wash them two three times a day with boric acid, while I wait for ema to make cure. But when end of two weeks comes they not sore any more. That ema work very good."

CHAPTER XXVII

Our Difficulties with the Language—The Questionable Humour of Broken Speech—
"Do You Striking This Man for That?"—"Companies, Scholars, and Other
Households"—Curious Correspondence—Japanese Puns—Strange Laughter—The
Grotesque in Art—Japanese Colour-Prints—Famous Print Collections—Monet's
Discovery of Prints at Zaandam—Japanese Prints and French Impressionism

The complete dissimilarity between the Japanese language and our own,
referred to in an earlier chapter, of course adds greatly to the difficulty of
communication in all its various forms.

In Tokyo and other cities I attended many luncheons and dinners organized
for the purpose of discussing relations between the United States and Japan,
and promoting a friendly understanding between the two nations, but though
Japanese statesmen and men of affairs spoke at these gatherings in fluent and
even polished English, I never met with one American who was equipped to
return the compliment in kind. The Americans, even those who had lived for
years in Japan, always spoke in English, whereafter a Japanese interpreter
who had taken notes on the speech would arise and render a translation.

The linguistic chasm dividing the two peoples is not, however, entirely a
black abyss. If one wall is dark, the other catches the sun. Practically all
Japanese students now study English in their schools, our language being
considered next in importance to their own. And though, as I have said, many
of them have perfectly mastered English despite the enormous difficulties it
presents to them, there are many others whose English is imperfect, and
whose "Japanned English," as some one has called it, achieves effects the
unconscious grotesqueness of which startles and fascinates Americans and
Englishmen.

To be honest, I have been in some doubt as to whether I should touch upon
this theme or not; for it has always seemed to me that humour based upon
the efforts of an individual to express himself in a language not his own was
meretricious humour, inasmuch as it makes fun of an attempt to do a
creditable thing. It is a kind of humour which is enjoyed in some measure by
the French and the British but which is relished infinitely more by us than by
any other people in the world, as witness entertainments in our theatres, and
stories in our magazines, depending for comedy upon dialect: German,
French, Italian, Irish, Jewish, Cockney, Negro, or even the several purely
American dialects characteristic of various parts of the country.

This dubious taste of ours doubtless springs, to some extent at least, from
the polyglot nature of our population; but whatever its origin it is a bad thing
for us in one important respect. We find the English dialect of foreigners so

funny that we ourselves fear to attempt foreign tongues, lest we make ourselves ridiculous. Wherefore we are the poorest linguists in the world.

Even after the foregoing apology—for that, frankly, is what it is—I should still hesitate to present examples of "Japanned English" had I not discovered that Professor Basil Hall Chamberlain, perhaps the greatest of modern authorities on Japan, a man whose writings reveal an impeccable nicety of taste, had already done so in his most valuable book, "Things Japanese."

One of the examples given by Professor Chamberlain is quoted from a work entitled: "The Practical Use of Conversation for Police Authorities," which assumes to teach the Japanese policeman how to converse in English. The following is an imaginary conversation intended to guide the officer in parley with a British bluejacket:

> What countryman are you?
>
> I am a sailor belonged to the Golden Eagle, the English man-of-war.
>
> Why do you strike this jinricksha-man?
>
> He told me impolitely.
>
> What does he told you impolitely?
>
> He insulted me saying loudly, "the Sailor the Sailor" when I am passing here.
>
> Do you striking this man for that?
>
> Yes.
>
> But do not strike him for it is forbidden.
>
> I strike him no more.

One curious aspect of the matter is that so much of this weird English creeps into print, appearing in guidebooks, advertisements, and on the labels of goods of various kinds manufactured in Japan.

Thus in the barber shop of the ship, going over, I found a bottle containing a toilet preparation called "Fulay," the label of which bore the following legend:

> "Fulay" is manufactures under chemical method and long years experience with pure and refined materials. It is, therefore, only the article in the circle as ladies and gents daily toilet.

And on a jar of paste I found this label, which will be better understood if the tendency of the Japanese to confuse the letters *l* and *r* is kept in mind:

> This paste is of a pureness cleanliness and of a strong cohesion, so that it does not putrefy even when the paste grass is left open. Though written down on paper or the like immediately after pasting, the character is never spread. This paste has an especial fragrance therefore all of pasted things after using this are always kept from the frys and all sorts of bacteria, and prevents the infectious diseases. This paste is an indispensable one for the banks, companies, scholars and other households. Please notice for "Kuchi's Yamato-Nori" as there are similar things.

The circular of one firm, advertising "a large assortment of ladies' blushes," might have been misinterpreted as having some scandalous suggestion, had it not gone on to discuss the ivory backs and high-grade bristles with which the "blushes" were equipped.

Another circular was that of a butcher who catered to foreigners in Tokyo. After stating that his meats were sold at "a fixed plice" this worthy merchant mentioned the various kinds of beef he could supply. There were, "rosu beef, rampu beef, pig beef, soup beef, and beard beef"—which being interpreted signified roast beef, rump beef, pork, soup meat and poultry—the word "beard" being intended for "bird."

In the admirable hotel at Nara I saw the following notice posted in a corridor:

REMARQUE

> Parents are requested kindly to send their children to the Hotel Garden for when weather is fine. When it is bad weather I will offer the children the small dining-room, except meal hours, as playing room for them, therefore please don't let them run round upstairs and downstairs at all. Please kindly have the children after dinner in a manner quiet and repose.
>
> MANAGER, Nara Hotel.

From a friend, an official of a large company, I got a number of letters revealing the peculiarities of "English as she is wrote"—at least as she is sometimes wrote—in Japan. All these letters are authentic, having come to him in connection with his business.

The first one, written by a clerk to the office manager, refers to an admirable Japanese custom which in itself is worthy of brief mention.

Throughout Japan there is housecleaning twice a year under police supervision. Certain districts have certain days on which the cleaning must be done. The shoji are removed, the furniture is carried out, and the mats are taken up and beaten. The streets are full of activity and dust when this is going on, and there is a pile of rubbish in front of every residence. Meanwhile police officers pass up and down, wearing gauze masks over their noses and mouths to protect them from the dust, and at the end they inspect each house to see that the work has been properly done, after which they affix an official stamp over the door.

Wherefore wrote the clerk to the office manager:

> MR. S——:
>
> Excuse my absent of this morning. All of my neighbourhood have got instruction to clean out nest.
>
> SIDA.

A more serious dilemma is revealed in the following:

> TO GENERAL MANAGER.
>
> DEAR SIR,
>
> My wife gave birth this noon and as it happened nearly a month ahead than I expected, I much rather find myself in painful situation, having not yet prepared for this sudden ocurrence.
>
> Up to this day, unfortunate enough, I am destined most unfavourably for the monetary circumstance, and consequently have no saving against worldly concerns, I am forced to ask you for a loan of ￥ 25.00 to get rid of the burden befallen on me by the birth.
>
> I know it is the meanest of all to ask one's help for monetary affair but as I am being unable to find any better way than to solicit you, I have at last come to a conclusion to trouble you but against my will. I deem it much more shamefull to advertise my poor condition around my relatives or acquaintances no matter wheater it will be fruitfull or fruitless.
>
> Yours obediently,
> Y——.

The subjoined was received from one of the company's agents in another city:

DEAR SIR,

We have the honour to thank you for your having bestowed us a Remington typewriter which has just arrived via railway express. We will treat her very kindly and she will give us her best service in return. Thus we can work to our mutual satisfaction and benefit.

Thanking you for your kindness we beg to remain,

Yours very truly,
O—— I——.

The porter in a Japanese office not infrequently sleeps on the premises. But he must have the necessary equipment, as the following letter from an agent to a principal reveals:

DEAR SIR,

In accordance to your esteemed conversation of other day for lodging the servant at this office, we consider we must provide to him the bed or sleeping tools. Please inform us that you could approve the expense to purchase this tool.

Awaiting your esteemed reply we are, dear sir,

Yours faithfully,
T—— A——.

The next letter is from a man who wished to establish business relations with my friend's company:

DEAR SIR,

I am a trader at Kokura city in Kyushu, always treating the various machines or steels and the architectural using goods.

I have known of your great names at Tokyo. Therefore I want to open the connection with each other so affectionately. Accordingly I beg to see your company's inside scene so clearly, please send me the catalogue and plice-list of good samples of your company. I am a baby on our commercial society, because you will lead me to the machinery society I think.

I trusted,

Yours affectionately,
I am,
K—— M——.

One thing which sometimes makes these letters startling is the fact that they are couched in English which is perfectly correct save in one or two particulars. Thus the errors or strange usages pop out at one unexpectedly, adding an element of surprise, as in the case of a man who wrote to my friend applying for work:

> DEAR SIR,
>
> I beg leave to inquire whether you can make use of my services as a salesman and correspondent in your firm. I have had considerable experiences as a apparatus, and can furnish references and insurance against risk.
>
> Awaiting your reply, I am
>
> Yours respectfully,
> K—— S——.

I have often been asked whether the Japanese possess the gift of humour.

They do—though humour does not occupy a place so important in their daily life as it does in ours.

A light touch in conversation is uncommon with them, and those who have it do not generally exhibit it except to their intimates. Yet they are great punsters, and some of their puns are very clever. A case in point is the slang term *narikin* which they have recently adopted to describe the flashy new-rich type which has come into being since the war.

To understand the derivation of this word, and its witty connotation, you must know that in their game of chess, called *shogi*, a humble pawn advanced to the adversary's third row is, by a process resembling queening, converted into a powerful, free-moving piece called *kin*. The word *nari* means "to become"; hence *nari-kin* means literally "to become *kin*"—which gives us, when applied to a flamboyant profiteer, a droll picture of a poor little pawn suddenly exalted to power and magnificence. The pun, which adds greatly to the value of this term, comes with the word *kin*. *Kin* is not only a chessman; it also means "gold." Which naturally contributes further piquancy in the application to a *nouveau riche*.

Moreover, through a play on the word narikin there has been evolved a second slang term: *narihin*—*hin* meaning "poor"—"to become poor." And alas, this term as well as the other is useful in Japan to-day. War speculation has made some fortunes, but it has wiped out others.

My friend O——, a truly lovable fellow, once spent the better part of an afternoon explaining a lot of Japanese puns to me, and I was hardly more pleased by the jests themselves than by my friend's infectious little chuckles over them. At parting we made an engagement for the evening, but about dinner time O—— returned to say that he could not spend the evening with me.

"I have just heard that my best friend died last night," he said, "It is very unexpected. I must go to his house." So speaking he emitted what appeared to me to be precisely the same little chuckle he had uttered over the puns.

The suppression of one's feeling is a primary canon of Japanese etiquette. To show unhappiness is to make others unhappy; wherefore, when one suffers, it is good form to laugh or smile. The foreigner who comprehends this doctrine must, if he be a man of any delicacy of feeling, respect it. But if he does not grasp the underlying principle he is likely to misjudge the Japanese and consider their laughter, in some circumstances, hard-hearted, apologetic, or inane.

The supreme proof of Japanese humour is to be found in the grotesqueries and whimsicalities of Japanese Art. You see it revealed everywhere—in the shape of a gnarled, stunted pine, carefully trained to a pleasing deformity; in the images of cats left in various parts of Japan by Hidari Jingoro, the great left-handed wood-carver of the sixteenth century; in the famous trio of monkeys adorning the stable of the Ieyasu Shrine at Nikko—those which neither hear, see, nor speak evil; in a thousand earthenware figures of ragged, pot-bellied Hotei, one of the Seven Gods of Luck, sitting, gross and contented in a small boat, waiting for some one to bring his abdominal belt; in the countless representations of the Buddhist god Daruma, that delightful egg-shaped comedian who will run out his tongue and his eyes for you, or, if not that, will refuse to stay down when you roll him over; in figurines without number, of ivory or wood; in sword-guards embellished with fantastic conceits; in those carved ivory buttons called *netsuké*, treasured by collectors; and perhaps most often in Japanese colour-prints.

The hundred years between 1730 and 1830 was the golden age of wood-engraving in Japan.

During the lifetime of this art it was regarded as distinctly plebeian. Many of the fine prints were made to be used as advertisements or souvenirs. Some, it is true, were issued in limited editions, and these cost more than the commoner ones, but generally they were sold for a few cents.

Unfortunately, before the art-lovers of Japan perceived that the finest of these prints were masterpieces representing wood-engraving at its highest perfection, the best prints had got out of Japan and gone to Paris, London, Boston, New York, Chicago, and other foreign cities, whence the Japanese have lately been buying them back at enormous prices.

From a friend of mine in Tokyo, himself the owner of a very valuable collection, I learned that the collection of 7,500 prints assembled by M. Vever, of Paris, has long been considered by connoisseurs the finest in the world. This collection was recently purchased intact by Mr. Kojiro Matsukata, of Kobe, president of the Kawasaki shipbuilding firm. It is said that Mr. Matsukata paid half a million dollars for it. My Tokyo friend tells me that the collection belonging to Messrs. William S., and John T. Spalding, of Boston, is probably next in importance to the Matsukata collection, and that it is difficult to say whether the Boston Museum collection or the British Museum collection takes third place. For primitive prints, the Clarence Buckingham collection, housed in the Chicago Art Institute, is also very important.

How does it happen that it was in Europe that Japanese prints first came to be highly appreciated as works of art?

Octave Mirbeau, in his delightful book of automobiling adventures, "La 628-E8" (which, I believe, has never been brought out in English) tells the story.

The great impressionist, Claude Monet, went to Holland to paint. Some groceries sent home to him from a little shop were wrapped in a Japanese print—the first one Monet had ever seen.

"You can imagine," writes Mirbeau, "his emotion before that marvellous art.... His astonishment and joy were such that he could not speak, but could only give vent to cries of delight.

"And it was in Zaandam that this miracle came to pass—Zaandam with its canals, its boats at the quay unloading cargoes of Norwegian wood, its huddled flotillas of barks, its little streets of water, its tiny red cabins, its green houses—Zaandam, the most Japanese spot in all the Dutch landscape....

"Monet ran to the shop whence came his package—a vague little grocery shop where the fat fingers of a fat man were tying up (without being paralyzed by the deed!) two cents' worth of pepper and ten cents' worth of coffee, in paper bearing these glorious images brought from the Far East along with groceries in the bottom of a ship's hold.

"Although he was not rich at that time, Monet was resolved to buy all of these masterpieces that the grocery contained. He saw a pile of them on the counter. His heart bounded. The grocer was waiting upon an old lady. He was about to wrap something up. Monet saw him reach for one of the prints.

'No, no!' he cried. 'I want to buy that! I want to buy all those—all those!'

"The grocer was a good man. He believed that he was dealing with some one who was a little touched. Anyway the coloured papers had cost him nothing. They were thrown in with the goods. Like some one who gives a toy to a crying child to appease it, he gave the pile of prints to Monet, smilingly and a bit mockingly.

"'Take them, take them,' he said. 'You can have them. They aren't worth anything. They aren't solid enough. I prefer regular wrapping-paper.'"

So the grocer enveloped the old lady's cheese in a piece of yellow paper, and Monet went home and spent the rest of the day in adoration of his new-found treasures. The names of the great Japanese wood-engravers were of course unknown in Europe then, but Monet learned later that some of these prints were by Hokusai, Utamaro, and Korin.

"This," continues Mirbeau, "was the beginning of a celebrated collection, but much more important, it was the beginning of such an evolution in French painting that the anecdote has, besides its own savour, a veritable historic value. For it is a story which cannot be overlooked by those who seriously study the important movement in art which is called Impressionism."

CHAPTER XXVIII

Living in a Japanese House—The Priceless Yuki—The Servants in the House—The Red Carpet—Our Trunks Depart—Tokyo's Night-time Sounds—Tipping and Noshi—The Etiquette of Farewells—Sayonara

My last days in Japan were my best days, for I spent them in a Japanese home, standing amid its own lovely gardens in Mita, a residential district some twenty minutes by motor from the central part of Tokyo.

Through the open shoji of my bedroom I could look out in the mornings to where, beyond the velvet lawns, the flowers and the treetops, the inverted fan of Fuji's cone was often to be seen floating white and spectral in the sky, seventy miles away.

After my bath in a majestic family tub I would breakfast in my room, wearing a kimono, recently acquired, and feeling very Japanese.

While I was dressing, Yuki sometimes entered, but I had by this time become accustomed to her matutinal invasions and no longer found them embarrassing. She was so entirely practical, so useful. She knew where everything was. She would go to a curious little cupboard, which was built into the wall and had sliding doors of lacquer and silk, and get me a shirt, or would retrieve from their place of concealment a missing pair of trousers, and bring them to me neatly folded in one of those flat, shallow baskets which, with the Japanese, seem to take the place of bureau drawers.

Thus, besides being my daughter's duenna and my wife's maid, she was in effect, my valet. Nor did her usefulness by any means end there. She was our interpreter, dragoman, purchasing-agent; she was our steward, major domo, seneschal; nay, she was our Prime Minister.

The house had a large staff, and all the servants made us feel that they were *our* servants, and that they were glad to have us there. With the exception of a butler, an English-speaking Japanese temporarily added to the establishment on our account, all wore the native dress; and there were among them two men so fine of feature, so dignified of bearing, so elegant in their silks, that we took them, at first, for members of the family. One of them was a white-bearded old gentleman who would have made a desirable grandfather for anybody. If he had duties other than to decorate the hall with his presence I never discovered what they were. The other, a young man, was clerk of the household, and enjoyed the distinction of being Saki's husband.

Saki, the housekeeper of some Japanese friends we visited, obligingly posed for me. The mattress is stuffed with floss silk, the pillow is hard and round, and the covering is a sort of quilted kimono

Saki was the housekeeper, young and pretty. She and her husband lived in a cottage near by, and their home was extensively equipped with musical instruments, Saki being proficient on the samisen and koto, and also on an American melodeon which was one of her chief treasures. She was all smiles and sweetness—a most obliging person. Indeed it was she who pretended to be asleep in a Japanese bed, in order that I might make the photograph which is one of the illustrations in this book.

Four or five coolies, excellent fellows, wearing blue cotton coats with the insignia of our host's family upon the backs of them, worked about the house and grounds; and several little maids were continually trotting through the corridors; with that pigeon-toed shuffle in which one comes, when one is used to it, actually to see a curious prettiness.

Sometimes we felt that the servants were showing us too much consideration. We dined out a great deal and were often late in getting home ("Home" was the term we found ourselves using there), yet however advanced the hour, the chauffeur would sound his horn on entering the gate, whereupon lights would flash on beneath the porte-cochère, the shoji at the entrance of the house would slide open, and three or four domestics would come out, dragging a wide strip of red velvet carpet, over which we would walk magnificently up the two steps leading to the hall. But though I urged them to omit this regal detail, because two or three men had to sit up to handle the heavy carpet, and also because the production of it made me feel like a bogus prince, I could never induce them to do so. Always, regardless of the hour, a little group of servants appeared at the door when we came home.

Even on the night when, under the ministrations of the all-wise and all-powerful head porter of the Imperial Hotel, our trunks were spirited away, to be taken to Yokohama and placed aboard the *Tenyo Maru*, even then we found it difficult to realize that our last night in Japan had come.

The realization did not strike me with full force until I went to bed.

I was not sleepy. I lay there, thinking. And the background of my thoughts was woven out of sounds wafted through the open shoji on the summer wind: the nocturnal sounds of the Tokyo streets.

I recalled how, on my first night in Tokyo, I had listened to these sounds and wondered what they signified.

Now they explained themselves to me, as to a Japanese.

A distant jingling, like that of sleigh-bells, informed me that a newsboy was running with late papers. A plaintive musical phrase suggestive of Debussy, bursting out suddenly and stopping with startling abruptness, told me that the Chinese macaroni man was abroad with his lantern-trimmed cart and his little brass horn. At last I heard a xylophone-like note, resembling somewhat the sound of a New York policeman's club tapping the sidewalk. It was repeated several times; then there would come a silence; then the sound again, a little nearer. It was the night watchman on his rounds, guarding the neighbourhood not against thieves, but against fire, "the Flower of Tokyo." In my mind's eye I could see him hurrying along, knocking his two sticks together now and then, to spread the news that all was well.

Then it was that I reflected: "To-morrow night I shall not hear these sounds. In their place I shall hear the creaking of the ship, the roar of the wind, the hiss of the sea. Possibly I shall never again hear the music of the Tokyo streets."

My heart was sad as I went to sleep.

Fortunately for our peace of mind, we had learned through the experience of American friends, visitors in another Japanese home, how *not* to tip these well-bred domestics—or rather, how not to try to tip them. On leaving the house in which they had been guests, these friends had offered money to the servants, only to have it politely but positively refused.

Yuki cleared the matter up for us.

"They should put *noshi* with money," she explained in response to our questions. "That make it all right to take. It mean a present."

Without having previously known noshi by name, we knew immediately what she meant, for we had received during our stay in Japan enough presents to fill a large trunk, and each had been accompanied by a little piece of coloured paper folded in a certain way, signifying a gift.

In the old days these coloured papers always contained small pieces of dried *awabi*—abelone—but with the years the dried awabi began to be omitted, and the little folded papers by themselves came to be considered adequate.

Fortified with this knowledge I went, on the day before our departure, to the Ginza, where I bought envelopes on which the noshi design was printed. Money placed in these envelopes was graciously accepted by all the servants. Tips they would not have received. But these were not tips. They were gifts from friend to friend, at parting.

The code of Japanese courtesy is very exact and very exacting in the matter of farewells to the departing guest. Callers are invariably escorted to the door by the host, such members of his family as have been present, and a servant or two, all of whom stand in the portal bowing as the visitor drives away.

A house-guest is dispatched with even greater ceremony. The entire personnel of the establishment will gather at with profound bows and cries of "Sayonara!" the door to speed him on his way Members of the family, often the entire family, accompany him to the station, where appear other friends who have carefully inquired in advance as to the time of departure. The traveller is escorted to his car, and his friends remain upon the platform until the train leaves, when the bowing and "Sayonaras" are repeated.

Tokyo people often go to Yokohama with friends who are sailing from Japan, accompanying them to the ship, and remaining on the dock until the vessel moves into the bay. How Tokyo men-of-affairs can manage to go upon these time-consuming seeing-off parties is one of the great mysteries of Mysterious Japan, for such an excursion takes up the greater part of a day.

To the American, accustomed in his friendships to take so much for granted, a Japanese farewell affords a new sensation, and one which can hardly fail to touch the heart.

Departing passengers are given coils of paper ribbon confetti, to throw to their friends ashore, so that each may hold an end until the wall of steel parts from the wall of stone, and the paper strand strains and breaks. There is something poignant and poetic in that breaking, symbolizing the vastness of the world, the littleness of men and ships, the fragility of human contacts.

The last face I recognized, back there across the water, in Japan, was Yuki's. She was standing on the dock with the end of a broken paper ribbon in her hand. The other end trailed down into the water. She was weeping bitterly.

Wishing to be sure that my wife and daughter had not failed to discover her in the crowd, I turned to them. But I did not have to point her out. Their faces told me that they saw her. They too were weeping.

So it is with women. They weep. As for a man, he merely waves his hat. I waved mine.

"Sayonara!"

I turned away. There were things I had to see to in my cabin. Besides, the wind on deck was freshening. It hurt my eyes.

THE END

Milton Keynes UK
Ingram Content Group UK Ltd.
UKHW012312040624
443649UK00007B/556